# ESCAPE INTO DARKNESS

### The True Story
### of a Young Woman's
### Extraordinary Survival
### During World War II

# ESCAPE INTO DARKNESS

## The True Story
## of a Young Woman's
## Extraordinary Survival
## During World War II

*Sonia Games*

SHAPOLSKY PUBLISHERS, INC.
New York

# A Shapolsky Book

Copyright © 1991 by Sonia Games

For any additional information, contact:
Shapolsky Publishers, Inc.
136 West 22nd Street, New York, NY 10011
(212) 633-2022

1 2 3 4 5 6 7 8 9 10

Library of Congress Cataloging-in-Publication Data

Games, Sonia, 19—
    Escape into darkness: the true story of a young woman's extraordinary survival during World War II. Sonia Games.
        p. cm.
    ISBN 0-944007-76-7
    1. Jews—Poland—persecutions. 2. Holocaust, Jewish (1939-1945)—Poland—Personal narratives. 3. Games, Sonia. 4. World War, 1939-1945—Underground movements—Poland. 5. Poland—Ethnic relations. I. Title.
DS135.P63G36  1991
940.53'18—dc20                                    90-41886

Typography and Design by Woodmill Press, Somerville, NJ

Printed and bound by Graficromo s.a., Cordoba, Spain

*This book is dedicated to those who
have perished and whose stories
will never be told. The
book includes a diary of recollections
that capture an instant in time.
The substance of the present and the future
is an endless chain of continuity, and every
tomorrow is a harvest of yesterday.
Tomorrow means hope.*

# CONTENTS

1.  Layers of Time                        1
2.  Identity                              9
3.  The Flow of Life                     18
4.  The Last Days of Summer              27
5.  The Countdown Had Begun              39
6.  Goodbye Praszka                      51
7.  The Children of Death                61
8.  A Night to Remember                  70
9.  Twenty Garibaldi Street              80
10. You Cannot Stay                     101
11. The Plaster Saint                   118
12. Russian Roulette                    132
13. The Action                          145
14. A Train Person                      153
15. The Last Time I Saw Warsaw          165
16. My Cousin Isidor                    173
17. The Farm                            184
18. The Dog Pound                       193
19. Just Shoot Her                      203
20. A Game of Chess                     212
21. Passport to Life                    227
22. Education                           235
23. Happy Birthday                      250
24. Freedom                             258

# 1

# LAYERS OF TIME

*Have you ever tried to remember the first impression registered upon your consciousness? The very first picture engraved upon your mind — the first page of your story as it sprang seemingly from nowhere into being. Somehow it is important why your mind, in its awakening, chose this particular picture, a feeling, an instant to store for remembrance. The first deposit into a vault of memories. What was it? Try hard... Back there, upon a layer of time, I exist. I am.*

*I am in a baby buggy. Its interior is soft and white. It is a joyous day. I am being wheeled, and I can feel a balmy breeze on my face. There is a diffuse green canopy above me, the leafy branches of trees. I love the color. I am very happy.*

*My nanny, Irene, is pushing the buggy up an incline in a park. I can see her face in my memory. We have reached the summit, and I can see the lane winding down. It seems so steep to an infantile mind.*

*Suddenly, Irene gives the buggy a push and lets go of the handlebar. Alarm! No control! The buggy is picking up speed. I want to stop it, but cannot. I am angry, afraid, but more than anything else, helpless. I brace myself for a fall. I yell. The leaves above are rushing fast overhead. Oh! — I am going to crash!*

*The buggy slows down at the bottom of the hill and comes to a stop. I didn't like it at all. I hated it. My earliest memory is of helplessness.*

*From then on, memories are beginning to accumulate, like pictures on a film. The colors of nature. A meadow, green and rolling, dotted with daisies and buttercups. I am fascinated by trees, shrubs, and butterflies; the gooseberry bushes and currants, red and white. I can see bees moving upon the blossoms. On the river's edge are swamps, excitingly ominous and forbidden world of pussy willows and high grass, from where the croaks of frogs drift, piercing the dark stillness of a summer evening. On the water float lilies, so tempting and inaccessible. From my window in the morning I can see the first buds of leaves opening up in yellow sunshine like a promise of such delight, of a waking day and balmy spring breeze.*

*Mother and I walk in the forest together. It is a mysterious fairytale land. Such treasures! Cones, ferns, moss and berries, squirrels and birds.*

We are picking mushrooms. How impressive it is to be smart enough to tell the sinister poisonous ones from those we will fry in butter for dinner or string like beads and hang in the kitchen to dry.

The fall is a breathless time. Harvest. The wheat field undulates in the wind like an endless yellow wave. It is taller than I, and dense. Here and there are cornflowers, very blue and sometimes the color of wine.

In the evening we sit in the field and bake potatoes under a bonfire. The smell is very special. Sparks fly against darkness. When the flames turn into red, glowing embers, it is time to eat a feast fit for a king under the stars.

Winter comes on strong and heavy, a cold Polish winter, fierce with wind and snow. In the morning the windowpanes are opaque with ice, and upon them frost creates spectacular flower designs. No artist could outdo nature. They are lacy and thick, each different; and from without, light streams in, subdued, crystal white.

We have ceiling to floor tile fireplaces in each room. They radiate heat, and when the ornate cast iron doors are open, the coals glow blood red. It is cozy.

We get snowed in and Christmas is near. Evenings are spent making decorations for the tree. Cones are painted silver and gold. We make angels and chains out of colored papers. Nothing is purchased.

In my hometown of Praszka, there are not many stores. We do not buy our clothes. One can only purchase the material. The dressmaker comes to our home for a week at a time and makes everything we need. She sits at the footpedal sewing machine and dresses emerge. We knit our own sweaters. The shoemaker comes by and measures our feet, returns for a final fitting, and completes the job in his small hovel, which smells of leather, hot wax, and shoe polish. The butcher brings our meat when the snow is high.

We have no electricity or running water in Praszka. There is no plumbing, just a cold wooden outhouse in the courtyard. Our lamps are the kerosene type, very ornate, with a wick one can screw up or down. The town idiots are the water carriers; this is how they earn their keep. They bring in water from a pump which stands in the center of the town square.

On a wash day, the laundress comes in and works in a steamy laundry room until everything is clean. She hangs the wash on a line and returns again to iron. The iron is a steel contraption, hollow inside. A chunk of iron is heated over hot coals until it turns red. Then it is inserted into the hollow. A small latch is locked and the iron is hot. The chunk of iron is called dusza, which in Polish means "soul." I am fascinated, for, like a person, the iron has a soul. Hot and glowing at first, then cooler and paler until it becomes lifeless, drab, cold, and is removed. Much like the process of life.

Our food supplies are usually stored for the winter in the basement. There, beneath our home, is a labyrinth of passages and rooms. It is musty and dark. You enter carrying a candle, which flickers eerily, casting shadows here and there, leaving corners pitch-black where its light does not reach. There we store our potatoes, coal, and everything else. Butter is stored in large, densely packed crocks, whose surfaces have been sealed by a layer of wax.

There are heaps of carrots, barrels of sour cabbage and pickles in brine, weighted by a stone. There are wooden crates filled with sacks of beans; crocks of sugar, flour. Everything is covered snugly to protect it from rats and mice. One storage room is full of homemade beer in brown bottles and endless rows of preserves and homemade wine. Traditionally, at a certain time of the year, wine is made.

I remember lying on my back, my face against the fragrant, cool wine barrel, which usually has a small leak. My mouth is open and sweet drops of the ciderlike fluid drip in one by one. I am so relaxed, hidden from the bustle around me. Slowly, there comes a dizzy sensation, and the room seems to spin like a carousel. I remember becoming deliciously drowsy and waking later on my bed, not knowing how or when I was brought there, my head still spinning, feeling light and empty like a balloon. I didn't feel so good, but somehow it was well worth it.

Sometimes, I am sent on subterranean missions to the basement to bring something needed. Mother gives me a ring of keys, a candle, some extra matches, and a smile of encouragement. I need it, for I am scared of the basement. I can never admit to it, oh no! My honor is involved, and my mother knows it. I walk down the stairs as if into a dungeon, my heart pounding like a drum. What if suddenly there was a sound or a ghostly gust of wind blew my candle out!

Part of the basement that is not in use is locked off. No one has been there as far as I know. It used to be an escape passage a long time ago, during a war, one of many that swept through Poland. I am certain that something lurks in there. No, not a ghost. After all, ghosts are just people who died. Something much more sinister and grotesque. I do have an idea what it is, which I have not confided to anyone. They might be foolish enough to laugh, thus perhaps offending the beast and making it angry.

I imagine that down there, somewhere in the blocked off, pitch-black passage dwells a Basiliscus, the mythical serpent of death. It has a monstrous beak, clawed feet and glowing doleful eyes. It is mute, a creature of such intense venom and malevolence that the condensed hate reflected in its gaze kills any creature its eyes fall upon. I know because

*on my father's bookshelf sits an old book in a gilded jacket with a draw-
ing of the Basiliscus in it.*

*Each time I go to fetch a bottle of wine, or a jar of preserves, it be-
comes a feat of magnificent bravery on my part. A conquest of fear. And
when I emerge victorious into the light of day, candle in hand, oh, how
proud I feel.*

I must have been very young the time when the gypsies came
to town. It was a day of great excitement. In Praszka there was no
movie theater, merry-go-round or any sort of recreation other
than what we provided for ourselves. How exciting then to have
someone else entertain us, and the gypsies did! They put on a
show, played violins, told fortunes and came to our very own
courtyard looking for pots and pans to repair or scissors to
sharpen. Their faces were dark and exotic, hair black, whereas
in Praszka mostly everybody, including myself, was blond. Their
women wore bright skirts, they pitched tents and cooked strange
dishes.

It was then for the first time in my life I understood that it was
possible to leave Praszka and venture out into the world. True,
my father traveled 20 kilometers each day to his office in nearby
Wielun. My brother was away in medical school in Poznan. But
school was a place everyone eventually left for as they grew older,
and the gypsies were different. They could go anywhere, didn't
even have to return. Their little world was mobile, a world within
a world. I loved the gypsies!

I confronted my mother, demanding to know why we could
not be like them, purchase a tent and go wherever we pleased. I
was inconsolable. I remember standing in the kitchen, no taller
than the edge of the table. There was such longing in my heart.

"I want to go with the gypsies!" I shouted. Mother tried to
reason with me. Told me about all the good reasons for staying
put, like the people who loved me, my dog, my bed. In any case,
I should consider waiting a little bit longer before leaving town.
But I was adamant. "I want to go with the gypsies!" I remember
stamping my feet. "I have decided."

"All right." Mother calmly walked over to the cupboard, cut
up some bread, made a sandwich, put it in a small brown bag
and gave it to me. "You might also like to take an apple. It might
be a long time before you come back. . ." I nodded. She hugged
and kissed me goodbye. "I guess it's time for you to leave," she

said. "Of course, you know that I will miss you, but if you must go, then you are, of course, free to do it."

My honor on the line, I trudged down the spiral staircase into the hallway and out the door. Suddenly the world seemed very large, bigger than Praszka. Bigger than I ever imagined. I walked the length of the square where the road began, then turned around and came back home. I sat on the doorstep for what seemed like a very long time, bitter tears streaming down my face. No one came down to see if I really left. Oh, well. I consoled myself by eating the apple and when finished went back upstairs. Mother was getting dinner ready and the maids were setting the table. Mother returned the uneaten sandwich back to the cupboard. "Maybe next year," she said matter of factly. I brightened up, my honor was saved. "Maybe. . ."

The town square was perfectly symmetrical, each side two blocks long. All the homes were two stories high, with wrought iron balconies decorated with planters, bright with petunias. In the center of the square was a hill made into a small park, shaded by walnut and chestnut trees. On top of the hill was a statue of St. Florian, the saint of fire, because once upon a time the city, Praszka, burned down to the ground, and now it was up to the saint to prevent its ever happening again. The two water wells were just outside the park.

Our home, like the others, faced the square. A short distance to the west flowed the river Prosna, a thin, insignificant stream, winding its way past the town into a swampy meadow. But the Prosna was important because it divided Poland from Germany. On the other side, the small German village of Grenzwiese, dotted with red-roofed houses, slumbered peacefully. Each morning, if I opened my window or stood on the balcony, I could hear the high school band playing on the German side. The flutes and the drums were a familiar sound and I knew the melody by heart.

There were no cars in Praszka; only horse-drawn wagons clattered occasionally across the cobblestones. The bus to Wielun, 20 kilometers away, left each morning and came back at five with my father aboard. The square sported a tavern, the general store, the doctor's home, and the apothecary.

The tavern was a place of great interest to everybody. Each evening from time to time, its door flew open and a citizen or two was unceremoniously tossed out on the cobblestones. Sounds of great ribaldry usually accompanied this procedure, and after a while, a shamefaced wife came to pick up her wayward spouse. In Praszka there was no crime. Of course, anything that was not nailed down could be counted upon to be stolen, but the citizens wisely took all precautions. There were many fights between the more virile and energetic men, but this was a welcome distraction in a dull routine.

The apothecary held keen interest for me. I wandered there many times to see the fancy jars and canaries in cages suspended from the ceiling. In Praszka a child wandered freely all over town, knowing everybody.

The pharmacist was a rotund, bald little man with a rubicund face. He was as jolly as his prune-faced wife was mournful. They had no children, and she sat in her apartment by the window for hours on end. She never helped out in the pharmacy, which was beneath her social position in life, so I often visited with the pretty young girl who was employed there.

One day, I pushed the door open during my visiting rounds and froze in horror! There, on a couch behind the counter, was the pharmacist on top of the young clerk. They appeared to be pretty active, didn't notice me at all. Well, I did not like whatever the pharmacist was doing to the girl, and let my sentiments be known by starting to wail. Up bounced the pharmacist and his young victim, he pulling up his pants, she straightening her skirt. Both were frantically doing their best to shut me up, probably because the Missus was by her window in her apartment adjacent to the store. I was picked up, bounced, crooned to, and carried to the cage with the canary.

"There is the birdie. . ." cooed the girl, trying to distract me. I was tickled under my chin and a piece of candy was instantly stuck in my mouth.

It shut me up, but only temporarily, and I hurried home bristling with indignation. Let the fat pharmacist wait 'till I told my mom about it. She could always be counted upon to punish the guilty. I was not about to permit such a thing happening. The pharmacist was hurting the friendly lady. Imagine bouncing up and down on top of someone! Something had to be done. Preferably, he should die, I decided. Maybe, if the wind blew out his candle during a parade, it would be a bad omen and he would soon be dead. I had no doubt about it. Perhaps mom and I could even make sure by managing to somehow blow out his candle! This would surely do it!

I firmly presented my case to Mother, expecting full coopera-
tion. The yearly parade, called *Capshick*, was due on Sunday. The
men would be on horseback and the ladies would carry flowers.
In each window and on every balcony there would be a candle.
Mother and I would sneak in and. . . But I was cut short. "You
didn't see anything in the pharmacy worth mentioning" said
Mother. She wouldn't listen at all. How could it be? I stayed away
from the pharmacy and waited patiently for the *Capshick* Parade.
Now dear God would have to take over. I had no doubt that justice would prevail. I was very excited when the parade began and
cast malevolent glances at the pharmacist's window.

As it happened, he died suddenly a few weeks later, as I
believed he should. I remember his funeral and his prune-faced
widow dressed in black. "You see— someone must have blown
out his candle," I told my mother, "and that was good!"


I was growing. Mother taught me how to read and write
before I went to school when I was five. I immediately embarked
upon improving the invention of the alphabet and promptly
created my own. Now I could put things down on paper that no
one but I could read. It created a furor in our household. It was
decided that I was a genius. I felt terrible. It made me feel like a
freak. I decided to be more cautious, but Mother was wise to me.
She found out that I could memorize her operettas completely,
both music and words, Polish and Russian, if she played them for
me a few times. Everybody was flabbergasted.

Mother made me sit by the piano and sing. Corks were inserted between my fingers to stretch my grasp. I would be a
musician, a pianist, just like Mother. I had the ability, and the lessons started in earnest, every day. But in spite of the corks, my
hands were too small. I struggled to reach the keys. My life was
no longer my own. I had to make a stand. My so-called talents
were ruining my life, interfering with my freedom and my happy,
solitary, prowling routine. I refused to cooperate. I wanted to
please my mother, but there had to be a limit.

"All right, you are free." It was her way to make me happy and
I loved her fiercely for it. I now became a girl who never slept;
how could I after discovering Tarzan? It was the first book I ever
read from cover to cover, the wick of my kerosene lamp turned
up all the way. If only I could be like Tarzan, live in a tropical

jungle, swing on lianas from tree to tree. But damn, I was a girl! Well, I could always hope to be Jane.

I developed a mania for climbing trees, and worked out on the bars by the hour. I became an expert. No other child could do nearly as well. I taught myself how to do somersaults. Mother just sat on the balcony and calmly watched as I fell off branches, skinned my knees and repeatedly fell on my head. I decided that it was better to have brawn than brains, to swing from branch to branch like Tarzan, rather than memorize Russian operettas. From now on I would just be smart enough to play being dumb.

# 2

# IDENTITY

At a certain point in childhood, there develops a sense of self, an identity. It is a combination of many things. First, my name, Zofia Roza Sieradzka; my father's name, Arnold; and my mother's, Esther. My self-image, a face considered very pretty, light reddish-blond hair, blue eyes with long lashes, turned-up nose and perfect teeth. I felt myself to be much loved, considered myself to be very agile, and could do everything better than my friends. I was best at gymnastics, ran fastest in my class, and sang very well. I had complete recall for music, loved to ice skate and dance. And most importantly, I wrote poems, a source of great joy for my mother. I was completely satisfied with my image, except for a sprinkling of freckles on my nose. Mother ordered some cream from Germany to fix this shortcoming, but it just made my nose red. It peeled a couple of times and we decided that I could live with this small imperfection.

Equally important was my self-image as a person, young as I was. I expected myself to be very good and kind, but above all, honorable. Honor to me was the true measure of a person and their worth. I cannot remember how, or when, this was ingrained and became a part of my personality. It must have been very early, but it was the central part of my developing character. "Honor," in my developing mind involved a long list of values. Bravery was a part of it and any sacrifice had to be made to uphold it.

The rules went something like this: One does not flinch and there is no room for compromise where honor is concerned. It is more important even than life. One must make a stand for one's principles and if you once give something, you can never take it back, especially your word of honor. If you are obliged to do something for your country, or what you stand for, it has to be done at any cost. If someone did you a wrong, or if you suffered an insult, the score had to be settled no matter what, sooner or later. You had to be kind and give other people their rights and the benefit of the doubt, play it strictly fair, and always hold up your side of the bargain. You had to be very giving.

My identity, as it began to emerge, was fiercely uncompromising, perfectionistic, idealistic, inflexible and self-demanding. This proved to be a burden to carry later on in life. It became difficult to live up to and hard to change because so early it became a part of my person. It caused me a lot of grief. It also was most probably the reason behind my survival.

I imagine that the Japanese Kamikaze, suicide pilots of World War II, were imbued with similar conditioning. I well understand how they were able to do what they did, and how they felt. I am certain that I owe my indoctrination to my mother—she was a romantic, an idealist and very much a rebel—and also in a great measure to her friend, Doctor Szczepanski.

The Doctor and his wife had no children of their own, and both were very close friends of my parents for about twenty years preceding my birth. The doctor, like my mother, was a fine musician. They lived across the town square, and almost always shared meals with us. Each day, after dinner, the doctor came up to my room to tuck me in and spent a while telling me fairytales and tales of adventure before I went to sleep. My father never did this, he was not inclined that way. He preferred to read, listen to music and just relax.

Father was fifty years old when I was born, and my mother was very much younger. He had an office in another small town, Wielun, in a great big house which at one time belonged to my maternal grandparents, and in which my mother was born. He was a businessman and a scholar. His library contained books in four languages.

He was educated in Germany, lived in London for a while and supposedly was a genius in mathematics, quite the opposite of my mother who went to school in Russia, where she studied music and literature. His hair was snow white and I used to call him grandpa and called the doctor who was nearer in age to my mother, daddy.

I always felt as if I had two fathers, and was actually closer to the doctor. It was he who took me along on his rounds in the countryside, where I proudly took care of the horse while he went into the houses to see his patients. The doctor's wife, a beautiful lady, was somewhat aloof. I always felt that she did not much care for me, pleasant as she was. I rarely spoke with her. My mother and the doctor spent much time together, took me along on picnics and walks. I remember to this day running breathlessly ahead of them through the meadows.

The doctor was a Polish aristocrat and a Catholic, but not very religious. My parents were Jewish, but my mother considered religion to be just a form of mythology, not to be taken seriously. The doctor somehow prevailed upon her to bring me up as a Catholic, but she made it a point that I was not to be christened until I was sixteen and had a say in this decision.

In the interim, I took classes in Catechism from the nuns and went to Church with the maids on Sundays and holidays. In this respect there was a schism in my identity, the father figure and religious adherence. I was told that the doctor picked out my name but did not deliver me. This was done in our house, as was the custom, by an uncle who was my mother's brother-in-law. Even at such an early time, the doctor already was shaping my identity by having given me the name of his sister.

I did not really know that I was Jewish until one day my brother, who was in medical school and away most of the time, came home for a holiday and told me. At first I did not believe him, did not want to, but when told by mother that it was true, I had to. At that point, however, my self-image was certainly not Jewish. We had no Jewish friends and did not celebrate holidays. My prayers, and each child is inclined to pray, were to Jesus.

My self-image, so perfect to begin with, was now blemished. I was confused. I can well understand why my brother forced this issue into the open. Poland is a profoundly anti-Semitic country, and he came dramatically up against this in medical school, where there actually were pogroms and Jewish students were beaten up. In Praszka, until I went to the little schoolhouse, I was quite insulated from this. Yet, it was good that at least I was somewhat prepared, because as soon as I began to attend, I saw Jewish children beaten up daily.

Now I owed my loyalty to children with whom I had never before identified myself. The issue of honor became more than just a rule; it came to a test. I felt obligated to make a stand, agonized about it, and in all fairness had to stand up for the Jewish children when they were harassed. They were a timid lot who mostly ran, but I was conditioned to make a stand. I did, and got beaten up for the first time in my life.

I remember sneaking up the stairs full of scratches and bruises, trying to avoid mother at all costs. I soon found out that the bruises would not be the last and they became emotional as well as physical. I was in the second grade, when once having overslept, I arrived a few minutes late for class. The teacher called me forward.

"The Jewess is late again. . . " she snarled. I had to hold out my hand and was beaten with a ruler. It was the first time that I had ever been late for school.

My identity developed a serious crack. What was I? I was an excellent gymnast and was chosen by my class as best. There was a parade and since I won the first place I should be marching in the forefront. I was to do somersaults at intervals and I practiced for days.

A few days before the parade the principal came to my class and made an announcement. "Jewish children will not be permitted to attend the parade."

I was very fidgety that day during Catechism class, much as I liked the nun who taught it. The bruises were more than skin deep. I could no longer keep it to myself and had to confront my mother, who was a staunch Polish patriot. I did not cry or go into details of how I felt but simply told her that as of this day I no longer considered myself to be Polish. I watched the parade from behind a curtain and for the first time in my life, there came upon me the feeling of estrangement. It was a terrible feeling, as if a door had been slammed in my face. It was my first experience of rejection. I was not good enough. There was something wrong with me, even if I did not think so. I was not accepted.

I went to my room and did my homework. It was an essay. The next day I read it out loud in class. I made my public declaration of renouncing my Polish citizenship. I went on to say that as soon as I was able to, I would leave Poland and go to live in America, preferably in Baltimore, where Tarzan's wife was born. It was a very unpatriotic and rebellious essay, and as punishment I had to stay locked up in the school room after everybody had left. Once alone, I opened the windows and poured the ink out of every inkwell. Then I proceeded to pee into the inkwells, which was not an easy task because the openings were small. I don't remember how well I managed. I was in second grade then, and had made my stand, not just against the other children, but against the whole world, my world, which was Poland.

My sense of identity was very bruised. The nun who taught me Catechism tried to soothe my feelings. All that was needed was for me to be baptized. She promised to talk to my mother at her first opportunity. Two nuns came to tea shortly thereafter, and my mother told them that as soon as I was sixteen years old, she would have no objections. But what if I died before reaching this magical age? I would then, of course, never go to heaven. Now the door to heaven was, at least temporarily, also closed to me. I had an identity crisis. No Jewish child, unless baptized, could join the Girl Scouts. Another closed door. But I still went to Church every Sunday with the maids. The doctor would have been very upset if I had not. If our maids were not available, their maid, Veronika, led me there by the hand.

It was Easter, and I remember carrying my basket to be blessed. I dipped my finger tips in holy water and crossed myself. I surely did not feel very Jewish, but enough to have all these doors already slammed shut in my face, at least until I turned sixteen. Somehow, I knew already then, that it would be much too late. I never confided these things to the doctor. I could not, it would hurt him and I loved him too much.

I recall my father discussing this situation with my mother. Perhaps I should get a book on the history of the Jewish people. I remember him saying that if I suffered for it, I should at least have some knowledge of what it was that I had to pay such a price for.

A young woman by the name of Miss Schapiro was hired to go over the book with me. She was very pleasant and I remember her to this day. Like several Jewish people in my hometown, she had one blue and one brown eye. I remember thinking that actually I should also have one brown eye to demonstrate my blood line, because somehow I considered myself to be only half Jewish. My features and coloring were definitely Nordic. I was as typically Polish as anybody could be. My mother was a Semitic type and had hazel-brown eyes. I wondered why I did not have at least this small trait.

I slowly began to make friends with some of the Jewish children. Mostly because I was curious. In Praszka, there were very few educated people like my parents. The rest of the population were simple peasants. I had a friend by the name of Stephanie Urbach, whose father owned a lumber mill. I went to her house from time to time and observed a Jewish family. The food was different, kosher, and it smelled very good. On the dresser was a menorah. My identity now was in conflict. What really was I?

At school, things did not go very well. I was bored. While the other children were just learning to read, I wrote poetry and read most of the Polish classics like the works of Or-Ot or Mickiewicz. I had already finished the Polish version of *Faustus*. Aside from math, which I hated, there was little I could learn in school other than the lessons of self defense. Because of my sense of values, I simply could not get beaten up and meekly go home. I felt obligated to beat up anyone who raised a hand against me. I developed devious ways of paying my debts. I attacked from behind, jumped someone when they least expected it. I began to use stones, and imagination.

There was one boy in particular who had it in for me. I finally finished him off from behind with a two-by-four by dropping a coin on the ground and waiting until he would bend down to pick it up. He had a few stitches put in his scalp and never bothered me again.

Once my brother came home for a few day's vacation. He happened to look out of the kitchen window and saw me being pursued home by one of my enemies. By the time he made it down the stairs to help me, the boy caught up with me and I tore at his lip with my fingernails. It was ripped and bleeding. He, too, needed stitches and turned out to be the last of my tormentors. After that incident I was one kid nobody bothered, no matter what my religion was. I was very frightened, but I held my own, it was a matter of honor. Do or die. . .

My identity, however, was scarred. That was not how, or what, I wanted to be. It was not me at all. I wanted to be kind, to write poetry, to sing and to dance. I wanted to excel and be praised, but not for tearing lips or cracking heads. It actually surprised me that my former tormentors later made efforts to befriend me, that I even became popular. Was it because it was safer or more fun to be friends with a bully? I only became one because I had to. I was forced into it. An enemy was so forever as far as I was concerned. In my inflexible mind, there were no grey areas, only black and white. My attitude towards school was just as rigidly set and my animosity extended to anyone connected with it, especially all teachers. Due to my past experience, I expected the worst from them.

## RECOLLECTION

*The following year, in third grade, I get a new teacher from out of town. I view this stranger with suspicion, since by now I am allergic to teachers in general. I transfer my sentiments naturally onto him. My new teacher turns out to be one of these gentlemen who regularly fly out of the tavern door on weekends.*

*Aha! I am inspired, and write a three-page poem on the subject. I poke fun at my new teacher to my heart's content in fine rhythm. I go to great lengths about his flabby belly and bloodshot eyes, ringed by bruises from the latest barroom brawl. I spare no detail about his spectacular exits, headfirst on the cobblestones. One of my classmates decides that it would be great fun to steal my literary masterpiece and present it to the teacher. Now everybody is waiting to see my head roll. Of course, I expect the worst but the day goes by and nothing happens.*

*After school, the teacher passes by our house and corners me at the door. "Ah, here you are, little one. . . come and sit with me," he says with a grin. I follow him reluctantly. We find a bench in the park in the center of the square and sit down. Here it comes, I think to myself, expecting to get an earful. But instead, the teacher picks up my hand and plants a mockingly chivalrous, Polish- style kiss upon my finger tips, just like the grownups do. It is the first time such a thing has ever happened to me.*

*He looks at me with a smile and says: "May I kiss the hand of a very talented budding poet. I wish to ask your permission to let me keep your very fine poem."*

*He pulls the three, clipped-together pages out of his pocket and hands me a pencil. "Please autograph it for me." I feel my face burning with guilt and embarrassment and solemnly affix my signature with a shaking hand. "Have a good day". The teacher puts the poem in his pocket and walks off in the direction of the tavern. My conscience is black and blue, as I go home to talk about it with mother.*

## RECOLLECTION

*In the third grade I am one of the tallest children in the class. I sit in the last row, since children are seated according to height. This is ironic because I eventually grow to be only five feet tall, and stopped growing at the age of ten. I am very good at sports, gymnastics, tumbling, and distance racing. I am very active, and much to my parents concern, require only a few hours of sleep. I spend most of the night reading, but it seems to agree with me.*

*Aside from being very thin, I am very healthy. Now that I have dis-covered the classical Polish poets, I completely memorize their books. I daydream that I could someday write like my idol Or-Ot (short for Artur Opman), or Mickiewicz. I am fascinated by the flow and rhythm of words and am now seriously writing lots of poetry myself. My mother is very im-pressed and so is my teacher. I am again accused of being a genius, but make up for it by being a poet by night and a little bully by day.*

*I love the countryside. During the summer, I help take the cows to pas-ture and love to spend the day out in the meadow. But when I feel like being alone or want to ponder serious matters, I usually go to the old Jewish cemetery on the hill. I like to bring a book with me, sit on an old grave and read. The other children do not bother me here; they are afraid of ghosts. What nonsense! The only thing that scares me is the thought that there might be no ghosts at all, that this is all there is. How reassur-ing it would be to meet a ghost!*

*Mother knows that I come here; she prefers it to my roaming around the swamps. Sometimes she jokes about my grandmother, Roza, her departed mother-in-law:*

*"This is one grave you should approach with great care," she warns me. "And do not be surprised if grandmother Roza reaches out her hand and grabs your ankle while you are passing by. Surely merely a few feet of dirt cannot suppress the spirit of that lady or keep her down."*

*I am told that the day she died, a whole lot of things happened. Her portrait fell off the wall at my uncle's home in Germany. Then a border guard who owed her some money returned it white-faced the next day with a tale that her spirit visited him while alone on duty and made no beans about it: "Give it back, buddy, or I will come to see you every night."*

*Of course, I cannot vouch for how authentic it all is, but, of course, having heard all this, I hopefully do my reading on grandmother Roza's grave. One day I hear a sound, something is moving in a berry bush at the foot of the grave. I sit transfixed, book in hand, waiting. Slowly the foliage parts, a snake slithers out, raises its head and looks up at me for an instant, then unhurriedly moves on. Oh well, grandmother, you tried.*

I remember so well standing on that hill in the late afternoon as the sun was setting over Germany in the west, glowing over the red roofs, under which windows looked up at the Polish hill like sleepy eyes. There are probably no ghosts, I thought with disap-pointment. The Basiliscus does not exist either. I didn't known then, of course, but the windows of the German country homes gazing upon that Jewish cemetery may well have been the Basiliscus' eyes.

It was not unusual for girls in my particular part of the world to mature and menstruate early. I did at nine years of age. I knew nothing about this physical phenomenon; somehow, no one remembered to prepare me for it. I arrived home after my usual strenuous day of activities and discovered the symptoms. It was too horrible a happening to discuss with anyone. I was losing my life's blood. I would probably be dead in no time at all. What if it was an injury I had sustained? I found some iodine on the shelf and tried to cure myself with rather grim results. I did not come out of my room for two days. Finally, when I was still alive after this, I bypassed mother and went straight to the doctor. At least he would not faint, being a man. He found me sitting unhappily in his waiting room and ushered me in. I resignedly told him why I was there. I am certain he must have explained it sometimes during his practice to someone, but wasn't able to help me at all. Instead, he called my mother.

"Esther," he told her urgently, "get here as soon as you can, the little one has grown up on us!" That day it was explained about what was involved in being a woman. For weeks afterwards I regarded all boys in town as possible future husbands, now that I was a "grown woman." It was an absolutely sickening thought and I soon put it out of my mind.

# 3

# THE FLOW OF LIFE

Family life in Praszka, as in all small Polish towns revolved around the church for the Catholic population and around the synagogue for the Jews. The church was situated prominently on a small hill behind the city square. The white, pointed steeple was a reminder of one's responsibilities. Every respectable person was expected to make an appearance in a House of God. One had to have a religion, a sure and unshakable faith, in order to avoid going to hell when one died, where "life" eternal, thereafter, was reputed to be rather grim. It was indeed a very small price to pay to be assured for one's self a comfortable residence in heaven where the climate was surely superior.

The cross and holy water were indispensable to a person's safety and well being in daily life. To mention a few examples, there was that haunted bridge one wouldn't dare cross after dark without a handy crucifix to fend off the ghostly spirits which frequented this particular small spot upon the map of Praszka. Of course holy water prevented the devil from playing all kinds of dirty tricks upon a person. There were at least a dozen places in Praszka where frightful things happened if one forgot to make the sign of the cross, like the field behind the cemetery wall where the suicides were buried. These souls took it upon themselves to illegally enter heaven before the grim reaper issued a formal invitation, and when denied entry, hung around and made a general nuisance of themselves. Moonless nights were particularly dangerous around these parts.

Thus, even after I found out about my being Jewish, I prudently continued to wear a small, silver crucifix suspended from a chain around my neck. I felt definitely safer just in case I ever needed to rely upon its magical powers. Our three maids surely cautioned me often enough. Children who did not heed this advice asked for all kinds of trouble, especially Jewish children, who were not in God's good graces to begin with. I wonder how it was possible for me not to question these things, but then even to question meant trouble in itself.

The Jewish community also observed all kinds of intricate rituals to assure their members of a pleasant hereafter and a measure of respectability. First and foremost was, of course, faithful attendance at the synagogue and observance of prescribed days of the calendar. There were also the strict dietary laws not to be trifled with. One wrong bite of a non-kosher food and someone above in heaven was certain to have noticed and placed it on a permanent record. The rabbi's wife would be guilty of an inexcusable offense if she did not hide her hair under a wig. It appeared that "Dear God" and his helpers, of whom there had to be at least a score, kept very busy keeping track of the citizens of Praszka on both sides of the religious fence. It was then only right for us to help out and to keep a watchful eye upon each other.

I still remember the day when two uncomfortably smiling ladies called on my mother to remove her unkosher, offending dishes from the community bakery ovens, where slow cooking foods were placed to simmer over low heat overnight. They even offered to bring us some food requiring this type of preparation as a gift, so we would not feel denied or slighted.

But then, all living creatures follow rules of sorts; it is a characteristic of life. The dog howls at the moon, the cat grooms itself and the ducks fly in definite formation. One could go on and on recording this behavior, from lemmings to elephants. Thus it stands to reason that God favors the following of rules, especially by humans who have it all down in writing, after all.

It therefore had caused deep consternation to every one that my mother did not attend religious services of any kind, and neither did the good Doctor Szczepanski, when he could avoid it. These offenses, however, though serious, came to be overlooked if not forgiven after a time. After all, the doctor was respected, loved and responsible for the health of all the surrounding towns and villages. He had no professional competition in a rather large rural area, that is, with the exception of my mother.

She, too, practiced a medical science of sorts, though without a license. There was usually a steady stream of citizens coming to our door for help. Her specialties included arthritis pains, stomach ulcers, and sometimes also stubborn infections of the skin. These were tended with homemade remedies. I often participated in the gathering of ants which were soaked for a time in pure alcohol for a rub down of stiff joints. Later in life, I discovered that they were a source of formic acid, indeed a curative ingredient.

For the stomach ulcers, mother made a barley preparation which was condensed, dried and dispensed to sufferers as a soothing coating for the stomach lining. I still remember certain plants we used to gather, which seemed to work wonders in curing a nasty boil if applied properly as a poultice. There were also certain mushrooms gathered for this purpose. These were, of course, the days before Penicillin was discovered.

If someone had a tenacious chest congestion which responded to nothing else, not even prayers, mother was often called upon to help. She had a set of small glass cups which she applied to the patient's back to "draw away the bad blood." First the air was burned out of the cups by the flame of a candle. Then, they were plunked down quickly upon the skin. This created a suction and the skin under the glass became elevated and red. After a while the cups were pried off one by one making a popping sound as they came off. The treated area then looked as if it had been hugged by an octopus. It was all very interesting to observe. There never was a charge for any of the treatments but we did receive baskets of berries, loaves of butter, or fresh fruit. I have undergone this treatment, usually under protest. But mother did have a way of insisting and even the doctor was coerced to subject himself to the glass cups cure when he had a cold, in spite of loud objections.

Many people in the countryside suffered from eye infections and on Wednesdays our home served as an eye clinic. These infections were treated by the doctor. Mother usually helped out and served soup to the patients. Some of these eye diseases were considered contagious and on Wednesdays, I was not permitted to touch the banisters until they were disinfected. It is indeed interesting that my brother went on to become an ophthalmologist later in life. It also explains why mother was usually forgiven for some of her eccentricities. She also dispensed advice when needed and refereed family squabbles.

Once every week part of our house also served as a dental clinic. A Doctor Boms usually spent that day filling and pulling teeth and for a while also joined us as a guest at the dinner table. Mother eventually put a stop to this hospitality because the good doctor had poor table manners, like picking up a piece of chicken with his fingers or moving the fork from one hand to the other.

I, however, liked Doctor Boms very much. I was permitted to watch him work and was fascinated by the way he mixed the quicksilver in a tiny dish to make a filling. I usually hovered over the dental chair, staring straight into the mouth of the patient with no objections from Doctor Boms. The pulling of teeth was particularly spectacular.

In Praszka, everybody knew everybody else and I could just roam around all day, visiting fascinating places like the cobbler's hut and observing him at work. I did not need to go home when hungry; people usually offered some clabbered milk, a potato or a piece of bread. Life flowed gently in Praszka, unpleasant school adventures notwithstanding, and I grew and developed fast.

Like many of the local girls, I developed very early. At nine years of age I was almost as tall as I would ever be; five feet even. I tended to be quite slender and small-boned and in this, there was an unexpected bonus. In order to fatten me up, mother usually paid me to eat. It was a dime *(ten groszy),* for a glass of milk or a sandwich. I remember that an egg went for five *groszy*. I somehow never actually liked food for its own sake, perhaps due to a bout of diphtheria which left a bad taste in my mouth. This is also probably why I was always slender later on in life. I permitted myself to be bribed quite happily and saved enough money in my piggy-bank to purchase a bicycle and a neat pair of skates. These became my prized possessions and well worth the trouble of having had to eat.

I owned a small wooden treasure chest, where I kept a small collection of stamps, ribbons, glass marbles and a ball made of silver foil collected from candy wrappers. I kept these little treasures very neatly arranged. This was where I kept my most important possession of all, a leather bound and embroidered notebook into which I deposited my innermost thoughts and dreams; my poems. I never kept a diary, was much too perfectionistic for that. Words were not to be simply put on paper, they had to have music; had to rhyme.

The ninth year of my life heralded momentous changes in every aspect of my existence. My brother graduated from medical school and married our first cousin, Irena, who was the daughter of my mother's brother.

Mother had mixed feelings about his choice. She considered the close relationship to be genetically unhealthy, but I sensed that there was much more to it.

Mother had two sisters and a brother in the city of Wielun where she was born, only twenty kilometers away. Each had adult children whom I had never met until then. I can only speculate about the reasons for this estrangement.

It must have happened long before mother had me at the age of forty.

My brother's wedding was an elaborate affair which took a lot of planning. Gowns had to be tailor-made, and I received a pink silk taffeta dress with a huge bow. Now, all of a sudden, I began visiting Wielun. The bus trip took less than an hour and I always traveled with a small bucket in hand. Motion and gasoline fumes never failed to make me sick to my stomach, but I loved these trips in spite of it.

Wielun, unlike Praszka, had electricity and running water. It was practically a century ahead in development. There were cars on the streets, it had a hospital and people even dressed differently. My cousins made a fuss over me, and were very glad to see me. I was awed by the light switches and toilets which flushed.

My maternal grandparents house was very large. It had a circular, cobblestone courtyard which was shaped like a horseshoe. It housed several families in each wing, all of them relatives, both their residences and offices. My father's office was also located there and it was the first time I have ever seen it. It was furnished with large black leather chairs. A painting of a fierce looking tiger hung on the wall. My uncle Doctor Weltman's office as well as private quarters were located in one wing of the house. He told me about the day he came to deliver me, on one of the coldest winter days in years. He made the trip to Praszka by a horse-drawn sled, the only possible way to travel when the roads were clogged with snow. I arrived before he did, which did not matter anyway because his hands were so badly frozen he could not help at all. Doctor Szczepanski, who lived just a few houses away did not do the honors, but instead only waited anxiously, I was told, in the living room.

By the time I was nine, I spoke rudimentary German. My mother spoke it well but didn't like the language and taught me Russian instead, just enough to understand the countless ballads and songs she sang in that language.

Mother had a very beautiful voice and loved to sing. She had attended school in Russia for many years. Father enjoyed very much the years he had spent in England and consequently decided to give me English lessons. I thought it was an exotic language, very gutteral and sounding somewhat like monkey chatter. I thought that it did not lend itself at all to poetry. It was much too choppy. However, I did learn two English songs at that time. They were "God Save Our Gracious King," and "It's a Long Way to Tipperary" which I added to my multilingual repertoire.

This was also the year I first visited a fairly large city, a big step into the world. My mother's brother, whose daughter my brother had just married, took us on a one-day trip to the city of Czestochowa.

Little did I know as we drove around sightseeing in his Rolls Royce convertible, driven by a chauffeur, that in a few years I would be here again and live through the most tragic and dramatic time of my life. How strange it is that sometimes we have a glimpse of the future, but never suspect it. But then it was just a fun trip.

There were no cars in Praszka and I was the envy of all my friends as we drove through the town square. We promptly collided with a wagon full of straw. The car sustained no damage but I can still see the irate farmer chasing after us with a horse whip and yelling at the top of his voice.

The word Czesto-chowa means literally translated, "Often-Hiding." It was so named because of the hilly terrain around it which made the city appear and disappear from view as one approached near. I still remember eating a chocolate covered ice cream popsicle, the first time I ever saw such a delicacy, while we drove around the historical and famous medieval cloister called *Jasna Gora*. The translation of the name means "enlightened-mountain."

The cloister looked very mysterious and forbidding to me for I had heard a lot about it. Every year, in August, people from all over Poland came here on a pilgrimage to pay homage to the holy and famous painting of the Black Madonna which hung in the chapel. The painting was ancient and it is not known who actually painted it. Legend has it that it was St. Luke the Evangelist himself. It dated to the 14th century and was reputed to possess miraculous healing powers. It is the most holy shrine of Poland, reputed to heal the sick and restore sight to the blind. The painting bore a scar upon the face of the Madonna, inflicted by a Turkish sword during a long ago war.

I saw trolleys for the first time in my life, ornate movie theaters, spectacular (for me) shop windows and swarms of pedestrians on the sidewalks. It was even a bit frightening to imagine myself walking on such a crowded sidewalk.

Mother and I toured the city while Uncle Leizer Berkowicz attended to business and I wonder if perhaps we passed the very streets I was destined to know so well in the future. How good it is that we cannot guess the future or even imagine what it holds in store.

It was the year 1939 and the spring, like any other, spilled over the countryside. Life was more fun than ever and I was in the midst of reading a book on Greek mythology, and had just finished one by Sienkiewicz, *Quo Vadis.* My brother was doing his internship in a hospital in Wielun and mother busied herself as usual. I was beginning to develop my own opinions and ideas and thinking independently. I often took the long walk past the white and purple lilac trees lining the road leading to the Jewish cemetery. I used to like it there. It was peaceful behind the stone wall, where, on a hill in a place of honor, rested many generations of my ancestors. I found a certain fascination in wondering what they were like and what stories they could have told me about their lives and times.

From the hill I could see deep into Germany. The small town of Grenzwiese with neat, red-roofed houses, just as peaceful as Praszka, basked in the sun. It was a fine place to write poetry. I still remember the words as they came to me, though in English they do not rhyme:

> Life is mysterious.
> Serious yet sometimes naive.
> Sometimes frivolous and gay,
> Sometimes full of romance
> Full of porcelain and finery
> And the sound of music.
> But sometimes it is tenuous
> As uncertain is if made of
> Spider webs.
> Sometimes with pain and
> Suffering it is endless

And bloody.
And sometimes simply pointless.
But all of you will pass
Through life, and how yours
Will be you shall discover.

I remember sitting upon the grave of one of my long-gone relatives as I closed my notebook. "And how was yours?" I remember asking the silent gravestone.

There was a certain undercurrent, an uneasiness in the air during that spring. At dinnertime conversations were about politics and names were dropped, like Hitler, Mussolini and a British diplomatic envoy by the name of Chamberlain who always carried an umbrella and vainly pursued ever-fickle peace. Jokes abounded about this comical figure during a dinner conversation. I remember father having been warned by some of his friends from the German side of the border that he must be cautious. Germany was not safe for him to visit any longer. It rather upset him and in one of his more creative moods, he dashed off a letter to Hitler. I wonder if it was ever received... My father had a citizen's complaint to present. He did business with Germany often enough, why should he not be welcome in that country any longer. It was a disgrace!

It was about then that I made another great discovery. It was my Uncle Leon Stecki's attic. Uncle Leon was my father's cousin who owned a liquor store on the other side of the town square. In Poland, it was a business assured of foolproof success for the Poles love their vodka so much that most would die happily if they drowned in it. Uncle Leon's store was an orderly, cool place with rows and rows of bottles lining the shelves. Uncle Leon was a quiet, small man. He had a startlingly pretty wife, Matilda, who bore him three handsome sons.

The store prospered and all his sons received fine educations. The oldest, Heniek, became a physician. Stefan chose an Army career and had achieved the rank of a captain. The youngest son, Isidor, was in Posnan (Posen) where my brother graduated from medical school; however, Isidor studied pharmacology. I actually knew only Isidor because he still came home during vacations from school and I liked him very much.

Now that Uncle Leon's sons were gone, the attic had become the repository of their favorite books. There, in the dusty hideaway swathed by cobwebs was a shelf full of magic. Almost everything written about ancient history could be found in those beautifully illustrated leatherbound tomes.

I practically moved in there for a while, into an undisturbed quiet place from where I could let my imagination roam across antiquity. I entered the mysterious world of ancient Egypt, the land of the Pharaohs, of Cleopatra the beautiful queen, the hauntingly stylish drawings of almond shaped eyes, exotic faces and hieroglyphics. I gazed with wonder at the pictures of the statues of Ramses II, and the deity Idris. Nobody bothered me in the shadowy attic as I let my imagination roam through the distant places, shrouded in the murky past. I imagined the lonely caravans of camels crossing the endless expanse of sandy desert. The amphitheaters of Rome, the distant drums of long ago wars, defeats and victories. What a world had been revealed to me in Uncle Leon Stecki's attic. It had filled me with this unquenchable longing to learn more about it, and maybe someday, if I were very lucky, to see those faraway lands in person.

# 4

# THE LAST DAYS OF
# SUMMER

There is something wistful in the way I remember the soft, lazy August afternoons of that year. I felt very grown up already. Before long, I was going to be actually ten years old, no longer an insignificant single digit person, a child. I can almost see myself as I then was.

### RECOLLECTION

*I have a million plans for the future. I flex my intellect and my muscles. I am almost as tall as I will ever be. There is a rounded curve under my blouse starting already to develop and in a closet drawer there is a brassiere hopefully tucked away. My hair hangs in two braids with bright yellow or red bows at the ends. I have learned to do triple somersaults on the gym bars in the middle of the town square park under the chestnut trees.*

*Father already decided that I shall go to school in England so I can learn the cool, sensible ways of the British. In the meantime, I keep very much on the go all day. I am on the ball team and I am a very good player. I wish mother would permit me to learn how to swim. But she is very firm and intransigent about it, won't give an inch. She had a dream once that I was drowning and she could only stand by and watch helplessly as my finger tips disappeared under the murky water. Mother had never learned how to swim and perhaps had transferred her fears on to me. Consequently, I have not been permitted to even go near the water. I do, however, break the rule every now and then and venture to the river bank to wade in the shallows, to catch crayfish in my net basket. These are considered a delicacy in Praszka.*

*There is always a bunch of kids by the river but no one ventures across. There is vague talk among us about Germany being now un-friendly towards Poland and the river is the official border. On the other* side lies Germany, the foe. It is possible that even the identical pussy willows on the other side are somehow different—German. We shake our fists at the German kids across the river and they patriotically do the same. This is also new.

Aside from this it is a very ordinary summer, the sky is soft and friendly, the breeze gentle upon our faces. I pay very little attention to the talk I hear, have no time for politics; I am much too busy. The days are never long enough. I like to read and write, I have other priorities. One does not become an accomplished gymnast without making a great effort. I do my reading now; when I go to the meadow by the swamp to help watch the cattle graze. It is not my job really, but it is fun. I love to curl up on the grass; it feels so soft under my cheeks. The dogs are very efficiently taking care of the herd.

War is just a word to me; I cannot imagine it at all and feel a tinge of annoyance when it is mentioned. The subject has become tedious. My parents do not seem in a panic over it either. We live in a part of the world which rarely knew peace in the past. My parents have lived through a war already and are none the worse for it. We have coffers of expired currency left over from various occupations.

True, the soldiers will have to fight if it ever comes to pass. Praszka had been an occupied territory before. In fact, when my brother was born it was under Russia and his birth certificate is actually printed in the Russian alphabet. Then, of course, I have heard many times how my father had to leave for England so he would not be drafted into the Prussian or Austrian Army. My uncle was not so lucky, and had to serve. He tried very hard to get out of it and supposedly swallowed a bunch of tobacco to speed up his heart beat or to appear sick, but it did not work, and he was drafted. He returned home wearing a German uniform and my grandmother Roza, who died long before I was born, refused to let him into the house until he took it off. She was particularly unimpressed by the iron cross he was sporting on his chest. In fact, he had to undress in the hallway to gain entry and received his welcoming hug from his mother wearing his underwear. Well, who knows, maybe I, too, will one day have a war story to tell, maybe an amusing one like this. But I cannot honestly believe it will come to that. The world has learned from World War I and is surely more civilized by now.

There is, however, a territorial dispute taking place over the port of Gdansk (Danzig), in Germany, and it is heating up. What if they do not settle it peacefully: Is it possible that there will actually be fighting in Praszka? It is a border town after all. I lie on the soft green grass and glance over at Germany. I imagine a fierce battle taking place. Hordes of warriors on horseback approaching from both sides, sabers flashing in the *sun, the clanging of armor, shouting, and the thunder of hoofs upon the cobblestones on the streets of Praszka. Doctor Szczepanski has an old picture of himself in the parlor, very dashing in an officer's uniform, astride a horse, a sword at his side. It is very impressive.*

*I am bothered by a nagging thought that both he and my brother will be drafted. But they are both physicians, would not be involved in a bloody battle; they would care for the wounded and the sick. . . The wounded? That means there would have to be blood shed. But I do have faith in the Polish calvary. I know they are fierce fighters and very brave. . . No, Germany would not dare to attack, they would get clobbered; surely they must know better. Fighting in the streets of Praszka. . . how absurd. . . I have so much to do and the war would interrupt everything. How irritating!*

It was the last day of August. I was practicing skipping my rope, swinging it backwards and sideways as rapidly as possible, my pigtails bouncing up and down. The air felt so nice and cool already, but the sun was shining brightly, a perfect day. In the early afternoon a car drove through the town square and stopped in front of our house. A car in Praszka... it was most unusual. I ran to investigate since it did not look like my uncle's. It belonged to a family by the name of Rosenthal. I knew that they did not own an automobile. Perhaps it was rented. Both the Rosenthals sat in the back and there was a chauffeur at the wheel.

Now, what was it all about? I stopped to say hello, but mother called me in before I had a chance. Her voice sounded very urgent and strange. She was packing a small suitcase, throwing in things hurriedly and carelessly. "Get dressed quickly," she said over her shoulder, "and put on the most comfortable shoes you have. We are going away!"

"But where?" I was confused, but sensed her mood and changed quickly. She made me put on a sweater and threw a coat over my shoulders. She seemed out of breath. "I will explain later," she said curtly as we ran down the stairs. We got into the car and there was hardly room for our small suitcase. The Rosenthals had a lot of luggage, as if they were leaving for a long stay. The motor started and the car began to roll. Soon the town square was behind us. It was very confusing. Just a few minutes ago I was skipping rope and all of a sudden I was riding towards

Wielun. Obviously something big was happening. The Rosenthals looked nervous and tense, and everybody was so silent. At last mother put her arm around me.

"We have to get away from the border," she said. "It is no longer safe. We are going towards the city of Lodz further inside Poland."

"Maybe it is just a false alarm," I speculated.

"If it is, we can always come back, but if it is the real thing, we have not a minute to waste." Mother's voice was very grave. Yesterday at dinnertime, it was just the old talk about politics, nothing really new. No plans were made to get away and father was not with us. What about him, I wondered. What about everybody? But mother explained that father will have to make his own way. There was no time left to even stop and look for him.

This was an alarmist thing to do, I thought. There was no sign of panic in Praszka as we left and father had gone to his office in Wielun that morning as if nothing new was happening. But mother and the Rosenthals seemed to know something that upset them very much. Oh, well, I thought as the car was rolling along the road. I have never been to Lodz before, but have heard a lot about it. It was a much bigger city than Czestochowa, an industrial center and it would be very interesting to visit.

Mother had two sisters in Lodz; Felicia Gustadt, who was married to a surgeon, and Gucia Stein, whose husband had been an industrialist, a very wealthy and successful man. He was no longer alive but she had a large apartment there and we will visit with her. Both of my mother's sisters have children I will be able to meet.

I tried to get mother into a conversation about all this, but she seemed distracted. It was totally out of character for her to behave like this. I knew that mother never liked to leave Praszka. It was her world. Mother was a very calm person. I had never heard her even raise her voice. She surely never behaved hysterically. All of a sudden I began to worry. A chill went down my spine. But the countryside looked peaceful and tranquil, the road to Wielun so familiar, and before long we were on the outskirts of the town.

The road we traveled passed by the hospital and my brother Wladek was standing there on the steps, waiting for us. He was dressed in his white doctor's coat and we could see him before he spotted us.

The car stopped by the curb and he hurried over. Mother leaned across trying to briefly touch his hand. They exchanged a few words and I fully expected that we would linger on long enough for me to talk to him also, but there was no time and we had to shout our goodbyes. Not even ten minutes to kiss each other! I felt tears roll down my cheeks. He was running along by the car as we drove, then behind it for as long and as far as he could, waving to us. We leaned back against the seat and huddled together. It was the last time he would ever see mother and we, of course, couldn't even imagine it then.

We passed Wielun without stopping again and soon were on the main road again. All of a sudden I knew it with clarity. I had no doubts or hopes any longer. There was going to be a war. The road ahead of us was suddenly crowded with people and the car slowed down to a crawl. We were not the only ones who knew something. There was a steady stream of refugees surging forward away from the border and deeper into Polish territory. There were wagons and horses and a few cars loaded with possessions, stopping and going and stopping again. There were people on foot, pushing baby buggies and carts overflowing with possessions. Suddenly, rapidly, the road was almost impassable. No wonder we were in such a hurry, and we were already too late.

Now I had a thousand questions. Was Wladek being drafted? What will happen to Dr. Szczepanski? Where were our cousins, our aunts and uncles? Surely Uncle Leizer Berkowicz, who had a car, could have gotten on the road already. What about Irena, my brother's wife? When did father leave Wielun? But there were no answers to any of these questions.

We literally inched ahead and probably would have made better progress on foot, but it was threatening to leave the comfortable seat of the car and plunge into the dense flood of humanity. People hung on stubbornly to their possessions as if their security and identity was linked closely to the bundles they laboriously dragged along. I kept looking for a familiar face in the crowd, hoping to spot the silver-white head of my father. If only he were able to find us somehow!

Then without a warning, the planes swooped down upon us with a horrifying roar, buzzing and screeching on their way down. Horses reared and people scattered looking for cover. Then came the staccato of gunfire, a terrifying rattle punctuated by the whine and thunder of bombs falling. The ground shook, shrapnel flew past our heads, dust rose upon the wind and sud-

denly there were craters in the road. Horses fell wounded and
dead, wagons overturned across ditches on both sides of the
road. The wounded cried for help in frantic voices or just
screamed out in pain.

When the dust settled we could see many corpses littering the
torn-up road. We abandoned the car, and suddenly the war was
upon us. Not at all like I imagined it to be. No fierce battle, no
cavalry, just great machines in the sky like monstrous preying in-
sects you could not run away from. They left as fast as they appeared and although it seemed like hours, the attack took just a
few minutes. It was the first salvo of the war, but we knew that it
was just the beginning and that they will be back. We were
stunned by the lightening speed of it. Whenever later I heard the
descriptive word *Blitzkrieg* (Lightning War), being mentioned I
could see before my eyes this terrible scene.

We pushed frantically ahead, hoping to outrun the front we
imagined must be just behind us. We lost the Rosenthals somewhere along the way and it was just mother and myself from
there on. Now we knew what to expect when we heard the
ominous rumble in the sky. We ran into the ditches or the
cornfields on the sides of the road, threw ourselves down and
hugged the quivering earth trying to melt into it. When they flew
on, we kept going again, those of us who could. We skirted the
craters where the bombs fell and tried not to look at the dead
lying like rag dolls in bizarre positions. We ignored the
wounded. We had no other needs but to somehow get to Lodz as
if in that city lay salvation. We did not even think about food or
rest, just safety. But was there such a place? We had no idea what
was happening. Was the Polish Army stopping the invaders? Was
there a front?

At one point just after a strafing, a man galloped in from the
field along the road. His horse was wounded and he had to abandon it, as it was wild with pain. He sat in a ditch with us and
rested for a while. He did have some information. Wielun was hit
pretty hard. It was burning and there were many dead and
wounded. He was looking for his relatives and friends. He told us
this was an air war, but there were no Polish airplanes above in
the sky, not a one. . . I kept asking mother if the hospital could
have been hit, as if she could answer that. I am sure she wished
she knew.. . .

It is strange how quickly a person gets used to the most
unimaginable. After a while, I began to look more closely at the

dead after the strafings. There was a macabre fascination in seeing these lifeless forms, who just a few moments before were human beings just like myself scurrying, terrified, trying to live. It could so easily be myself lying there. It did not take much imagination to know that. Right in front of me, a woman lay dead, sprawled across her suitcase which had flown open and half spilled its contents. Her hand was still clutching the handle and blood trickled from her head and neck into the open suitcase where she had a fluffy Teddy Bear which must have meant enough to her to take along. Now it was turning soggy with her blood. She must have been young but now it made no difference what she ever was. Her face was frozen, eyes unseeing, legs and arms askew, but still the lifeless hand hung onto the remnant of her possessions. She must have dragged this suitcase a long time, she must have been determined and strong. . .

From that day on, I saw possessions in a different way. They took on a different meaning. How very temporary possessions were, all we had and ever will own in life was just borrowed for an earthly interlude. Nothing truly belonged to any one for ever. Even we did not belong to ourselves. I, too, had a Teddy Bear I had left at home that meant a lot to me. I wondered if holding onto that suitcase had cost the woman her life, if she could not run fast enough to take cover. I caught myself thinking that I tried to find fault with her, as if to say if she only was smarter, or it was somehow her own fault that she died because she was being greedy. It was so senseless otherwise. Somehow it would have been a relief to find her at fault. It would have been a reason; her death would have made some sense, but not really. There were others there, many of them quite dead with no suitcases to blame it on. A bullet flew at random, it did not discriminate, sometimes it even hit the dead again as if killing them twice.

Later, when the planes came, it was only strafing. No bombs fell any longer. The pilots knew they did not need to waste them on us. The machine guns did the job efficiently enough. The pilots were already getting experienced and so were we. We did not walk upon the road any longer, but along its side, just close enough to keep direction. Now they had to search us out and they swooped so low that it was possible to see the pilot's faces, the faces of monsters who killed women and children along a dusty road, but still looked remarkably human. The blood spilled onto the thirsty Polish soil and soaked into it.

Mother and I eventually arrived in Lodz. We must have been utterly exhausted but that is not what I remember most vividly about our entry. The German Army had beat us to it and was already there. The road shook under armored vehicles, tanks and cannon. The enemy soldiers moved ahead, very orderly and organized. They were obviously completely unopposed, pushing east, maybe towards Warsaw.

What makes this memory so stark was that except for the German Army, the streets were totally empty of inhabitants. There were no pedestrians on the sidewalk. Windows were closed and shuttered, doors bolted. On this street, alongside the German Army, marching upon the vacant sidewalk were two lonely civilian persons, my mother and myself. We were going in the same direction as they. Mother marched on, undisturbed by all this might.

"Do not look at them at all," she admonished me, as if not looking made us somehow invisible. I could not help myself and my gaze strayed from time to time in their direction. They wore grey uniforms, had calm faces, were quite rested looking and they ignored us completely. A woman and a girl, dirty and disheveled, carrying nothing at all, presented no threat to the German Army. On both sides of the street, the houses were mutely silent. We seemed to have walked like that a long time undisturbed and I had a good look at the enemy; an invading army bristling with might. From time to time, motorcycles whizzed by on the edge of the road past the trucks. But nowhere at all did I see any horses, not a one! There was no flashing saber, no cavalry warriors galloping ahead, nothing like I ever imagined. It was a modern, motorized army, very unromantic but devastatingly efficient.

I wonder to this day how it was that my mother dared to be the only civilian on that street or why she chose to enter the city in such a way. She seemed quite unafraid as if she denied the fact that everybody else was lying low and hiding. There was no one to ask for directions and we eventually turned off into a side street, but that too, was deserted. Lodz is a big industrial city, with tall buildings and many factories. It seemed like we walked through it forever before we found the house of mother's sister, Fela Gutstadt. In fact, I cannot imagine how mother had managed to find it. I suppose that she had been to Lodz before. It must have been a feat of desperation. We seem to have been on the road for days.

How good it felt to be welcomed with open arms, to rest, and to wash up. I found myself actually again sleeping in a white, comfortable bed. Aunt Fela, and her physician husband had had a spacious and elegant apartment, more beautiful than any I have ever seen. Her daughter, my cousin, Lilka was just a couple of years older than myself and I immediately liked her. She had curly brown hair which was very thick, and soft brown eyes. She was very pretty. She and I spoke in whispers until late, tired as I was. The war could not be over, we speculated. It had just started. There would still be fighting. The Polish Army would try to recover the city. What if poisoned gas was used? Would we survive it? How will life be now? What will happen to us? In the morning Lilka and I watched from the balcony as German planes rumbled overhead, probably on their way to Warsaw. No bombs fell but we both fretted that we would still be killed and somehow Lilka kept worrying about that poison gas she had heard so much about. What did life have in store for us now?

As it turned out, Lilka did not survive the war. She died in Bergen Belsen concentration camp, like Anna Frank. She died at the very end of the war with liberation almost in sight, of dysentery and weakness. Her mother, my Aunt Fela, survived alone and eventually emigrated to Israel. Her husband never returned from the war either. Aunt Fela became a tragic figure, despairing the loss of her daughter. She had nothing. After the war, Aunt Fela worked in a hospital in Haifa and lived in a tiny room by herself. She did what she could, at first cleaning and scrubbing toilets, any manual labor she could find. Later on, she trained to be a dietitian and continued to work in that hospital until her death in the '60s. Her only goal in life was to save enough money to be able to donate a small room in memoriam, and in the name of, her daughter Lilka. All she had left of her daughter was one little snapshot.

I remember Lilka. I remember the pretty face and the voice whispering in the dark as the two of us faced the reality of war. "Do you think we will live through it? How long will it last?" It is good that the future is always around the corner, that we do not see it until we actually get there. How often, impatiently, we wish there was a crystal ball, a magical way to see what is in store for us, what is waiting around the bend. It is just as well we cannot know.

For the city of Lodz, the war was over — no surprises, no rescue from the invasion. Germany had won. The pedestrians appeared on the sidewalks again and people made an attempt to pick up the thread of their lives. Even the streetcars began to run again. Days passed. We had enough to eat, and sat at the elegantly set table trying to act normally. It was psychologically important. Lilka and I enjoyed each other's company as much as it was possible under the circumstances.

Mother and I visited her other sister, Aunt Gucia Stein. I met both her daughters, Paula and Lucia. They were beautiful women though completely different in appearance. Paula was a redhead with freckles and Lucia had shiny black hair and startling blue eyes. Lucia was married and had a seven year old son, Jasio, blond, blue eyed, much like her handsome husband. They lived much different lives than we did in Praszka. Their apartments were elegant with intricate parquet floors and fine paintings. All the amenities that wealth brought were obvious and present. My cousin Felix was a delicate young man, and clearly effeminate. I liked him very much because of his gentle manner, but he puzzled me until Lilka, who was more sophisticated than I, explained how he was. Lucia's husband was a very witty and worldly person.

It was a very different and new world I discovered and observed with a great deal of curiosity in spite of the situation we were in at that time. I was especially fascinated by Lucia who was flamboyant and outgoing. Her hands sparkled with diamonds and her dresses were exquisite. She was very warm and laughed easily. She smothered her son with kisses and hugs and put makeup on my face just for the fun of it. She seemed so oblivious to all reality, like a princess who was always sheltered and pampered and never wanted for anything in her life. Her husband obviously adored her. To them the war was something that was just going to pass, or go away, and was not to be taken seriously.

But then Lodz fell without a shot having been fired. It happened so fast, it was hard for them to imagine how very much all was changed and different now. I already had more wisdom and experience in this respect and more worries.

We still did not know what happened to everybody in Wielun and Praszka and it was not until about two weeks later that father knocked at Aunt Fela's door. What joy it was to see him! He had started towards Lodz after Wielun was bombed and by then the roads were completely impassable and too dangerous, so he travailed cross country through the woods and back roads. At one point he was caught in a small forest with the Polish artillery on one side and German on the other. Many refugees were caught in the cross fire and the forest was decimated, the trees reduced to splinters. Eventually, it caught on fire. There were many casualties and he was fortunate to have survived.

Eventually the Polish artillery was bombed out, retreated and the Germans followed in pursuit. It was probably one of the few battles where the Polish army managed to make even a feeble stand. They had no chance with their antique cannon and horses against the motorized, modern German army and the onslaught from the air. The few civilians who survived in that forest soon found themselves behind the front lines. They were afraid to venture out or to follow too closely. It took father a long time to make it to Lodz. He was very tired. He was sixty years old, after all, and the trip had been arduous. Now we only hoped to hear from Wladek. He was with the Polish army and could be just about anywhere.

It was not long before Warsaw fell. The *Blitzkrieg* (Lightning War), was over altogether. The German soldiers, (the *Wehrmacht*) were everywhere and soon following on their heels, the real occupation forces, the SS, began to arrive. Of course, at that early stage, we did not know the difference between the two, except for the color of the uniforms and different insignia. It was not long before we found out that it was the SS we needed most to fear. They were the real masters and oppressors. At first they didn't do much but settle in place in the cities and the small towns in the country side. They appeared everywhere right from the start but did not bother us much at first. It took them a little time.

We couldn't stay in Lodz indefinitely. It was not our home, and we decided to return to Praszka. We, too, needed to pick up our lives again and surely did not know what to expect. I said goodbye to my cousins and to Lilka and we started out for home.

We traveled slowly on foot, and did not even stop in Wielun which was in shambles anyway. We hoped that Wladek will somehow manage to get in touch with us. We seemed to have walked forever, resting only when absolutely necessary. We were now very anxious to get back.

At last we arrived in Praszka and it was unscathed. The town square looked exactly the way we left it, peaceful and very small, after having visited Lodz. It was early evening and the windows glowed with light. No battle took place at the Prosna river border.

It probably took the German Army ten minutes to drive through and past the town of Praszka. There was already the chill of fall in the air and the chestnuts were falling in the small park in the town square as we crossed it. We approached our house hopefully and gratefully, tired as we were. There was our house, and the familiar wrought iron balcony. We opened the front door and went in.

We were met at the stairs by the wife of the former mayor of Praszka. She and her daughter moved in during our absence because the city hall was now occupied by a German mayor (*a Burgermeister*). The previous mayor seemed to have disappeared without a trace. He could have been killed or taken prisoner. His wife told us anxiously about how worried she was. As it was, we were fortunate that she took refuge in our house because it was being methodically stripped clean during our absence. The furniture and my mother's piano were too heavy to be carried away and the curtains still hung in the windows.

We began to wearily take stock of what was left. Much of mother's antique china was gone along with the linens, furs and clothes. It seemed the mayor's wife arrived just in time to save some remnants of the silverware and much, if not all, of the food in the basement. There was a bin full of potatoes, a barrel of sauerkraut, some beans and onions.

There was even a crock of butter preserved by a layer of hardened wax and some cooking oil. It seemed that the looters still respected the presence of the ex-mayor's wife, probably out of habit. Most of the locks on the basement doors were broken in and needed replacing.

We collapsed gratefully on the bare mattresses to rest while the mayor's wife prepared dinner for all of us. I can still remember how good it smelled. The fireplace glowed with fire and the warmth of home spread out reassuringly. It was so good to sleep in my own bed again, bare as it was. I closed my eyes in the darkness and tried to imagine that it was all just a bad dream. There was no war. It did not happen at all. I will just wake up tomorrow morning and it will be time to go to school. Father will take the bus to Wielun and life will go on as before. I began to learn how to banish bad thoughts from my mind, insulate it, and to rest.

# 5

# THE COUNTDOWN HAD BEGUN

We woke up late on the first morning of our return home. The mayor's wife and her daughter had made some hot tea for breakfast and had sliced the homemade bread. We sat down, more rested now, to eat and talk about all that had happened to us. She informed us about what was taking place in Praszka. The City Hall, which was located in my paternal grandparents' home, now sported a German flag with a swastika on it. The mayor's wife was afraid to go back there, to the apartment her family once occupied, to pick up anything. The City Jail, also located there, was already full of people who had been picked up on mere suspicions or for no reason at all. Praszka had already acquired its new administration and they were all SS, dressed in black uniforms. The town also had a new name; it was to be called Praschkau from now on. The entire district of Polish Silesia up to the river Warta was annexed to Germany proper. It was not considered occupied territory but an integral part of the Reich and renamed Warthegau. The anti-Jewish campaign already began and the Jewish shops were being closed up; expropriated. The Jews were all scared, although the administration did not yet have sufficient time to start much harassment.

The mayor's wife and her daughter had taken it upon themselves to carry some of our things to Dr. Szczepanski's house for safe keeping. It was not much, but things of sentimental value they thought we would like to preserve, like picture albums, mother's embroidery and a little silver. Later, I also asked her to take my precious book of poems there for safekeeping. It was the most important possession I had. We were cautioned against going across the town square to the doctor's house. The new "Administration" kept a watchful eye on all comings and goings and it was fast becoming inadvisable to associate with the Jews.

We should act as if we didn't even know each other because the doctor was a prominent man and very much at risk. He had already been questioned by the SS and very worried, as was anyone considered part of the so called "inteligentia." The only reason he was still free was because his services were needed.

The mayor's wife, herself, was only waiting to hear from her husband, and was fast losing hope. She was planning to leave shortly for her mother's house on a farm in a nearby village. She felt unsafe associating with Jews now, as did everyone in Praszka.

We were astounded. So much had happened so fast. Praszka was already caught in a net, enslaved. We now lived in Germany. Anyway, much of its inhabitants were of German descent and had German names. Now all these folks have become German Nationals called (*Volksdeutsche*). They all strutted around proudly as if they owned the place. They were part of the master race now, and high above the rest of us, who were plainly scared. People behaved stangely, furtively, looked over their shoulders and tried not to attract attention to themselves, particularly the Jews.

In such a small town, we got to know our SS keeper's pretty quickly. There were five of them actually in charge and they had a retinue of assistants hand picked from among the local German Nationals and occupation personnel.

There was the new mayor (*Herr Burgermeister*), who was ensconced at the City Hall, just a few of houses away. There was a Lieutenant Cebula, who was a German but whose name was actually Polish, meaning "Onion" as translated, so he must have been of Polish descent somewhere along the line.

He was quartered in a house facing the town square, along with his wife and young son. There was also a Lieutenant Weiner who lived presently just two houses away from us with his wife and two young children. Another member of the "elite" whom mother called "the clique", was a hunchback, a single man of the same rank who also took up residence at the City Hall. We called him "Heuker" which in Yiddish means a hunchback. He was particularly vicious, a sour faced menacing little man. Then, of course there was the officer of the army, the *Wehrmacht*, who was less active in local harassment activities and was stationed nearby.

The German children were already playing in the park like any other kids, but mother instructed me to keep a distance from them. I could see the young boy, Lieutenant Cebula's son, out of my window riding his bicycle, dressed in short leather pants. Now

Praszka was swarming with men in various uniforms, the soldiers in gray, the SS in black and the local police dressed in green.

The town, after all, had to be restructured to fit into the German mold in a hurry. In this respect, we were again on the front line. What ever happened to the Jews in the rest of Poland later on, had already begun to take place in the annexed district of Warthegau, the formerly Polish Silesia. Still, it took the Germans a little while to feel their way about and became well organized.

In the meantime, our little family kept a very low profile and tried to be invisible. We ventured out only when absolutely necessary and for a while I obeyed this rule, but it was very hard for me. I was still a little girl yearning for some normalcy, however minimal it could be. There, in the center of the small park, were my favorite gym bars. I couldn't resist the temptation, and went out in spite of mother's orders to the contrary. Now what could they do to me if I had a little fun? Soon I was on the bars doing a knee flip and a backwards flip just like the good old times. Before long I was surrounded by the offspring of Lieutenants Weiner and Cebula. They admired my skill and wanted to play. Would I teach them?

It is amazing how unrestrained children are. They were very friendly, especially since I spoke a rudimentary German and before long we were playing together, no questions asked. At noon Lieutenant Weiner's daughter insisted that we all go to her house for lunch. Her mother would be very pleased if we did and I just had to see her new kitten. She practically dragged me there by my hand. In the kitchen Frau Weiner was peeling potatoes just like any other housewife. She served us lunch and we played with the big German Shepard dogs in the yard. Later on I was to fear these animals very much. They were especially trained to tear people apart on command and were much included in the process of the occupation and suppression. For days afterwards, little Anna Weiner knocked on our door asking me to play. She was about my age and offered to help me practice my German. But before long, it was not possible. There was a new rule that every Jew, children included, had to wear a yellow star sewn on the front and back of everything we wore so that everybody could tell from any direction that it was a Jew they saw. After that little Anna stopped knocking at my door.

We sewed the stars on our clothes as it was stipulated because now to be caught without the stars was punishable by *death* and they couldn't just be pinned on. This made it impossible for me to go out and play. I felt self conscious, like a branded animal. My ice skates were of no use to me any longer. There was a new rule: Jewish children could not play in the town square. Mother sold them along with my bicycle to a local *Volksdeutsche* who purchased them for his daughter. Now I could only look out of my window and watch as someone else rode my bicycle and wore my skates.

It was getting cold. The winter in Poland starts very early and by October it was snowing. The hilly lanes in the park were frozen solid, but I could not skate and did not even have my sled any longer. It, too, had been sold. It was necessary because we had no money at all. Our account at the local bank had been frozen, then expropriated by the Reich. The war came so fast we never managed to withdraw our funds. Now we were destitute.

The ex-mayor's wife moved away and one day the new Burgermeister, himself, came to our house and requisitioned two rooms for his secretary, a new arrival from Germany. He chose what furniture he wanted, which included my mother's piano. The young lady was musically inclined, he said with a smile.

Now incredibly we shared our home with the German woman. She was very pleasant to be sure, had no quarrel with us at all. All she was interested in were the young German soldiers and she did like them very young, fortunately for us. This excluded anyone from the SS clique but we did have a procession of privates and corporals knocking at our door at all times of the night. Of course, the curfew did not apply to them, but only to us. Father made the trips down to the door and ushered in the callers. She had her own entrance to these two rooms which led into the hallway but insisted that the downstairs door be closed so only those she invited could come up. After a while our house resounded with laughter and German songs; it was an ongoing party until the wee hours of the morning. However, now we were no longer so invisible. True, the corporals and privates were very jovial and friendly, but eventually some of the SS also began to arrive, not to miss out on the merriment at Freulein Luise's. It was very noisy and I began to learn some of the songs by just being next door in my room.

We now desperately needed money. Mother had some jewelry left she could sell, but Praszka was hardly a market for it. Everybody was pretty much broke and we were afraid to let it be known that we had it in the first place, or it would simply be confiscated. Father did not venture out at all, it was not prudent, so mother revealed herself to have some entreprenurial talents.

There were shortages of everything in Praszka, but naphtha, which we used for our lamps, was particularly hard to get. There was no electricity in Praszka and the evenings were long and dark. I was sent across what used to be the border, to Germany, to purchase candles and naphtha in Grenzwiese. Of course, if I were caught going there, especially without the Jewish star firmly sewn onto my clothes, I would be shot. Only the *Volksdeutsche* were permitted across to what used to be the old Germany. But we needed the money so I went almost daily, dressed in my best dress and wearing my most engaging smile.

I became known in some stores in Grenzwiese and was not asked any questions. They probably thought I was a *Volksdeutsche*. Then mother sold these smuggled candles to the local Jewish people who were unable to get them at all, and surely not from the *Volksdeutsche* who avoided any contact with Jews. It was my first experience with smuggling and we made a little profit. I am full of wonder at how calmly mother sent me on such dangerous errands. She simply never knew if I would get back alive, but she kept her calm. First, they would have to catch me, she said. She must have had boundless confidence in my abilities.

I became a girl with a cause. I could help my parents to survive. I almost never ventured out of the house wearing the Jewish star. It was best that my face was not seen associated with it for Praszka was a very small town, where the local keepers soon knew everybody by sight. There were not that many of us. Mother had some faithful friends among the peasants whom she had helped so much in the past and a small reservoir of good will. I had to sneak surreptitiously into the countryside to pick up some provisions, like butter, or some eggs from our friends. We sold some and kept some. It kept us going and it was good practice for what I had to do later on in order to survive.

I learned to suppress my fears. I had my own well-mapped-out route past the swamps, which were by now frozen, into Germany. I learned to keep up my stamina when I had to trudge for miles through the snow, always using back roads or cutting straight through the fields and meadows. I stayed away from the doctor's house, but one day I was instructed that they wanted to see me.

I sneaked in the back door very happy to have a chance to see him again. We had to be so very careful. It would be the first time I would talk to him since before the war. Praszka was like a fish bowl and we were the fish.

Dr. Szczepanski had very good news for me a letter from a friend with news about my brother. He was in a city called Bialystok under the Russian occupation and he was well. I visited briefly and told them what it was like for us. They gave me a package of food and I returned carrying the good tidings. Wladek and Irena were both fine! I still remember how happy I was. Shortly thereafter it was confirmed and we actually received a letter from him. He even managed to send us a parcel of food.

But happiness was short-lived, bright as it was in the darkness which enveloped us. Things began to change in Praszka much for the worse. The SS clique formulated its plans very carefully and with great imagination and began to put them in action. First, our house was searched. By now, they knew we were considered relatively well off. Perhaps we still had something they could take away from us. Several of them came, led by the Army Lieutenant. Our house was searched thoroughly from ceiling to floor. Pillows were ripped apart, mattresses cut open, floor boards ripped up. We stood there helplessly watching it all.

They found a bottle of wine, and mother smiled, went to the kitchen and brought out several glasses. "Would you like a drink?" she asked pleasantly. Well, — they did not mind at all. They sat down among the clutter and drank the wine. They also found my sapphire ring which mother had in her pocket and which was given to me at birth by the local Countess, Chmyzowska, a close friend of my mother's. They were less threatening after they drank the wine and did not push us around. Some other jewelry was also found. Mother's gold braisollette was confiscated. They even looked inside our mouths to see if we were hiding something under our tongues. The house was a shambles by the time they left.

A couple of days later, there was again banging on our door. This time it was not friends of Freulein Luise. It was the police. They came to get Father. No explanations were given; they practically shoved him down the stairs like a criminal. He was not permitted to take anything along.

Mother and I were now left alone and badly shaken. We had no money, not even personal jewelry we could barter with. They took Father to jail at the City Hall, ironically located in the very home where he was born and raised. His ancestral home now became his prison. We were not permitted to see him, even though we lived just three houses away.

Evening came and we knew that he was there behind bars, along with several other men. We knew they subjected all of them to questioning. We knew that the so called "interrogations" were terrible, that the prisoners were beaten. We sat alone by the light of a candle I recently smuggled from Germany. Just behind the wall, Luise was having one of her usual parties accompanied by all the singing and ribaldry. It was unreal. The night dragged on oppressively, neither of us able to sleep at all.

In the morning, mother resolutely put me to work chopping cabbage to press into the barrel for sauerkraut. She placed a whole basket full of cabbage heads in front of me. We must survive she told me. We have to eat. The effort must go on no matter what, or they will get the better of us. This was the only way we could fight back, by not giving in, or giving up.

Early next day, we found out that the prisoners were still in the City Hall jail and could not stand idly by any longer. We knew it was just a temporary set up and that they usually took those who were arrested elsewhere to a prison. At least we wanted to know how Father had survived the questioning.

At last mother sent me out to see what I could do. I approached the guards respectfully. Would they please let me see my father. They tried to shake me off, but I would not give up. I pestered them, I begged. Finally, one of them felt sorry for me and gave in. But I had only a few minutes and he was not supposed to let me go inside at all. . . I went in through the gate which led to the large cobblestone courtyard. The jail was immediately on the left. I could see the men crowded in there behind the bars. There were quite a few. I approached the bars and called father's name and at last his face appeared in the barred window. He looked very pale and his silver white hair was unkempt. His voice was tight and hoarse. He told me that they expected to be taken to a prison any time now. I wanted to at least touch his hand but the guard was standing impatiently behind me. Father told me in whispers that he was beaten, they all were, one by one. His voice became almost inaudible as he said it, as if he were ashamed to admit this to his daughter, but he wanted me to know, so I could tell the other families what was going on. The guard pulled me by the shoulder. . . "Beat it now!"

Later in the afternoon, the SS loaded the prisoners on a truck and it pulled away from the City Hall. I kept seeing father's face before me, the haunted look in his usually happy blue eyes. A man who never did anything dishonest in his life was on his way to prison. We watched from behind a half-drawn curtain as the truck passed our house and headed towards Wielun. We wondered if we would ever see him again, or when. But we worried in silence, there was nothing we could do.

About a week later, mother found out that they took father to a prison in Lodz. At least we had some family there, maybe we could do something to free or contact him. Mother still had her diamond earrings. She never did tell me how she managed to hide them during the search and it was the last of her jewelry, but they were large clear diamonds, worth quite a lot. Maybe it would be possible to bribe his way out of there. She spoke to a couple of local *Volksdeutsche* she had known for years, afraid to tell them too much but trying none the less. She was so secretive about it that even I never found out the details of her efforts. At least we were glad that Wladek was not under the German occupation. We heard that the Russians, though perhaps not exactly pleasant, were not nearly as cruel. At least they did not single out the Jews for punishment.

The winter was bitter and cold. We had to somehow get by. Life had to go on. We spun cotton into a thread on a spindle and knitted sweaters. Shoes were impossible to get unless one had a fortune, and I simply outgrew mine. Now I could not even try to go anywhere to smuggle food or naphtha. I simply had no shoes. My bicycle was long gone, and we sold most of our dishes and anything of value still left in our torn up house. Luise did not speak to us at all lately, obviously she had been warned not to.

Again mother came up with an ingenious idea. Soap was another unavailable luxury, so mother decided to manufacture soap at home. She had a formula on how to make it, if only we had the necessary ingredients; — mainly lard. I am still full of wonder at mother's ingenuity. I put on my too small shoes and hobbled over to see a *Volksdeutsche* butcher by the name of Herr Utta. He had always been very friendly with mother. To our joy and surprise, he promised to help. Oh, he remembered Pani Sieradzka, she did help him when he had such bad trouble with his ulcers. Yes, he would sell us the lard. We knew that he was really taking a chance in doing so. Again, it was my job to make these trips for lard.

Off came the Jewish stars and I sneaked to the butcher shop, careful not to be noticed. I had to go across the river, to Ger-

many, for the other ingredients. My feet ached in the tight shoes
and froze in the cold snow, but we assembled all we needed,
though I developed painful ulcers on my toes. We used a wooden
box to form the cakes of soap. At first they did not come out
white enough, but we perfected the formula and even managed
to give it some scent of perfume. We were in business and it
turned out to be very profitable. Even the Poles bought the soap
from us.

Before long we had enough money to get me a new pair of
shoes from the local cobbler. What a relief that was! We were
making money hand over fist. Even Herr Utta liked to be paid
with mother's soap. We even managed to buy some gold coins
and a broach with eleven diamonds in it. We had a small home
factory working around the clock. I distributed the soap for
mother and there was never enough of it to meet the demand. I
still had to make a few trips to the old Germany from time to
time, but we were getting along just fine.

But again it was not to last. It seemed that the local clique, the
SS, were busy overtime thinking up ways to harass and demean
us. What better way to get at the local Jewish population than to
mistreat the children. Now every day all the Jewish children were
rounded up for so called "work." We carried stones at a building
site. We were whipped as we worked to carry more and to run
faster. The blows fell indiscriminately. The local Jewish women
and men were now also put to work but it was the children who
were mistreated the most. The idea was a brain child of the
Hunchback. He seemed to derive great satisfaction from watching us suffer. He could do it for hours.

One day Lieutenant Weiner took all of us to the school house
personally. We were to clear it out for the German children to
use. We carried out the small library's books and loaded them
into a wagon. Nobody needed Polish books any longer in Warthegau, and the Poles needed no education as far as the Germans were concerned. Warthegau was now Germany, after all,
and Praszka was being properly Germanized. The books were to
be used as fuel. We ran up and down the stairs with armloads
full, Jewish children carrying Polish books. "Faster!" yelled the
overseer, "faster!" Children were tumbling down the steps as
they were pushed and shoved, the stairs were full of tumbling
books and falling children, bruised and bloodied. We cleared the
entire school and then were told to begin moving the furniture.
It was bedlam. We simply were not strong enough. Suddenly and

as if from nowhere, my mother appeared. She simply walked up, took me by the hand and got me out of there. The local *Volksdeutsche* overseer was perhaps too surprised to stop her, or maybe he, too, remembered her and still respected her out of habit. Anyway, she simply took me home.

One day a woman came to our house. She was sent by Wladek, my brother, to try to smuggle us out of Praszka from under the German occupation to Bialystok in Russian occupied Poland. My brother had heard about the conditions in Silesia from some young people who made it across that border seeking asylum from the Nazi's. He paid the woman in advance to lead us across and bring us to him. We desperately wanted to go but it was a hard decision to make. How could we leave without father? Mother knew he was still alive in prison in Lodz. She could not do it. The woman picked up other people, while we sat with our backpacks ready, still agonizing over the decision up to the last minute. Finally the woman left. We stayed behind.

It was March, and the snow began to thaw. As usual, the roads were a sea of mud at this time of the year. Winter was over. We had made or had we?  All Jewish children were ordered to line up in the city square. Orders from the hunchback himself. We were each given an old spoon and were told to clean out the grass from in between the cobblestones. We were told to get down on our knees and had to pick at the mud and the dirt all day; there was, of course, no grass. A *Volksdeutsche* guard stood over us with a truncheon. We had to keep our heads down or were struck viciously. Our knees ached. It was nothing less than pure torture and was meant to be just that.

We only saw people's shoes or boots going past us as we "worked". We were not permitted to look up at all.  From time to time we heard laughter at such a spectacle.  The Polish kids were making fun of us shouting obscenities at us and were encouraged to do so by the overseer. It's amazing how infectious brutality is, how it brings out the worst in people. The torturous labour lasted all day. The pain in our knees was excruciating, not to mention the humiliation.

I dragged myself home muddy and aching at the end of that day, wondering what genius it took to conceive such an idea in the first place and wishing that mother and I had accompanied the woman scout across the border to the Russian Occupation Zone.

But mother was correct in her assumption that we needed to stay and wait, because one day, father appeared walking across the town square. He was ragged and barely limping along when we saw him from our window. We wanted to rush out to meet him, but were afraid to attract attention to all of us and just waited patiently by the door. He had walked again all the way from Lodz and we knew all to well how difficult that had been. Mother gave him a bath, and we put him to bed. He was in a terrible shape. He avoided going into details about his ordeal at the prison but we found out that the prisoners were beaten constantly. He had lost a lot of weight and thought he had suffered a heart attack or something that felt like that during one of the so called interrogations.

He had expressed regret that we had waited for him instead of accompanying the woman guide Wladek had sent to the Russian Occupation Zone while we had the opportunity. He would have been happy even if it had meant a separation for us. He had found out in the Gestapo Prison what we were really dealing with, what the Nazi's must have in store for us. He was at a loss for words to describe the bestial brutality he witnessed and experienced, but it was there, clearly imprinted in his face. He was no longer the same person. His eyes had the haunted look of someone who confronted pure evil. It was not even the fear of losing his life; the dead did not suffer after all. Father used to have a cheerful, jovial face, with almost cherubic blue eyes. He used to look quite a bit like Churchill, minus the cigar. Later on in life when ever I saw a picture of Churchill, I was immediately reminded of my father.

After his return from the Prison Camp, he had not the vaguest resemblance to his old self. His gaunt face was no longer capable of a real smile. His voice was hushed and fearful. Lodz, he told us, was a terrible place to be. The Jews were pushed into a ghetto and were under a siege. They were crowded in there, enclosed by a tall, barbed wire fence, and more people were brought in every day from surrounding communities. They were all concentrated in one small area of the city, twenty to a room. For some of the new arrivals there was simply no space at all. There was hunger there and disease and the Germans had them encaged like a herd of cattle ready for slaughter and completely at their mercy. Those who could buy their way, had left for Krakow or Czestochowa where they hoped conditions were better.

Among those who made it to the Czestochowa Ghetto was my Aunt Gucia Stein, both her daughters, son and son-in-law. They pursued the hope that perhaps the Ghetto of Lodz was an aberration, that in Czestochowa the grass was greener. But a Ghetto was a Ghetto, a place where grass could not grow. There was no space. It would have been trampled by the condensed, crowded Jews. Father was certain that the Germans had a plan. We were witnessing the implementation of only the first stages of it; there was much more to come and only they knew the full details.

There was nowhere to run, no place to hide. The Poles could not hide Jews among them. The few that might be sympathetically inclined were afraid and most simply did not want to. The penalty was execution on the spot, and deportation for any one even remotely connected with such a "crime." There was already a system of registration of all citizens of every house and every precinct. Everyone had to carry air-tight identification at all times. People were stopped and asked for it at random all the time, everywhere, especially those who did not have typically Polish features. Father most certainly did not appear Semitic, still he traveled through back roads, afraid to use any kind of public transportation or facilities. He had barely made it home.

We brought him up to date about our experiences during his absence and mother obtained some hair dye to darken his silver white hair so he would blend more into the background. It meant trouble to be noticeable or singled out. If only one could become invisible! There was always the specter of being apprehended for no reason at all and deported to a prison camp. Father knew that he could not make it if it happened to him again. I have no idea to this day how he got out of there in the first place. Miracles did not happen very often, but I knew that mother no longer had the diamond earrings. We huddled fearfully in our home afraid of today and tomorrow. The countdown had begun and it was well under way.

# 6

# GOODBYE PRASZKA

It was the spring of 1940; the sea of mud which accompanied spring in Praszka began to dry and the breeze was softer and gentle again. We had survived the first six months of the war, Father only barely so, and the future seemed murky and bleak. There was no end in sight, no end to our misery, not even hope. The German Army seemingly unstoppable, pushed ahead as if unopposed. In April, Norway and Denmark were invaded and the Allies were repulsed near Trondheim. In May, the mighty German *Wehrmacht* spilled like a tidal wave into the Netherlands, Belgium and Luxembourg. On the 14th, the *Luftwaffe* bombed Rotterdam and the Dutch Army surrendered. By the 15th there was a break through at the Meuse and by the 21st of the same month, the *Wehrmacht* arrived at Abbeville having reached the English Channel. Two days later Boulogne was captured and five days later Belgium fell and the British troops began the evacuation of Dunkirk. We read the newspapers in disbelief. Countries fell like pins in a bowling alley. The headlines shouted joyfully about the German victories, the local *Volksdeutsche* stuck them under our noses making sure we saw and heard the good news. The radios blared the German song "Tomorrow the World." Maybe it was true, but our little world had begun to shatter.

All the Praszka Jews were assembled in the town square and orders were given. We could take a minimum of personal belongings and had to leave our homes. The overseers made sure we did not remove anything of value. We were shoved and pushed and within an hour or two the Ghetto of Praszka came into being. It encompassed several small streets adjacent to the Jewish cemetery, which were vacated for that purpose. It was a dilapidated part of town consisting of old homes and shacks. A barbed wire fence sprung up, closing off streets, cutting us off efficiently from the rest of the world. Jews from surrounding hamlets and villages were herded in with us. Now the entire countryside was cleared of all Jews, including anyone of partially

Jewish ancestry. Records were searched for mixed births. The Ghetto became crowded, sometimes ten to a room, only enough space given each person to sleep upon. It was rat infested. We were forbidden to leave the enclosure; the punishment was death on the spot. The same penalty applied for unauthorized entry by anyone but the members of the SS Clique. Now they had us all concentrated and at their mercy, right under their boot.

Somehow, however, part of a road leading from the Old Germany through Poland skirted the Ghetto. We could see it clearly from our side and the traffic upon it, mostly military, tanks and trucks and the jolly smiling faces of the *Wehrmacht*, flushed with victory, our only contact with the outside world. We children watched them with fascination, sometimes we waved at them; children will be children, and often they waved back.

People get used to anything if they have to. The Ghetto began to evolve its own way of life. Everything in it revolved around survival from day to day. Food became the most important part of the struggle. We planted vegetables wherever possible; somehow obtained a few chickens. It became harder and more dangerous to smuggle food, but we did this also. My parents could not, they were too old, but I did for them and other children did also for their parents. We crawled through drainage ditches in order to get in and out. Once outside, we ran, our hearts pounding, to buy that bag of flour or potatoes. We had to chance getting killed for these simple staples. We knew we would be shot if caught but could not do without food either. The Poles were fearful of dealing with us, so if they did the prices were steep. There was no way to make money in the Ghetto, and off came the wedding bands, engagement rings and anything of value that would fetch a price. What will happen when we ran out of everything we could barter? How long will the war last? But it was just the beginning.

In time Italy declared war on France and on the 14th of June the *Wehrmacht* entered Paris! On the 25th France surrendered. In July, German air attacks against Britain had begun. In August, the *Luftwaffe* launched the greatest single day attack on Britain.

Uncle Stecki managed to get a newspaper now and then. We huddled gloomily reading the glowing headlines, England, a small island just across the channel was now our only hope. How can it ever brace itself against a power that conquered all of Europe in one clean sweep.

## RECOLLECTION

*The SS Clique is jubilant and very sure of themselves. They can now do whatever they want, need answer to none. They celebrate, get drunk, come to the defenseless Ghetto and torment us, shouting in the middle of the night Everybody rauss (out). They line us up and we must stand at attention. We are completely at their mercy. Anyone who dares to hide in the house is shot. They demand total obedience; we may not disobey an order. Women with small children, everybody stands for hours at muster. If they do not like the way you look, they strike at you with a whip across the face, wherever the whip falls. They stagger around drunkenly, guns pointing at us in drunken hands. The Heuker Hunchback is having his fun. A line of people stand, each with a yellow star sewn on the front and back; a line of yellow stars and frightened faces. When it is over, we go back to our hovels, humiliated, resigned that there is no hope for us anywhere in sight.*

*While we are out of the houses, the rats came out of their holes. They are everywhere. Under our beds. We try to kill the rats. Who knows, maybe soon we will have to catch them for food. It might come to that, anything is possible. It is quiet at last and we sleep, grateful to be safe for a few hours. Tomorrow they will be back, the SS in their black uniforms resplendent with insignia, wearing their black boots, short whips at the belts, death head and cross bones insignia to intimidate us.*

*Still, the next day we try to go on with lives, to hang on to sanity. Mother gets down on her hands and knees and scrubs the small, pantry sized room we share. We can at least have the small luxury of cleanliness. We try to be polite to each other, that, too, is important. We share what little we have. The rest of the world does not exist as far as we are concerned. We only have each other. We do not even have contact with other Jews in the other Ghettos. They might as well be in another country. We do not know what happened to our relatives in Wielun, only twenty kilometers away. They seem to have disappeared without a trace, not a word, as if they were dead and maybe they are.*

*But still Jews will be Jews and education is life itself. Even if it is against German law, and like everything else, punishable by death. Books are forbidden, but to a Jew a book is holy, like the cross to the Christians.*

I remember with wonder that we organized a school of sorts. It was taught by a teacher named Mr. Urbach. He had one useless, misformed hand but the good one turned the pages of a book like a Blackjack dealer's. The small class of which I was a part, met at the Jewish cemetery, of all places, by the grave stones of my own ancestors. There we sat on the damp ground, well hidden and we studied, a little spelling, multiplication tables, and read the forbidden books, just to keep in touch with humanity. Mr. Urbach tried so hard. He even fretted about teaching us a little Latin. One had to have some background in that! He read us stories, we had discussions. We stored our precious knowledge in our minds; notebooks were too dangerous to have and carry back and forth. They were contraband.

It was in the Ghetto that I first met Zenek Markowicz and his sister Celina. Mr. Urbach also had a son, a small, bright boy with a spirited smile; his pride and joy. The things we learned there were as important as the chickens and the potatoes. The human spirit, especially the spirit of a child had to be nourished to survive. I shall never forget Mr. Urbach.

Sometimes the SS brought friends to the Ghetto for an outing, an afternoon's diversion. They picked the most Semitic looking men or women and took pictures. There was old Mr. Matejas, the eternal Jew, with a huge hooked nose, sideburns, beard and an inevitable black Jewish frock, now in tatters. He was tall and very thin. The SS loved to photograph him as the classical Jew. He had to pray for them and smile and pose.

Lieutenant Cebula particularly liked to take pictures. He was a very talkative man when drunk, imagined himself to be profound and witty, and rarely spared his whip if we didn't look enthralled when he spouted like a two bit Shakespearean actor. The Hunchback liked to shout. We feared him the most.

In this atmosphere of oppression, we children were growing up nonetheless. It was fast becoming the only world we knew. The old one with its memories and impressions became distant and unreal. Was it possible that not too long ago we were just people like everybody else? That we had expectations and hopes? Now we were just Jews with no rights at all. It was becoming imprinted upon our attitudes. Now, if we went outside to smuggle, even though we consciously knew it had to be done, subconsciously we were experiencing guilt. Subconsciously we were already "being bad"; breaking the law... We began feeling guilty for having been born Jewish; not consciously perhaps... If someone keeps drilling into you every day while your mind is forming that you are subhuman, that you have no rights, if you see those you respect, your parents, those you obey, being humiliated daily and beaten, the young, just-forming ego, the self image of a child warps. It becomes stultified and weak. If not our parents, our teachers, then we should look up to God for justice, or even pity. And if even all-powerful God could not be relied upon to give us justice, that put the Germans beyond his law. Or perhaps even in his eyes we were "bad." He seemed to be on their side.

I remember having formless dreams about being bad. Not in words but in images. Dreams of feeling that I could not touch the lilac trees, that I reached out my hand and pulled it away, was not supposed to have such rights. There was something very wrong with a person who was not even permitted to touch a lilac tree, could not walk down the street past the barbed wire, who lived in constant fear of punishment. God would not permit it to happen otherwise. This feeling of being "bad", not good enough, subhuman, became a subconscious part of our egos, an oppressive stranglehold upon our developing personalities. Still, children will be children and the need for something positive is inherent in the young. We developed friendships based on common experiences. This was very important, and sometimes, incredibly we found something to laugh and sing about. My little friend Celina Markowicz sang us a song about the Sahara Desert. At least this seemed far enough away to sing about. Free of the Germans...

We had made it for a year and a half, though we hardly knew how, and this was a victory just to have survived. The war could not last for ever... Children have to hope.

The cemetery lessons continued, but we were more and more dispirited. How could you concentrate on spelling when the Germans were clearly winning the war?

In April of 1941, the Germans invaded Yugoslavia and Greece. On the 8th of that month, they were in Salonika, Greece. On the 13th in Belgrade and on the 18th, Yugoslavia surrendered. By the first of May, all Greece was occupied. "Tomorrow the World."

### RECOLLECTION

*Life is oppressive in the Ghetto. We hang on one day at a time. We have received news from my brother recently, a letter from Siberia! Even this cannot be as bad as the Ghetto. Still we feel very badly. There was nothing he could have done to warrant his deportation into that frozen, forsaken part of the world. He is just a young physician. Had Mother and I gone to be with him, maybe we would also be in Siberia. There is no place to run and really, there never was. The letter came just in time be-*

*cause a short time later we would have never received it. It is a miracle that we did, just by chance. Now, even a letter became as great a miracle as a loaf of bread, or an egg.*

*There is new and strange activity on the road from Germany which skirts the Ghetto. Huge processions of tanks and trucks full of Wehrmacht are passing through Praszka day and night. We hear the rumble echoing from the west. Something new is happening. We children look out from our fenced-in world at the spectacular convoys of armor. Sometimes the soldiers notice us and wave.*

*We also hear that a new policy is shaping against the Polish farmers. They are being deported and their farms are given to German Nationals. It is done at random, we hear, and not yet on a large scale. The only thing slowing the process is a lack of sufficient numbers of German Nationals ready to take over. The farmers only get permission to take a few pounds along and have to leave everything behind. They are ordered to clean and scrub their houses for the new arrivals, even to put fresh flowers on the table as a welcome. They are paid nothing, the farms are simply confiscated. It is all a part of Germanization of Silesia which now is considered Germany up to the river Warta. Occupied Poland is named the General Government under the rule of a Gauleiter (governor) Frank, who is ensconced at the Wavel, the castle of the Polish king in the city of Krakow. The Polish farmers are resettled into Occupied Poland. They also are suffering, if not as severely as we.*

*The local Clique of the SS seems lately to be strangely agitated. They are upon us more than ever. Lieutenant Cebula hints darkly during one of his drunken rantings: "A new wind is blowing a wind of change you just wait and see!" It cannot be a good wind, if it so pleases Lieutenant Cebula. We are very apprehensive. If the Poles are being deported, then what will happen to us? The Germans do not tolerate Jews on what they consider German soil; we already know that. They have deported their own German Jews. Germany is fast becoming what they call* Juden frei *(free of Jews).*

*The Hunchback has an itchy finger on the trigger during the so-called roll calls. I remember one of those in particular. It is a bright, sunny day but a harrowing one for us. It is a vicious roll call, and bullets begin to fly. Some of us panic and bolt, including myself. The hunchback is shooting drunkenly. I ran for cover across the street from where the line up is taking place. I know that there is a hole in a wall leading into a drainage ditch I can squeeze through.*

*I see to my horror that the Hunchback is right behind me in hot pursuit. "Halt!" he screeches firing his gun at me while he runs. I skirt around an open sewer pit. It is full of human refuse, it stinks and it is deep. He slows down as he reaches it. I ran behind it along the fence and hear a bullet zing past my head, but the Hunchback is too drunk and cannot aim very well. I dive into the hole and ran along the drainage ditch, completely out of breath. Of course the Hunchback does not follow me there, he has lots of easier targets. I slump to the ground exhausted, listening to the yelling from the street. I am safe, but I worry about my parents and my friends because I hear shooting. At last it is quiet again. I sit and wait to be sure.*

*It is a lovely June afternoon. There is an old newspaper by my feet, perhaps blown off the main road by a breeze, discarded by a soldier from the convoys. I read the headline in amazement. The gothic script forms large bold print. "Russia Invaded By Victorious German Army. The Troops Surge Ahead Unopposed, Shattering All Resistance." I continue reading, hardly believing my eyes. But the two countries had a pact! They both attacked Poland and divided it. I thought they were friendly towards each other. It cannot be true. I gape at the words as they filter into my mind. "The Russians are retreating with the Wehrmacht in hot pursuit". For a moment I forget about the line up and the Hunchback. Hope washes over me like a wave. I know how huge Russia is, how vast. Mr. Urbach had taught us about Napoleon, read to us about his defeat on the steppes of Russia. Didn't Hitler ever hear of Napoleon? Maybe he did not have a Mr. Urbach to teach him about it. Suddenly, I am glad that my brother and his wife are in Siberia, a long way from the fighting. I cannot imagine an army, any army, making a "clean sweep" through Siberia. They would drown in the snow.*

*I fold the dusty newspaper and hide it under my blouse next to my still fluttering heart. After a while, my legs still a little weak from the terrifying encounter with the Hunchback, I cautiously emerge from the hole into the Ghetto street. I ran home anxiously, but my parents are alright, just frightened and shaken by the violent line-up of today. We hug each other and then I spread the newspaper before them. Father reads it carefully and the news soon spreads throughout the Ghetto. People come around to see it for themselves. We speculate about it. Maybe it means hope. I have Father draw me a map to see how far Irkutsk, Siberia is from the front lines. We never thought we would rejoice about Wladek having been deported to Siberia, but now we do... Maybe he at least is safe from the Germans!*

*The small ray of happiness filters into our grim lives. We wonder what it all means. No wonder the SS Clique was lately so vicious. Maybe even they are a little bit worried about having taken on the Russian Bear. Maybe the picnic is over and the Wehrmacht will get mauled a little. In a way, we think they deserve each other. The Russian Occupation was far from benign. We have heard that many Poles have been deported to Siberia for nothing more than having been an intellectual or a prominent person, or anybody who could be a possible leader in the community. It was clearly, simply an effort to subjugate and control the Poles. Wladek was deported for just being a physician. Yet, sometimes, an ill wind blows in a small bit of good fortune.*

*The Praszka Ghetto is bursting at the seams with people brought in from adjacent areas. We are concentrated in this one spot and Father believes it is done for a definite reason. Now they can just swoop down upon us while we are caged in like cattle. Something is afoot. We children have been particularly listless and hungry most of the time. I have not even seen the town square in ages, even though it is just a minute's walk away. It might as well be in another country as far as we are concerned.*

*I am told that the* Volksdeutsche *Butcher Herr Utta now lives in our house. He occupies our apartment, both wings of it, and has been remodeling the main floor to set up his shop, where before we had two tenant shops. At least he was nice to us when we needed his help. I often try to imagine our apartment. I day dream about the high tile fireplaces radiating warmth, our cozy whitewashed kitchen. Will I ever enter it again? Maybe never, not the way things are going. The Germans have been bragging that by August they were advancing on Odessa in the Ukraine and by September had reached the outskirts of Leningrad! Maybe there is no stopping the German Army after all. Nobody can do it. They must have some superhuman strength. It means there is no hope for us in the Ghetto. In time, we will perish from hunger alone.*

*In Poland the fall swiftly turns into winter. A frigid wind howls outside, it is the coldest, most bitter winter in years. Snow is already beginning to pile up on the roof tops and the fields are white. It will not begin to melt again at any time until next spring. By December we are even freezing indoors, but it could be worse. It can always be worse! And one day it is.*

*We are called to assemble in the town square this time. Immediately we know that this is different. The entire population of the Ghetto is marched out and all of a sudden I am standing with the others in front of our house. I get to see it again at last, but under such bitter circumstances. The windows look like eyes, the drapes behind them eye lids. The face of my house gazes upon me as if with sadness.*

*This is not an ordinary line up. The entire Clique is represented, guns at the ready, the black uniforms in sharp contrast to the snow. We do not speak to each other. We must stand rigidly at attention and the whip swings constantly. I almost get hit across the face but Mother moves in front of me and absorbs the blow. She also receives an extra one for having stepped forward. I feel terrible but she whispers when she can "it hurts me less this way." In a way, it hurts me more. It is bitterly cold and the snow crunches under foot. None of us have high boots or even very good shoes.*

*We are being counted and one half of us is separated from the rest. The group we are with is lined up four abreast and marched back to the Ghetto. We are counted again and our names are registered. Then we are given five minutes to go to our apartments to get what warm clothes we can put on or a blanket. We are permitted to carry five kilo per person. We are counted again at another roll call and when all are present, the order is given: "Forward March!"*

*I wonder where they are taking us or what will happen to the other half of the Jewish population. We never manage to find out. Last look at the Ghetto... at the little rat infested room we called home for so long. The Jewish cemetery on the hill which served as my schoolhouse, all my ancestors sleeping eternally and peacefully under a white blanket of snow.*

*The dead, I think, are better off than the living. We are surrounded by dogs and guards and march once again through the town square, past our house and Father's ancestral home, now the City Hall, bedecked with a German flag. The sky is heavy and gray. It is snowing again and I see it fall softly on the wrought iron balcony of our house and on the sloping roof. I can see the heavy lace drapes in the windows, so familiar. I remember every handstitched design. I know just how it feels inside each nook and cranny. The smoke is rising from the chimney. I know my parents are glancing at the house which was their nest for all of their married life, and thinking their thoughts. Or do we even think any longer, or do we just feel?*

*We file silently past the small park in the middle of the town square. It looks like a Christmas card scene. The chestnut trees and my familiar gym bars are laden with snow. I send my thoughts home once again, let my imagination roam from room to room and say goodbye. We turn into a side street from where I can see the steeple of the old church. We march down the Kowalska Ulica, over the familiar bridge, and towards Wielun. We are silent. It takes all our strength to trudge through the snow. We continue for an hour, then turn off the main road and take another. This, too, is familiar, leading to a small forest. There are tall willow trees along the drainage ditches on both sides.*

*I think of my friends and wonder if I will ever see them again. None are a part of this group. Perhaps I am here because I am so completely developed and fully grown, they might have thought me to be older than I really am. I do not see Mr. Urbach, teacher, or the Markowicz family. In fact, most of the people marching along with us are Jews from the sur-*

rounding villages with only a small number from Praszka. There are several hundred people at least, but it is hard to count. I wonder why I do not have a sense of fear, why I am so numb. It is strange. I have this feeling of not really participating in all this. I am just an observer. It is not my body which is freezing, I am inside it and I can see through its eyes, but it is as if I were a different entity which is hiding. The feeling is disturbing and very real. I glance anxiously at Mother and Dad. He looks very tired and her face is expressionless. It takes all their energy to keep up with the silent column.  Only the German voices are being heard, prodding us ahead—"Mach schnell!!" (hurry).

We veer into another forest road, where the snow is thick and undisturbed. The world is black, white and gray.  There are fur trees at both sides of the road.  We grow more and more tired with each step. Finally, in the late afternoon, we arrive at a clearing in the woods. In its center stands a Polish farm house and a couple of barns.  The clearing is surrounded by a barbed wire fence. It is a camp maybe a labor camp, we speculate. To our surprise, there are people here already; Jews we have never met from some other small town Ghetto in Silesia. Unfamiliar faces are milling about, confused, indifferent eyes looking blankly at us. They all appear very depressed.

"Fall out!" Even our guards are tired. We mingle with the other couple hundred Jews who stand around much like cattle. We don't know where to sit and some of us just collapse in the snow. The guards clear one barn of people already settled there and assign it to us. They leave with the same dazed docility taking their blankets along. As we find out later on, they leave many of their lice behind. It is getting darker and bluish shadows fall upon the whiteness of the snow. For what reason are we here? The others cannot tell us, they do not know. They have been here for weeks already. It is everybody's guess that this is the beginning, the seeding of a labor camp to be established, because some of the men have been put to work cutting trees.  The barn is so crowded we have to take turns resting. Those with no space to lie down stand against each other inside the barn to escape the biting wind. Inside my mind a small voice is whispering, "It is bad, oh, it is bad!"

# 7

# THE CHILDREN OF DEATH

### RECOLLECTION

A person's self-awareness encompasses many things. One has a name, is an inhabitant of a certain place, an apartment, a city, a country. One is a daughter or a son, a father or a mother, a friend of someone. Then come the things we do, simple things like work, or personal care and the ritual of it. Here, in the clearing of a forest, in a still-nameless camp, all this is suddenly stripped away from us. None of the rituals apply, we have no possessions and our attachments to others are threatened. It is disorienting; we become quickly depersonalized, we become nonpersons. This is why the people here look so listless and dazed. Hundreds of us are clustered in one farm house and two barns. We cannot undress at any time, do not even have a place on the floor we can call our own. One has to take turns to lie down. Buckets of soup are brought out and deposited in the cold snow. Again we have to take turns because there are just a few bowls. After each person licks theirs clean, the next person is waiting to rinse it with snow and repeat the process. It all takes time and soon the soup is cold.

At the edge of the clearing is a simple hole in the snowy ground where we can relieve ourselves. It is difficult not to fall in. It is very cold and everything is frozen, otherwise there would be a stench. There is no chance for modesty here for either women or men. We are stripped of all our dignity. We own nothing; we have no task but this which will be forcefully assigned to us. Our time does not belong to us. There is no soap, no towels, no place to dry wet clothes or wash what is dirty.

We speculate that we are here because the Germans plan on constructing a labor camp or a concentration camp. Otherwise, we would not be milling around this enclosure. We would have been already eliminated unless they have use for us. We have heard of small Ghettos where all Jews were simply executed en masse. The instinct of self preservation is so basic

*that we experience relief at this thought in spite of the fact that we know it
will be only a small reprieve. Nobody can survive such conditions for very
long. Hunger and disease will kill us just as surely. The barbed wire
fence is not electrified as yet but even if one could escape there is nowhere
to run. The Poles would never take the chance of hiding anyone. The
frigid, below zero temperature would kill in a matter of hours. There is no
food to sustain a person, and anyone caught outside is brought back to
the "camp" and shot in front of everybody as an example. It is like trying
to run away from a burning ship in the middle of an ocean full of
sharks. There is no hope. The only thing we have plenty of is lice.*

*I walk out of the barn into the clearing to catch a breath of fresh air.
All around me the forest is very still, the trees heavy with snow. I am
struck by its beauty. An enchanted forest around a place of such horror.
Maybe this is why I am so moved by its beauty. The contrast between what
nature created against this creation of man. Still, it has a calming effect
on me, I am filled with actual pleasure of being able to see and smell the
forest as if my senses were enhanced and sharpened by impending death.*

*I meet a girl in the clearing who tells me she is sixteen years old and
from a Silesian town Ghetto, almost a replica of Praszka. She is very pretty even under these conditions, blond curly hair and cheeks pink from the
cold. She has been here for a couple of weeks and tells me that each day is
harder. I remark about how pretty she still is.*

*She smiles bitterly, "Not for long, we will rot here very fast." She has
been separated from her family, does not know where they are. All that
she knows is that her parents were simply marched away with a group of
people. I am suddenly confronted by the possibility that I, too, can be
separated from my parents. I feel terribly sorry for the girl. She looks at me
with resignation, "We have no home. . . " she tells me in a low voice. She
is very depressed but does not cry. "Nobody cries here anymore." she tells
me. I can understand what she means. A person cries to express sorrow so
someone will hear. We have no one to cry to any longer, we are all in the
same boat and nobody cares about us. Around us is the purity of the
snow and the clean scent of pines. How can the world be so beautiful?
How can there be such a pocket of sheer misery within an enchanted
forest.*

*I return to the crowded barn and find my parents who are resting on
the floor. We have little to say to each other. Later, during the night, I
literally feel the lice crawl all over my body. We do not undress and it is
hard to scratch the burning itch. We try to rest thinking how palatial our
tiny pantry-sized room in the Ghetto was. I never believed it would have
been possible to miss it, but now I wonder with envy if the other group
had been allowed to return there. I think about the food we left behind*

and how hungry we are; if only we had it now! We spend a wretched several days in that camp and I become aware that there are no children here at all.

Again a couple of SS men come accompanied by some guards. All the Praszka Ghetto Jews are lined up again, four abreast. We are counted and all accounted for. "Fall in!" yells a guard. "Forward march!" We leave the camp in the clearing and our barn behind. We do not know where we are going, all we feel is resignation and fatigue. It was hard to sleep well enough to be rested. We feel dirty. Some of us have rubbed our faces with snow but we had nothing to dry us with. Lips are chapped and eyes are red. Our stomachs feel empty and queasy from the slop they gave us under the guise of soup. Death is no longer so frightening, life seems almost worse. We do not have the spirit or the energy to fight to live; our survival instinct is blunted. Again we march through the crunchy snow. I am concerned about Father; he has been completely silent for days. Mother tries to maintain her composure. What can we say to each other? That it will get better or to have hope?

It is hard to tell without a watch how long we march but it is not very far. We make very slow progress because of the deep snow. We leave the forest and the narrow road winds itself through a snowy field. There, on a slight elevation stands another farm house. It appears to have been readied for us, it is encircled by a barbed wire fence. It is smaller than the other one was and there is no barn. We walk up the narrow path leading to the gate and enter. The house is very small, has dirt floors and is roofed with straw. Its interior is all prepared for us. It is layered by shelf like tiers made of wood. Each shelf is uninterrupted and extends all the way from the back and side walls towards the front of the room. There are a couple of meters of empty space at the entrance. There are two shelves under the low ceiling and each one is like a cave. There is a brick hearth in the front room with one large pot sitting on top of it. Next to it is a barrel of potatoes and carrots. Someone has gone to a lot of trouble to prepare this place for us, but we do not know who. There is a hole in the ground to use as a toilet just as in the other camp.

We are also greeted by the unmistakable sight of blood in the snow and surmise that the preparation work was done by Jews and that they were beaten. It must have been done while we were in the other camp. We wonder if there are several such camps scattered around. We are expected to sleep on these shelves but there is not enough space to accommodate all of us even if we are stacked like wood tightly against each other. Again we will have to take turns sleeping. Now even the barn we left in the other camp seems nice by comparison. This place would also be harder to break out of because it is surrounded by an open field rather than a forest. That is if anyone had the strength to run for it and a destination. It is so cold that even the SS lose their zest and are mostly anxious to get back home. They stomp their feet and rub their gloved hands to keep warm. They finally leave in a horse-drawn-sled and we are left in our new camp in the middle of the naked snowy plain. The frigid wind is howling unrestrained by the windbreak of a forest, blowing crisp hard snow against the walls of the house.

There is a frantic stampede to get inside where we can warm up after the march. We crawl onto the shelves and the people who got in first find themselves pushed hard against the wall. It is hard to describe the sleeping conditions. The shelves are covered with human beings tightly pressed against each other. There is not enough space to lie on one's back. When one person turns the others must also move. When any person other than the one on the edge has to get up and out, the entire row of people has to be disturbed. There is not even room enough to scratch as the lice bite. The space between the shelves is not high enough to stand up, we can only crawl. We spend our first night in our new camp. It is a small scale prototype of the huge concentration camps to come in the near future. Nobody attempts to escape. The temperature outside is below zero but inside it is warm. If you pack human bodies as tight as sardines, they will generate their own heat.

In the morning, the women boil soup upon the hearth. It is a mixture of potatoes, carrots and snow. In front of the house is a well, but it is frozen solid. We have no shortage of water, however, it is provided by melting the snow. We wonder who has thought out such a plan and quickly recognize the style and touch of the Clique. They must have stayed up nights to plan it. We are told by the Germans that we will be put to work but the weather has paralyzed everything. It is too cold even for them to direct us. We have a little rest from them at least and we do the best we can. Everybody tries to cooperate, to help each other. There are no arguments. We feel sorrow for each other, for what is being done to us and deep down we know that we cannot survive for very long. We all face death sooner or later.

Somehow we are ashamed to talk to each other. We feel like cattle; no longer human. We have not a semblance of human dignity. The feeling of shame is so overpowering we can hardly look one another in the eye. We know that whatever the Germans are planning, it will only get worse when the weather lets up. At least those who did not get enough rest at night, who had no space on the shelf can rest a little during the day. How could anybody work after a night of such discomfort? People cough and sneeze, some are sick and running a temperature. It is very hard to sleep. The place smells very bad.

Eventually the weather lets up enough for the Germans to return and we are visited by the Clique. They arrive on a sled, well bundled up. The horses snort from the cold and are covered with blankets. The SS jump off jauntily, very pleased with their accomplishment, and examine the setup. We are lined up and stand at attention. Even the Hunchback is smiling. He bares his teeth like a dog. His pointy nose is red with cold. Weiner and Cebula are both large and bulky men who resemble each other. They wear well-lined leather coats; very elegant. The haven't forgotten their warm gloves, either. The  Burgermeister is not with them, but the army lieutenant is. They walk slowly past us, stopping from time to time.

"How do you like your new quarters?" bellows Cebula. "You can see that we have new plans for all of you. A new wind of change is blowing as you will soon find out." He selects several men, including my father, and makes them responsible for keeping order. If anything goes wrong around the camp, such as an escape, they will be held responsible and shot, even if the escapee is caught. He wags his finger at my father. "Herr Sieradzki," he addresses him mockingly, "now you have an important job befitting a man of your position in life. Be sure you carry it out!" They leave without beating anyone today and we let out a sigh of relief, but are left with a worry. Father is now literally a hostage.

The weather lets up a little bit and work is assigned to us. A working party is selected and marched off to repair a nearby railroad track. Those of us left behind now have a little extra space during the day. Mother is put in charge of making the soup. She is also responsible for the provisions, which include a new supply of carrots and potatoes. I help in the kitchen, but there is not much to do. We do not peel the potatoes or the carrots, it would mean too much wastage. We rub them clean in the snow, chop and cook them.

We feel totally cut off from the rest of the world. The isolation is complete. We have no idea what is happening in the other camps or in the Ghetto, let alone in the world. I am so lucky to be together with my parents. Some are separated from their families and worry about what had happened to them. We know nothing about Praszka Ghetto. Has it been liquidated? And what about the group we left behind when the Germans marched us away? We have no way to find out. The guards answer questions with a blow across the face.

It is very difficult to keep track of time. The days blur together, but I know it is a Sunday when the guards are off and there is no work detail. It is a grey morning under a leaden sky. Around noon we hear the jingle of bells in the distance. The sled is winding its way from the edge of the forest, up the incline, towards the camp. I feel a tightness of apprehen-

*sion, a sense of entrapment. The Clique is coming again. Will there be shooting? Whom will they mistreat today...*

*We all line up in anticipation of a roll call as we know they expect us to do. All three are here today: the Hunchback, Weiner and Cebula, accompanied by a couple of guards. We can sense immediately that this is not a routine visit. Something is up. They count us and Cebula confronts us angrily. One person is missing! Did we know that! We stand mutely looking straight ahead. Father is called and ordered to step forward.*

*"Sieradzki!" screeches Cebula, "you are responsible for making sure that nobody runs away from this camp!"*

*Father stands at attention. "I did not realize it Herr Lieutenant."*

*"Well you should have!" shouts Cebula. I feel fear for my father. Will they beat him? Everybody is holding their breath, standing very still. Who could it have been? I feel a blind rage at whoever did it. Who is responsible for my father's predicament? Who dared to run away? "Let me tell you all about it!" Cebula yells at the top of his voice. "The pig was caught yesterday on the way to Praszka and shot by a patrol."*

*He must have tried to make a run for it and they shot him on the spot, I think to myself. Otherwise he would have been brought back here for a public execution. We soon find out that the fugitive was Beniek Krawiec, a seventeen-year-old boy who had been particularly fretting about the fate of his family. Poor kid could not stand it any longer. Suddenly I do not feel angry at him any more. I would probably have done the same.*

*Lieutenant Cebula slowly peels off his gloves, puts them in his pocket and takes his gun out of the holster. He savors his moment of power, obviously enjoying every minute of it. All eyes are fixed on him, he is the center of all attention and he loves it. The other members of the SS just stand around and watch. They let him have the stage. He tells Father to stand aside, next to the frozen well in the center of the yard, then turns to the assembled prisoners.*

*"Where is the town idiot?" he bellows. He knows us all pretty well by now from the innumerable previous roll calls in Praszka. He knows who is who. The town idiot, a severely retarded man, is pushed forward and stands in front of Cebula, totally confused, grinning, his eyes vacant. Cebula gives him a kick and shoves him towards my father.*

*"There, Sieradzki, is your companion. You will enter the other world with an idiot at your side. We would not want you to die alone!" The idiot now stands next to Father looking bewildered. Cebula laughs at his own joke; the gun is pointing at Father who stands very still, resigned to his fate.*

*Suddenly I cannot control myself any longer and begin to cry. Cebula turns around and looks at me. "What is the matter with you? Why are you crying?" he shouts at me.*

*"It is my father. . . " I tell him. "Sieradzki is my father!"*

*"Very well,' let's see what we can do about that," grins Cebula. "The more the merrier, ha, Sieradzki? No reason why your daughter should not join you also if she feels so badly about your being shot."*

*I am ordered to step forward and hurriedly walk over to my father's side, still crying. Mother follows me and walks over to me ignoring the lieutenant. She raises her hand and lightly strikes my face.*

*"Do not ever cry in front of a German!" she tells me in German so they too would understand. It sobers me and I calm down instantly. Then she moves to my side and stands next to me.*

*"We are now ready Herr Lieutenant," she tells him in a calm voice, "my husband, my daughter and I."*

*It is very quiet for an instant and I look at her. She stands very straight and defiant, looking straight ahead. Her Semitic face is as Jewish as a map of Jerusalem and to me she is suddenly very beautiful. There are no tears in her eyes and I am very proud to be her daughter. If we must die at least my mother gave me back my dignity. I understand that Cebula wanted to humiliate Father as well as kill him by bringing forward the poor idiot. Maybe we changed his script a little but we are still completely in his power. He holds the gun — it is still his show.*

*"Well, well, Frau Sieradzki," he addressed Mother with mocking courtesy. "It is just fine with me. It makes no difference anyhow. . . There is a new policy now, a new decree, and you Jews are all* The Children of Death*!" He smiles theatrically at us.*

*Mother looks straight at him, ignoring the pointed gun. "In the end, Herr Lieutenant, we are all the Children of Death, sooner or later. . . " She is totally calm.*

*Lieutenant Cebula gives it a little thought. He can see that we are not afraid of him any longer. It takes away his pleasure. He orders me to walk over to the side of the house near the door and stand against the wall. I walk there calmly and lean against it. It is just a few meters away. Cebula turns towards me and points his gun at me.*

*I try not to look at him or at my mother. Instead I look at the snow-white plain under a grey cloudy sky and down the incline towards the line of the forest. I am going to die, I think to myself, in front of my parents. They will have to watch it happen. Somehow, I retreat within myself; the world does not matter. I feel so isolated standing there, so lonely but I feel no fear. Nobody controls time. This is just an instant and whatever happens next, it will pass. The present will inexorably become a yesterday. It is Sunday and tomorrow will be another day. Tuesday will come no matter what. Time is relentless, it flows ahead and this moment will be soon left behind. It cannot be frozen forever. It will pass no matter what will happen next. I am only aware of the sky heavy with snow. The calm greyness around me. Is this the last picture my eyes will see? The last thoughts my mind will record? I hear a sharp report but no pain. Instead a few splinters of wood fall on my head. The bullet hit a few inches above it. I can hear the Lieutenant laugh.*

*"Now we will see, Frau Sieradzki, if I am a good shot, how well I can aim. Just relax and enjoy the show."*

*I wonder what my parents feel at this moment. I can see my mother behind the bulky figure of Cebula who is partly obscuring Father and the idiot. She is motionless; still. I see the gun in his hand pointing straight at me, the little round hole at the end of the barrel and I cannot stand to look at it. My body jerks and recoils with each report as he slowly and leisurely empties the clip. Surely he will finish me off with the last bullet. Snowflakes drift gently to the ground before me. Everything is happening in slow motion. Strange, I am still alive. . . I try not to move as the bullets hit the wooden wall around me. Then it stops, the gun is empty. At last he turns away from me. . . has changed his mind. He is not going to kill me anymore. Instead, he turns his attention again to my parents.*

*"Now," he screeches, "Sieradzki, you and your Frau will have to patrol this camp at all times. You and the others are responsible, but you are in charge. If one more person is missing next time we take count, you can be sure of what will happen to you! Next time I will aim to kill, of this you can be sure."*

*I can see Cebula put the gun back in his holster and pull on his gloves. They are walking away towards the sled and climb in at last. The sled moves ahead, the bells jingling. The gate slams shut. I am still standing against the wall, not daring to move.*

*At last Mother comes over and leads me into the small kitchen. We say nothing to each other. No joy, no jubilation at being alive. It is only a reprieve. It is harder to be alive than to be dead. I feel very, very tired. I am the first to get my bowl of soup. People speak in hushed tones as we eat standing around whereever we can.*

*The snow keeps falling, thicker now. Large fluffy snow flakes fall into the soup. I am overwhelmed by deep sadness for my parents, for all of us. If only he would have aimed to kill. I would be out of all this, it would have been all done with. Now I will suffer for a little longer, that's all. . . I wonder what date it is, but we lost count and can only tell it is a Sunday It could be December or January. Not that it matters. . . It could already be 1942. The New Year slipped in while we were not even aware of it. I wonder vaguely what is happening in the outside world. For all we know Germany might have already won the war. But then Cebula would have announced it. He would have found it too irresistible not to brag about it. We would surely have heard about it.*

*In the meantime, unknown to us on the other side of the world, on December 7th, Japanese carrier planes attacked the U.S. Naval Base at Pearl Harbor in Hawaii and nearby Army bases. On the 8th, they swooped down and attacked American air bases in the Philippines. On the 10th, they landed in the Philippines at Vigan, Aparri and Luzon. The Battle of Wake Island took place and on the 23rd, the Japanese were victorious. Now America also is embroiled in a war and Yankee blood has been spilled. There are many casualties. Closer to home, the Germans push ahead. The Manstein's offensive in the Crimea began on October 29th. In November, the Germans captured Kerch on the 16th, Rostov on the 22nd, and Kharkov on the 24th. They have been steam rolling ahead, but then the merciless Russian winter set in. On the 5th of December, the German offensive halted at Moscow. On the 6th, the Russian Winter Counteroffensive had begun. On the 11th, Germany and Italy declared war on the U.S. and vice versa.*

*But we do not know anything about these events as we huddle in the enclosure of the camp. The dense white snowflakes drift endlessly from the grey sky and pile up ever higher upon the frozen ground. For us it has already been more than two years of war with no end in sight.*

# 8

# A NIGHT TO REMEMBER

*RECOLLECTION*

*Mother, Father and I have a conference. It has been several days since Cebula made Father responsible for making sure that nobody runs away from the camp. It is an impossible task and we know it. He did not shoot to kill the last time for his own reasons. It is just another way to play with our lives, to make us squirm until he is good and ready. He is toying with us, but now that he has singled us out, we can guess the outcome. We do not have a chance either way, whether there is an escape or not. Eventually all of us will be killed, but now, if they are forming a camp, they need inmates, for the time being anyway. We are their job, their kingdom. We are the subjects; they cannot rule over the dead. Maybe letting us live a little longer appealed to the lieutenant's theatrical fantasies, his sense of drama—who can tell? The Hunchback would have shot to kill. We were just fortunate it was Cebula's show that day.*

*It is decided that now we have nothing to lose. I will be sent to Praszka to see Doctor Szczepanski. I will have to make it there somehow. It is our only chance. Maybe they can somehow provide a horse and a sled so we can get to the border of the Occupied Poland, the General Government. It is a very long shot and a very slim chance but the only one we have. We cannot make it on foot, that is certain. Mother will remove the yellow stars from my jacket and Father will have to dig a hole under the barbed wire for me to get through. It is all hard to do. Mother has no scissors, but there is a knife used to cut potatoes in the kitchen. She will have to somehow manage to remove the stars without attracting attention. We have nothing to dig with, but a tin bowl and our hands. Father decided that he must do it alone while he patrols. Otherwise, others will notice and they will fear that if the "Clique" discovers anyone missing, all will be punished. The others would stop us. I am instructed to rest. I will need to use all my strength to make it through the snow and I will need to travel after dark.*

*I am sent to rest on the "shelf" while there is some space when a number of the men and women are on a work detail. It will have to be done during the week because on a weekend the "Clique" usually descends upon us. We can expect them. They will arrive in their sled, feet snugly wrapped in warm blankets. A Sunday excursion to have some fun with the helpless Jews. They will warm themselves up along the way with schnapps, their guns loaded, waiting for murder.*

*I think about it all, while I am trying to sleep, and my imagination will not let me. I know the routine. They will beat and terrorize us to make it more exciting. They will leave right after breakfast and their wives and children will stay behind in the cozy warm homes they have confiscated from us. The "Frau" will get back from church just in time to put the Sunday cake dutifully in the oven so that it will be ready when the "breadwinner," the papa, comes back home all decked out in his resplendent black uniform after a hard day's work killing Jews, even on Sundays. Papa will romp in the snow with the children. Later on, he may even build a snowman. All the while in a converted farm house are several hundred Jews behind barbed wire, sleeping in shifts, covered with lice. The bodies of those they shot will be buried in shallow graves in the frozen earth. In the snow will be a red stain of life's blood having frozen fast. It stays bright and red until more snow falls over it. Among the living, the bruises from the blows will ache for a long time.*

*It is hard to sleep in anticipation of my mission to Praszka and the lice make me itch all over, but I am more excited than scared. Mother is right, we have nothing at all to lose. I wonder if the doctor will be able to help us, if I make it at all. Mother gets me up before the work party returns. The stars have been removed from my jacket. Father did most of the digging last night and camouflaged the spot with fluffy snow. The guards who delivered the work party leave and the evening is changing into night, first bluish grey, then dark. Still there is enough glare from the snow to see a short distance ahead.*

*I get started as early as possible. We do not kiss or hug. It would make us too sentimental. Nonetheless, the love we feel for each other seems to flow between us. We need only a look, a touch of the hand. I crawl under the wire and Mother kneels and gives me a shove forward. The snow is so cold it feels dry like salt. I come out on the other side of the wire and look back just once at my parents. It is possible that I will never see them again.*

*I trudge through the snow as fast as I can, anxious to leave the field and the camp behind me and enter the sheltering forest. At least there I will not be so visible. I can hide. I remind myself that I must walk rhythmically erratic progress will wear me out too soon; I know this from experience. I feel terribly alone and unsure of myself as I enter the forest. There are no stars tonight, it is overcast and probably it will snow. The* wind picks up snow off the ground and swirls it around in occasional gusts. It whistles between the trees. The snow is bluish and white and the sparse scrubby forest is dark and shadowy.

Dangerous as it is, I must follow the road. Otherwise, it would take too long and I would run out of strength. There is not a soul anywhere, but I can tell where the small groupings of farmhouses are by the sound of dogs baying in the distance. I realize that the road has patrols here and there and small outposts in the woods, where they could warm up occasionally. They sometimes have dogs along also, well trained and watchful. It is a sensitive area right on the border of old Germany. I am probably walking right along it right now.

So very much depends on me; I must make it! If I do not, we will perish, but worst of all, I might be killed before my parents eyes. How must they feel, how does Father feel, not to be able to protect his daughter? The wind begins to pick up as I near Praszka. It is knocking the breath out of me and I realize that I am walking against it. It is past curfew time and I can be picked up easily, but it is quiet. Nobody ventures out in such weather, not even a dog.

Now there are houses on both sides of the road and I go over the familiar bridge on Ulica Kowalska. The steeple of the church must be on my right. The Town Square is empty and quiet as the houses slumber peacefully on all four sides. The small park where I played all my life is shadowy. My own house is dark. Who is sleeping in my room right now? There is the wrought iron balcony. I know that the high tile fireplace must be radiating warmth. Suddenly I feel a sharp twinge of homelessness, an insane desire to go to my door, to touch it. But there is no time for that.

I am lucky to get to the doctor's house undetected and now must make it past the dog. The pharmacist's wife has this huge German shepherd. It usually sleeps in the hallway by the stairs. I have developed an irrational fear of dogs, since I have seen the Germans use them to attack prisoners. It is a horrifying sight. People fear dogs more than guns. I have to force myself to open the main door. The dog is there. I halt and let it sniff at me until it is satisfied. I walk up the stairs with the dog right behind me and rap at the door of the doctor's waiting room and wait.

"Who is there?" It is Veronika, the maid's voice. I tell her in a loud whisper.

"Are you alone?" she asks suspiciously.

God, they are afraid, I can tell. After a while, the doctor's wife, Pani Szczepanski opens the door and peers into the hallway to make sure I am not being followed.

"Did anyone see you come here?" I reassure her that it is safe and only then is the door opened wider. I am ushered in and it is closed again has-

*tily. There is no hearty or happy welcome. . . I follow her through the familiar rooms. This was almost a second home to me for as long as I can remember. The study is dimly lit by a flickering candle. Then I see the doctor sitting in his chair fully dressed, as if he had expected me. I rush to him. Oh, how I have missed him! He cares for me, he loves me, he is like a father to me; always was. I am overcome with emotion. But there is no response from him, not a word. He is impassively silent, like a wooden statue.*

*"It's me," I whisper urgently as if I were talking to a blind person. "It's Zosia" (diminutive for Zofia). Pani Szczapanska pours some hot tea out of a samovar, and gives it to me. Now I am aware of how cold I am. There is almost no feeling in my feet and ankles. I tell Pani Szczepanski and she pours hot water into a rubber compress bottle and gives it to me. She orders Veronika to get me a pair of woolen hand knitted leotards which stretch to fit every size. I change into them and give my old dirty ones to Veronika. I feel very guilty because I know they are crawling with lice.*

*We sit together by the flickering candle and I try to explain how it is for us. I have so little time to make them understand the incomprehensible. I try hard to be calm and articulate. They know nothing except that "they took the Jews away," but they do know the Germans. How else could you explain the unimaginable in a minimum of time. I find myself talking to the doctor. I hope he will comfort me, I love him so much. But there is no response from him at all, as if my words fell on deaf ears. Finally, I lose control and confront him. I lean urgently forward, "Please, do not be so afraid, oh please! Why are you struck dumb with fear? What is the matter with you?"*

*A little girl like myself does not understand catatonic depression. I have never seen it before. I try to get through to him with such desperation, but he only nods his head ever so slightly and when he finally speaks in a very low voice it is only to ask again if anyone had seen me come. It makes me very angry. "If I am not afraid, then why are you?" I practically shout in frustration. "Please, please do not be so afraid!" Could it be that the man I idolized so much is only a coward?*

*Pani Szczepanski motions me to follow her to the kitchen. "It is no use. . . " she tells me curtly. But she, at least, is intact and responsive. She does not put her arm around me, but then she never did particularly like me.*

*But she is going to help. There is a house near the camp. She knows the occupants well and is certain they will help us for a price. She will pay it whatever it is. All we need to do is get ourselves there. She will supply the sled and the horse. It will cost a fortune, but it means our lives, she knows. It will be done.*

*I explain that it must be tomorrow. The Nazis can come any day. They will kill Father if anything goes wrong at the camp. He is a hostage. She understands but she impresses upon me how dangerous it is if they were discovered helping us. She, too, is putting her life on the line. I have little time even to thank her. There is a snowstorm building up and I hear strong gusts of wind slamming against the windows. I wonder how I will ever make it back so many kilometers through the woods. She offers me some food but I am now too tense to eat it. There is no time. All I crave is some sugar, though I don't know why. I shove some cubes of it into my pockets.*

*Oh, yes, there is one more thing I want very badly; my leather bound book of poems! I left it with the doctor because I loved him. It is my most prized possession. It is my soul. Now I know I will never come back to their house again. I can sense it. I do not want him to have it. . . He had let me down, he is a coward. . . I cannot leave my soul in his hands.*

*Pani Szczepanski takes it out of a desk drawer and I insert it under my sweater against my body, where I know the lice are crawling. My most precious possession.*

*It is time to leave and Veronika impulsively offers to walk with me a little way, but we know it is too dangerous. . . What a silly suggestion. If she were caught with me, it would involve the Szczepanski's. I thank them for my parents and myself and go to the door. I cast one last glance at doctor Szczepanski. There is such pain in my heart. . . "Goodbye. . . " He sits woodenly in his chair in the flickering light of a candle, and does not say a single word.*

*The door slams shut behind me and the wind almost knocks out my breath. I hurry through the town square through the swirling snow. It seems to come from all directions as the wind picks it up from the ground and blows it from place to place. I am submerged in a sea of snow. I feel safe; nobody would venture out in this weather, not even the Nazis. It is fortunate that I do not walk against the wind, now, but am almost propelled by it.*

*I pass my home again and see it for the last time ever. I know this instinctively and steal glances at it as long as I can. I remember the basement and how afraid I was to go down there. Afraid of the Basiliscus and its evil eye. Goodbye Basiliscus good hunting! The wind carries me forward and I am now very anxious to get back to my parents. Mission accomplished. Maybe I have misjudged Pani Szczepanski over the years.*

*She is a good friend and a faithful person under that cool exterior. We now have a chance to escape. I have such good news for my parents!*

*Before long, I am in the forest. It is terribly cold, as if the wind reached its icy fingers all the way to my bones. I know I have to hurry if I am to survive. I throw all caution to the winds; surely no one will patrol tonight. But I am wrong. They are. . . At first I think I imagine it. Surely it is only the howling of the wind.*

*"Halt!" They are behind me. I turn around and see their shapes against the glare of the snow. There are two of them and a dog. Just off the road and out of sight a sled is parked. How could I have missed it. It is like a blow of a hammer, a sinking feeling, a stab of despair. It leaves me too weak to run. My legs are so terribly cold they feel numb, won't move. I stand still and they walk over to me. I cannot see their faces very clearly but can recognize their uniforms. They are the green clad* Shutzpolizei *(police) on patrol. They are not the SS who are probably keeping warm tonight. But I will be delivered to them in due time, of this I have no doubt.*

*They ask to see my papers and I just shake my head pretending not to understand. What is the use; I have no papers anyway. They tell me it is past curfew, as if I did not know it. They do not even pull their guns out of the holsters. They have a dog and I must look very small to them. I know I am finished. . . Now that the horse and sled, our salvation, will be available to us tomorrow, I have failed. I have not delivered, and all is lost. I walk ahead of them towards the sled in the vicious wind and it is a little quieter behind the trees. The horses are covered with blankets, but they could not have been here long. Just my luck! If only I had started out sooner or had left a little later. If I had walked through the woods instead, if only. . .*

*"Where are the rest of you?" the German wants to know and when I make believe I do not understand one of them repeats the question in Polish. I guess that he must be a* Volksdeutsche, *a German national born in Poland. I tell them I know of no one, that I am walking alone.*

*"Where are you going?" is the next question. I name a small village just ahead, but know they do not believe me. It is a winter storm, the middle of the night and after the curfew. It is so cold they give up questioning me. The dog climbs onto the sled. It must be trained to do it, and the men talk to each other in German. I can catch only a few words because of the howling wind. They obviously are on the lookout for some smugglers they expect to pass through here. They also mention an outpost.*

*The* Volksdeutsche *motions for me to follow him. There is a narrow path leading into the woods. It is a little quieter and warmer among the trees. The other patrolman stayed behind with the dog. I fish out a cube of sugar and put it in my mouth. My ears hurt from the cold even though they are protected by a shawl. A short distance away, among the trees, stands a small shack. It is a tiny, square, portable wooden structure. Its windows are wooden shutters. The flashlight makes a yellow circle on the snow as we approach the shack. We go in and the patrolman lights a kerosene lamp. There is a small iron stove in the center and it is still hot. It is very warm compared to the freezing temperature outside.*

*The patrolman shines the flashlight in my face and examines it, then indifferently pulls a chair toward the stove and sits down. He stretches his hands toward the stove. I can see handcuffs suspended from a small hook on the wall. Soon, I think, he will put them on my wrists. I am overwhelmed by despair, I tried so hard. . . but the German pays very little attention to me. My small, ragged person is no threat to him. He is obviously very cold and is much more interested in warming up a little. It is lousy duty and he probably hates it. I envy him being able to warm up his hands; my own are numb from the cold. I stand very still, not daring to move.*

*By the wall stands a small bench but I cannot sit on it. There is an old fashioned cast iron coal holder on top of it. I have seen this kind before and I know that it is very heavy. It is shaped like a flat basket with a handle and one side of it is made into a pointy spout. They are very handy for pouring coal straight into the opening of the stove. I look at it with nostalgia, it reminds me how nice it was to be in a warm, cozy place on a winter night.*

*The German is still preoccupied with his personal comfort. He removes one of his boots and rubs his foot, then thrusts it forward towards the comfortable heat. Then he begins to work on the other one. I am forgotten for the moment, I surely can be dealt with a little later.*

*Suddenly he stiffens. Above the sound of the wind, or perhaps carried upon it travels the distinct sound of a gunshot. The German jumps up and opens the wooden shutter, then swings open the door to hear better. A strong gust of wind sweeps into the shack. We can hear the dog barking and loud voices. Again a shot. The German curses and sits down on the chair again to put on his boots. I can see his face bent down with the effort.*

*Now he will handcuff me, I think, and my eyes fasten on the empty coal basket. . . My hand touches the handle and my fingers curl around it. A gust of wind rattles the wooden shutter and makes the lamp flicker. I do not think at all. My mind is a blank, but my body moves as if of its own accord. My hands clasp the iron handle and raise the heavy basket. I feel my back stiffening with the effort as I swing it high and forward and the spout connects with the head of the German at the temple. His hand reaches up to his face and I swing again, catching his fingers and part of his nose this time. He makes a growling sound and lurches for the door with me right behind him. I swing the heavy basket upside down but am unable to reach his head and catch him on the side just above his belt as he stumbles out the door and into the snow. He falls on one knee clutching his face as his other hand gropes for his gun.*

*It is hard to swing the basket with much speed, but I manage to hit him again across the face. He grips his face with both hands and I continue to strike. The yellow light of the lamp filters out of the open door illuminating a dark spot on the snow; blood. . The German is crouching in the snow and I can see that his gun is half out of his holster. I grab at it and pull it out. I point it at his head and frantically pull the trigger, but nothing happens. The safety is on. From the road come the sound of voices, yelling and the yelping of a dog.*

*I try to run but cannot. Instead, I return to the German and resume hitting him. It feels like striking a melon, a muted sound. I raise the basket as high as possible and bring it crashing down. I pick up the gun again and fumble with the safety. I do not know what to do with it, so I take it with me along with the basket.*

*I run through the forest until I reach the road further up. I let the wind propel me and lose the iron basket in a snowdrift. I keep running with the gun in my hand. Occasionally I stumble and fall. Out of breath, I let myself rest in the snow, then get up again and move as fast as possible. I feel a surge of adrenalin inside me, my heart pounds. Somehow, I find myself near a small group of farmhouses, I can hear the dogs barking. There is a hay barn at the edge of the field. I have been running the wrong way, but I have an idea where I am. The camp is just across the forest from here. I bury the gun in a snowdrift by the farm and have to go back against the wind to find the narrow path which leads across the forest to the open field on the other side. I do not feel my feet or my ankles. They are completely numb. I eat the rest of the sugar cubes and force myself forward.*

*It is getting lighter by the time I reach the field. I can see the outline of the camp on the incline. I follow the narrow road not to leave footprints, which is foolish, because the wind would probably cover them quickly enough. But I remember being told "must not leave footprints. . . "*

*I feel very disoriented. Something has happened to me. I am not Zofia any longer. I am someone else. Zofia cannot exist. It hurts me to think about her. I cannot tolerate her name. It fills me with the most aching, most profound sadness, a mourning. My parents must never know about the iron basket. It would only worry them. They would fret that the Nazis will connect it to us, swoop down upon us and wreak a terrible revenge.*

*It is almost daylight, a blue dawn; the wind has died down. My legs refuse to bend. Just a few meters further, just another small effort. I can see the figure of my father by the barbed wire waiting for me. I crawl into the burrow under the wire, now filled with soft fluffy snow. I can feel Father's hands pulling me forward. I lean upon him and we walk into the room with the hearth.*

*Mother is melting snow upon it for water. She takes off my shoes and leotards. She rubs my feet and my ankles with snow to restore circulation. Then she warms them up slowly. I have suffered frostbite and later developed permanent purplish spots on my ankles. I tell my parents in whispers about the arrangements Pani Szczepanski has made for our escape.*

*Mother looks at me sadly. "I sort of hoped that they would keep you, or maybe find a way to hide you. . . ." I tell her that they were even afraid to open the door for me at first. I tell her just a little about the doctor, not enough to worry her, and then I tell her that I brought back my book of poems with me. She seems disappointed.*

*"You should have left it there. The doctor would have kept your poems safely until the war was over. . . "*

*I reach my hand under my sweater where I inserted the book but it is gone. . . Lost somewhere in the woods or on the road. It would remain buried and rot in the snow. It was my soul and I have lost it. Zofia is lost forever. When did I last feel it against my heart? My only possession that mattered. I was so very cold I did not even feel it slip away.*

*I cannot bear to think about what happened in that shack either. I cannot understand it. It was as if some other "creature" took over. My will played no part in it. It was not my choice. I did not even think of doing it, would not have dared to.*

*We wait an extra day so that Pani Szczepanski would have sufficient time to make the arrangements. On the second night, all three of us crawl under the barbed wire one by one. Then we go to the designated farm house. My parents hide and I knock on the door. A young farmer greets me. I can tell by his friendliness that all is well. I tell him I am a friend of Pani Szczepanski and he ushers me right in and asks where are my parents. He tells us that he already has the horse and the sled ready, but we cannot leave immediately. The roads are watched carefully because there has been trouble. The Germans are on the prowl.*

"They fought it out with some of our men," the man tells us full of patriotic pride. I want to know what happened to the Polish smugglers and am informed that both have been killed. "So were the Germans," he tells me.

"Both of them?" I ask astounded. "We hear there were two of them," the farmer tells me, "But they don't tell you much, we don't know for sure. . . ." He hopes it had to do with a partisan activity, but this is questionable. Silesia is now Germany and there is little partisan activity here. The "Krauts" have made sure of that. He tells us how gradually the Polish farms here have been confiscated and handed over to German Nationals, many of whom came from the Ukraine and other Eastern Territories, where there were German settlements. Those newcomers are called Ostdeutsche (East Germans) and Silesia is full of them.

The Polish peasants mostly go to the General Government (Occupied Poland). Some of the deportees go berserk with grief, cannot bear to lose their homes and land. The Ostdeutsche do not feel at ease to have them around even as labor. They import others to do the work, who are strangers. The whole district up to the river Warta is changing its population pattern.

The farmer takes us up to his barn where we will stay in the loft until the tensions subside and we can make a run towards the border between Warthegau (Warta District) and the General Government. He will then leave us there and we will have to shift for ourselves.

He tells us that he also expects to lose his farm soon even though it is very small. It happens to be too close to a concentration camp for the Jews. He is already in the process of smuggling out some of his livestock and belongings. He has a young family to look after and they have to eat. This is probably what the smugglers the other day were caught doing. They were stealing their own belongings and this is punishable by death. The Germans want the confiscated farms intact, clean, with flowers on the table to welcome the new arrivals. They want nothing missing.

The young farmer smiles bitterly, "We can only take our clothes. Eventually there will be no Poles left here at all except for those who are needed, like craftsmen and professionals, they cannot replace."

We listen to this tale in amazement. There were all those changes taking place we never even heard about. We were not the only ones affected by this "new wind of change," as the good Lieutenant Cebula put it. We luxuriate on the clean straw in the loft. After the camp this is undreamt-of comfort. We can stretch, it is quiet. Such a peaceful evening. We feel incredibly lucky and grateful to Pani Szczepanski. The farmer brings us some thick nourishing soup made with chunks of bacon. It is a celebration. In a way we need this delay. We are exhausted. This is the *first comfortable sleep we have known in months. We don't even mind the lice. At least we can scratch as much as we need without disturbing others. We bury ourselves in the straw and it is warm after a while. We still cannot wash up or leave the loft until it is time to depart.*

*The Polish family is anxious to see us go. Every minute we stay here means danger to them. But we get a real breakfast; grits and milk. There is a small round ventilation hole in the attic and we can look out and see the road. It is Sunday and around noon we hear the bells of a sled.*

*The "Clique" is passing right in front of the house on their way to the camp as usual. We can see them. We worry what will happen when they do the roll call count and notice us gone. Will they take their wrath out on the others? Has anyone else attempted to escape? We know that some of the young men were making plans to do so while it was still possible. When the camp is enlarged eventually, no escape will be possible. They will need sentries when it gets warmer and fugitives won't freeze to death in the woods. They will then have to make the camp escape-proof, as only they know how to do*

*In about two hours the "Clique" passes again down the road on their way home. We cannot help imagining how the roll call went. We are still too close to that camp; cannot shake it loose from our minds. Our hearts are still with those we left behind, who have no chance to survive. We have such fervent hopes that in the General Government things will be better because it is Poland. Occupied of course, but it is at least not a part of Germany. If only we had left sooner, while we still had some things to barter. . . but better now than never. We talk until late and then sleep. It is our last night in Silesia, and near Praszka.*

*I lie buried in the straw and wonder how I have survived the last ten days. What has happened to me. I am changed no longer the same person at all. Something is very wrong with me and I dare not even mention this to my mother. I am puzzled about what happened in the guard post shack. Somewhere there is blood frozen in the snow. There is a leather-bound book of poetry rotting in the woods. There are bullets lodged in the wooden wall of the camp and there, down the road ten minutes away, is the camp itself. The lice are crawling all over my body, and I am Zofia no longer. The last night in Silesia passes slowly.*

*We rest one more day and the next evening after dark we climb into the sled. It is a long ride to the border. We do not dare take the main roads but Warthegau is a flat country. The fields are frozen and hard. The sled moves easily and the Polish farmer knows the way having traveled there before. It is night, but the snow glare makes it possible to see and we make progress. The further away we are, the safer it will be. All the happenings fall like stones into the depth of my consciousness and sink to the bottom.*

*Under the cover of darkness we are leaving Silesia my home. But before we are out of there, the local Poles manage to say a final goodbye. Suddenly as if from nowhere, a group of men come out of the darkness. The sled comes to a halt and we are surrounded.*

*At first we think they are Germans. They search us for valuables and take away the little money Father still has in his pocket. They are very disappointed until they find Father's pocket watch. It is gold and they cheer up somewhat. We feel even grateful they do not take the time to turn us in. Maybe even they are a little fearful of the Nazis after all. It happens to be past curfew time and they also would be in trouble. Strangely, they do not search our driver or threaten to take his horse away. In fact, we have the distinct impression that they seem to know him.*

*At daybreak, we are deposited in a small town at the border of the General Government. All we have now is the filthy rags, crawling with lice on our backs. We do not even have change in our pockets. Father writes a note to Pani Szczepanska with a code word to tell her we are safe, that the driver completed his task and he may be paid. He supplies us with the paper and pencil because we do not even have that. We are glad to be rid of him; we no longer trust him after our encounter with the Poles. We suspect that it was staged. They seemed to know exactly where to intercept us. We stand forlornly on the icy street. Now we must somehow cross the border.*

*This small town turns out to be a sort of cross roads. It has a small Ghetto and we manage to enter it. We ran into some Jews from Praszka there, also on their way to the sanctuary of the General Government. They share their food with us and tell us that Praszka Ghetto has been liquidated. It is no more. They know that some of the people we knew have been rounded up and shot by the Hunchback, Cebula and Weiner.*

*I ran into my little friend Stephanie Urbach. Her mother is not well and cannot manage to cross the border. But we have to take the chance. We have no money and our only hope is that my mother's sister, Aunt Stein is in Czestochowa. She will help us if she can, will share with us what little she has. Mother has no doubt about it.*

*We run the border the next day. It is not very tightly guarded. From time to time the guards catch and shoot a few people, but otherwise it is possible to get across. We are told that it fits the plans of the Germans to let some people filter into the big Ghettos in the General Government. It puzzles us at the time, but later on we discover the reason. It will make it easier to annihilate us after we are all concentrated in one spot.*

*We do not cross together, but one at a time and it is on a clear night. There is moonlight. Later on, perhaps just for the sport of it, the border guards shoot several people. We can hear the screams and the gun fire from the other side. Now we must walk the rest of the way. We see the Jasna Gora mountain as we approach nearer to Czestochowa.*

*We find that we are not the only Jews headed for that Ghetto. There are others. The Germans do not stop us, they know they will get us all in the end. They also know we have no where else to go. The Poles will not hide us. It is punishable by death and we have no money to bribe them.*

*We enter Czestochowa hungry and on blistered feet. We are in tatters. We see others who are like us in rags, trudging towards the Ghetto. Here it is, the promised land. . . Later on the Germans completely empty the surrounding countryside of all Jews and bring them in. The Ghetto swells with people until it contains at least 55,000. It becomes a city within a city. Then when it is done, the Germans close it up hermetically. We have arrived at our new trap. But at least, for the time being, we find a measure of comfort.*

*Mother was correct. Aunt Stein does have an apartment. Both her daughters live in it, her son-in-law and little grandson Jasio. There is also another family of four a couple and two young children. At last we disinfect our clothes and our hair. We bathe after months of being filthy. We are given blankets and a place to sleep on the floor. No more lice! We discover that the whole building is infested with bed bugs, but at least these live in the walls and not on our bodies. And they only come out and bite us at night.*

*To us, after the terrible camp in Silesia, it is a paradise. We even have an address once again. It is Czestochowa Ghetto, 20 Garibaldi Street, The General Government, Occupied Poland.*

# 9

# TWENTY GARIBALDI STREET

The Ghetto of Czestochowa was an amazing place for me. I have never seen so many people milling around in all directions. The sidewalks were so congested that walking was like pushing my way through a crowd. The Jews here did not wear the Yellow Star on the front and back of their jackets, sewn on permanently. Instead, everyone had to wear a white arm band with a blue Star of David in its center. This was much easier since it only needed to be slipped on the arm.

Twenty Garibaldi Street was a large building with an inner courtyard. All the apartments were very crowded with several families in each, but still it was not as bad as some buildings where there were ten people to a room. My parents and I slept in the small kitchen of our apartment. After the camp in Silesia, it was pure luxury.

The Czestochowa Ghetto, in addition to its local Jews, was populated by tens of thousands of arrivals from the many small towns of the surrounding territory. The Germans had liquidated most of the small town Ghettos in order to concentrate all Jews in a few designated areas.

The squalid old part of the city was jam packed with people from all over Poland. Everyone thought that things must be better somewhere else. We knew that it was a logical destination for people from Praszka because of its relative nearness, but it was impossible to track them down in this teeming cauldron of compressed humanity.

As soon as the process of immigration was completed, the Ghetto was sealed tight. Entry was forbidden to anyone unauthorized by proper authority under the penalty of death. Any Jew caught on the outside was executed on the spot. The streets leading to the outside were either walled off or blockaded. Each

entrance was manned by armed guards. The only people allowed
to enter were SS and other Germans who had a special pass issued for a specific purpose. Poles were not permitted to enter.
The teeming Ghetto was a world unto itself. It had its own Jewish
militia who were the order keepers. They were called the *Judenrat*
and answered directly to the Gestapo who were the ultimate
authority.

We ran into many Jews from Warthegau, the territory annexed to Germany, who, like ourselves, somehow found a way to
escape from there. People had terrible stories to tell.   The
refugees from the Warthegau were already the only survivors of
their small Jewish communities. We were already considered the
"lucky" few who made it; survivors already!

There was hunger in the Ghetto. People who came here with
nothing more but the tattered, lice infested clothes on their
backs, had no way of earning money. The only industry in the
Ghetto were the SS owned factories taking advantage of very
cheap labor. People bribed and paid to obtain these jobs. In addition to work, it meant security. We all knew from experience
that working for the Germans offered some protection from
deportation if it again came to it. It hadn't yet in Czestochowa,
but there were people from other Ghettos where having a
workers card provided at least temporary safety, especially if it
was considered employment "For the War Effort." Working for
the SS owned enterprises always fell under this category. "They
will not kill or deport you if they need you," people whispered.
That special pass with the red official stamp and swastika made
people feel a little safer. But these factories only employed a
small fraction of the population. Jews, of course, no longer had
the right to own or start any enterprises.   They could only do
business among each other on a very small scale.

There was a soup kitchen for those who could find no work at
all. The thin watery soup was served once daily, if available. A
bowl per person was all the food given to last the day. It was
served under the watchful eye of the *Judenrat* militia so that
nobody would get more than their ration.   Still, there was never
enough to feed all. People lined up early to be sure to get it and
waited for hours. Still, if one had enough money, food was available. It had been smuggled in various ways. A Pole could become
very rich fast if he cooperated, but there was always the terrible
risk of the death penalty and the prices reflected the danger.
Still, in the Ghetto, the Germans left us relatively alone. Alone,

perhaps to die of starvation and disease but anything was better than the constant torment we had lived through at the hands of the SS "Clique" in Praszka Ghetto. No daily beatings here; blissfully, no contact with the SS.

I was overwhelmed by the wonder of this small measure of freedom and by being able to walk for blocks and blocks. The Ghetto seemed so large to me compared to Praszka or the camp. What happiness it was being able to walk from one street to another! It was such a joy. The wonder of being clean! Why had we not come here before? What madness it was not to have tried at any risk. In addition, Aunt Stein still had money. She had been very wealthy once and managed somehow to keep some of it. She made sure we did not go hungry. She shared her clothes with us and her dresses were altered to fit us. Aunt Stein had prevailed upon her son-in-law to give Father a suit and some underwear. He, too, was glad to share what he had. At last we again looked presentable. Shoes were too expensive, but we could always wear wooden clogs.

We felt very guilty about eating the food given to us. Nobody could spare that in the Ghetto. We ate as little as possible. Eventually we were registered for a *Lebensmittelkarte* (food ration card). It made us eligible to purchase the 300 calories the Germans allotted per day, provided we could afford to buy it. At least we were now legal inhabitants of the Czestochowa Ghetto. But we had no money. Rent had to be paid and Aunt Stein had to provide it also.

Soon, I knew I would have to smuggle again, but Czestochowa was a strange territory for me. I have never lived in such a big city before; it was confusing. I didn't know where to start. First, I had to learn how to get out of the Ghetto without being caught. There was no room for error. Young or old, anyone caught was shot on the spot. I needed to get my bearings straight. There was no room for fear either; it interfered with judgment and I was afraid. I was very unsure of myself. Gone, at least temporarily, was my old bravado. This was not Praszka where I knew my way around. Besides, I could do nothing until I had shoes. Nothing was as likely to cost me my life as being conspicuous, and clogs would have been impossibly conspicuous. We were very emaciated and thin. And then there was the fatigue, even my mind was slow. On the Ghetto streets children were begging for food. It was not unusual to see someone dying of hunger in the middle of a sidewalk. Still, nothing was as bad as the camp we just left behind. At least here there was a little hope left, and, in spite of all else, we were recuperating and gaining strength.

Someone told Father that perhaps he could get a job working in one of the SS-owned factories. It was a very slim chance. He was too old to be a laborer. Still, one had to try. He borrowed a pair of shoes and went to apply anyway, early in the morning. He did not return until late in the evening and he was elated. He had presented himself as an accountant and they needed one immediately. He was taken to see a high ranking SS officer who was in charge of two factories. Father spoke perfect German and was able to compose and write business letters as well as do accounting. The SS officer took him around and showed him his books. Father made a few suggestions and was put to work.

Within two weeks, Father became an assistant to Herr Buhler, the SS officer. A drastic change took place in our lives. Suddenly we had all the food we could eat and more. According to Father, Herr Buhler turned out to be a very appreciative man. He was involved and interested mostly in political functions and the factories took up too much time to allow him to pursue his real ambitions. Father even assisted him with his private correspondence.

In return, Buhler provided him with a pass to leave the Ghetto so Father could report to him at his home or the factory, whichever was convenient. Now Father had the enviable opportunity to buy food and bring it in while he traveled back and forth. Herr Buhler was quite willing to look the other way as long as Father did not overdo it, and the German official vehicle was never searched.

It was a windfall. We now had more than enough to eat. In the Ghetto, food bought everything. I was given two pairs of shoes. A seamstress made me two dresses in the latest style. The material had a few holes in it, but the seamstress managed to camouflage them skillfully. It was the best to be had in the Ghetto. Mother bought a blue wool suit and Father one of tweed.

Later, Father purchased a sporty, maroon, felt hat. He was jubilant when he brought it home. Now he felt normal again, like a human being. He joked about how a man could hold up his head if he wore a decent hat on top of it. Then it was worthwhile because people actually had something to see.

Spring came and life was comparatively better, at least for us. Now that our most primitive needs had been met, my parents began to be concerned about my progress. I was growing, but my education had been interrupted. It really worried Father. I needed a tutor and a crash course in Latin and arithmetic. Father worked about twelve hours per day. He had no time to teach me and Mother did not know Latin. How would I ever catch up? Father was adamant on the subject. Every educated person should have knowledge of Latin.

One April day, I was taken to meet Moishe Altman. He was a very religious young man and a linguist. He wore a black coat and had sideburns called "peyses" in front of his ears. He hoped to study to become a Rabbi one day. He had chestnut brown hair and hazel eyes which betrayed his sense of humor. I thought he was very funny and liked him immediately. Father personally gave him a quiz and was very impressed. Moishe was indeed a scholar and knew his Latin declinations amazingly well for a young man of twenty.

Moishe needed the money very much and was an enthusiastic teacher. He was very disappointed that Father did not request that I be taught Hebrew also. He even offered to teach it for free. Father was very tactful about it. "A girl's mind should not be stretched too far. We should take it one step at a time." Now I was to spend three hours every day at the Altmans.

The apartment where they lived was also very crowded but Moishe and I had a little alcove by a window designated for my lessons. I put on my new lilac dress and patent leather shoes and made my way through the narrow, noisy Ghetto streets. I could almost block out the filth, congestion and squalor. I was going to school again, such as it was. I was elated. Moishe addressed me as *Panienka* which in Polish meant "Miss," and I beamed with pleasure. We got along well from the start and I did my homework to perfection. My mind was thawing out as if it had been frozen.

I began to write poetry again and embarked on an ambitious project. It was to be a fifty page poem about Rome at the time when Paganism gave way to Christianity. I researched the history with Moishe's help. It would make Mother very happy. It would cheer her up! Lately, in spite of our good turn of fortune, she was very depressed and quiet. In fact, she worried me. We had plenty to eat, but she did not gain an ounce. She remained very thin and frail looking. I worked feverishly at the Altmans apartment after my lessons. I had all the reference books at my fingertips.

The poem was about a young, handsome tribune, son of a Roman patrician, who falls in love with the statue of Venus. He goes daily to her temple gardens to commune with his love and to give her tribute. He remains faithful and devotes himself to her symbolic perfection. No woman can take her place in his affections. He makes Venus an offering of himself. But under Constantine, Rome is changing. The mob is restive and demanding an end to the worship of pagan gods. Angrily, it surges to destroy the temple of Venus. The Tribune hears the shouting and hurries to the gardens to defend the statue. He stands before it, a lonely man against an angry mob. He makes his last offering to her. The mob surges forward, trampling the flowers and stones begin to rain at the statue striking its face. The spirit of Venus must leave Rome forever. Suddenly, the statue begins to sway upon its pedestal under the blows, until it falls into the arms of its faithful Tribune. It crushes him to death and Venus departs this world forever taking with it the most lovely offering, the young life and the faithful love of the handsome tribune, the most precious gift of its reign on earth.

I showed my poem to Moishe and he gave me a sad smile. "It is a strange poem to write in the Ghetto," he said thoughtfully. Somehow I hesitated to show it to Mother.

For the first time since the war started, I had not seen a member of the cursed SS in months . They had not disappeared, nor had they become inactive. Moishe told me scary stories which somehow penetrated into the Ghetto. In the City of Wilno, there had been a mass execution. Jews were taken to open pits and shot by the thousands. There was a special outfit, a commando, which went from town to town murdering people. They were called the *Totenkopfverbaende.* They wore the death head and cross bones insignia on their caps.

In *Warszawa* (Warsaw) something terrible had begun to happen. People were starving in the streets but now there were also deportations. Trainloads of people were being taken somewhere, supposedly to labor camps. Labor camps! I sat up straight as a bolt.

Labor camps would simply mean a place where people have to work. But I knew better! I have been there already and to me they were *Death Camps!*

I did not discuss it at home. Aunt Stein was taken ill. She came to the kitchen one morning dragging her leg. She had suffered a stroke. It was progressive. She was very weak and Mother took care of her. Her daughters were shattered by her illness. One afternoon she asked me to sit by her. She wanted us to have a talk; it was her goodbye. She wore an elegant beige sweater, embroidered with cultured pearls, a leftover from her once exquisite wardrobe. She asked me to keep it. "I will not need it any longer. . . " she said. "It is my gift to you."

A rampant epidemic of polio was sweeping the Ghetto like wildfire. It fed upon the crowded and filthy conditions. The people, already weakened by hunger, had little resistance. My cousin Felix fell victim to it. Death was everywhere.

I began to grow restless. There was something stirring within me that I was powerless to stop. I began to circle the perimeter of the Ghetto, observing, looking for a suitable place to get out. I had to do it! Finally I decided on a spot which was probably most obvious; near the guarded entrance. The guards were busy checking passes at a certain time of day when a small group left to work on the outside. I slipped out right under their noses.

I spent the whole day roaming the city of Czestochowa. I found a street where Polish farmers sold sausage and butter on the black market. I even took a trolley to the suburbs.

I sneaked back into the Ghetto, just before curfew and missed my lessons with Moishe. I had to let him in on my secret, because otherwise he might alert my parents that I was absent. He was horrified. I tried to explain to him how it was for me. I couldn't help what I was doing. He was very sad, and did not understand at all. I could never bring myself to talk about the incident at the border guard station. It was like a stone dropped into deep water and had to stay there. I promised Moishe that I would make up my lesson, but he was despondent.

"It is useless," he said bitterly. "What good is knowing Latin, or anything else. We will soon all be dead." Moishe was losing weight. I couldn't help noticing it. His face was drawn and pale. His family must be running out of money to buy food on the black market. I suggested that he give me a little money so that next time I went out I could buy him some food.

His face turned chalk white. "I cannot do it, 'Panienka Zosia'. If you were killed bringing me food, I couldn't face it!" But I insisted. I was not going out for him, I explained, or for the food. There was something inside me like a creature needing to be free, that made me do it. I knew that the penalty if I were caught was death, but they could not kill me twice. . .

Father gave me money to pay Moishe every Monday, which made it easy. On Monday, I slipped out again, and took the trolley to the black market. I knew that Mrs. Altman would probably want to have a chicken, but I did not feel like carrying a dead bird around. Instead, I bought two one- kilo loaves of fresh butter. It took all of Moishe's money and some I borrowed from cousin Lucia. I re-entered the Ghetto and went straight to the Altmans.

Moishe was sitting in the alcove. He practically pounced at me. "You did it again!" he said accusingly. I gave him the two packages wrapped in cabbage leaves and paper for freshness. One kilo was his payment for my lessons. The other we would have to sell. It took fifteen minutes to sell my loaf for twenty times what I paid for it.

Smuggling was very profitable. Now I could pay back my cousin and have money left over for myself. Moishe collected twenty times his week's pay when he also sold his butter. I was going to help him out from now on. He was my hazel eyed friend and teacher.

As my smuggling activities continued, I began to lose interest in my lessons and never did show my poem to Mother. It would have made her too sad if I were killed after having made her especially happy. It would be sad enough as it was.

Moishe could not talk me out of it; nobody could. I had an irresistible need to leave the Ghetto as often as possible. I began to know Czestochowa very well. There was a little restaurant where, for a price, I could get a tasty lunch of white bread, bloodwurst and tea. It was a quaint place and the food was good. I particularly liked to sit by the window. The place was often frequented by Germans, *Wehrmacht,* and sometimes the SS with their dates. I casually squeezed past them to get to my favorite table. They never gave me more than a glance.

I often brought back butter and and sold it in order to have enough money for my escapades. The Altman's neighbors and people on the street began to refer to me as "Panienka Maslo" (Miss Butter). Moishe gave up on me altogether and he also worried that one day I would not make it back.

In the meantime, Aunt Stein died. Her daughter Lucia rejoiced. It was for the best, she said. At least the Nazis will not have a chance to kill her! At least she had the dignity of dying in her own bed.

The news was all bad. There was a blackout of silence from the city of Lodz. Not a word filtered out of there. It was as if everybody in that Ghetto had ceased to exist. We heard stories of mass murder often enough, so perhaps deportation was better. But where were those "Labor Camps?" They had to be huge to accommodate all these transports. A million people could not simply disappear. Ghetto after Ghetto went silent and not a word trickled back.

Depression and panic began to spread throughout Czestochowa. What is happening? Are we going to be next? We discussed these questions with neighbors. Did anyone have an opinion? A rumor surfaced that the Germans were planning to deport Jews to the island of Madagascar. Any explanation was a relief. People soaked up this rumor, eagerly wanting to accept it. At least it was a place. It was something. Within a week a song about Madagascar was composed and became very popular. It went like this:

"Oh, Madagascar
A wild country
A dark land
Hot and steamy
Oh, Madagascar
What are you like?"

Some half-hearted jokes were told about settling there. My cousin Lucia did not know what to think. Her instinct told her bad things. She fixed her black hair in an extravagant way and began to wear black dresses and a mourning veil. She was in mourning, but not for her mother; her mother was very lucky. She was in mourning for herself, her husband and little Jasio, for their young lives. . .

Father tried to cheer people up. Certainly there were killings and massacres, but there were three and a half million Jews in Poland. No nation could annihilate three and a half million people! Not even Hitler's Germany. It had to be Labor Camps and only for those needed to work there. It was as they called it, a "resettlement." Of course it was frightening, but it was only a "resettlement!"

Mother expressed no opinion. She was thinner than ever and very quiet. But I had something to say: There was only one place from where no one ever returned and it was a *mass grave!*

Eyes bore into me. Angry frightened eyes. "Do not say such things!" I was admonished. Must not even think this way.

My notebook sat untouched — no more poetry. The last poem was like a last gasp of a dying soul. Moishe and I met now mostly to talk. Like the others, he argued and could not accept my theories. He did not want to worry about dying so he began to worry about living. He fretted about not being able to pray in a "Labor Camp," or to observe the Sabbath.

"Moishe," I said and took his hand in mine. "You may not need to pray to God any longer. You might meet him face to face soon enough." I knew how the "Labor Camps" were. I was ahead of him a couple of steps. I remembered Herr Lieutenant Cebula delivering his theatrical, drunken harangues and waving his gun to make the point sink in. "You Jews are all the *Children of Death.* . . You will see. . . "

Father almost summoned enough courage to ask his boss, Herr Buhler, but decided against it. He was a high ranking Gestapo officer. It was best not to take a chance. And Herr Buhler continued to be very nice and pleasant. Here was proof that all of them were not bad. Some of the SS hierarchy were just interested in production, in the War Effort and labor was needed, after all. It simply made sense.

Besides, there was nothing we could do. The Poles would not dare hide us. If a Jew was found being sheltered in an apartment all the inhabitants were shot. If a Jew tried to get by with false papers and was found, the Germans still executed people just to teach them a lesson. Ignorance was no excuse. The Poles were on the look out, watchful. If they were at all suspicious, they notified the authorities.

The Polish resistance stayed clear of Jews. They had it tough enough. If a young Jew went into the woods trying to join, he was found the next day on the side of the road with his throat cut, by the Poles, not by the Germans by the Polish Patriots The *Armja Krajowa* (National Army), the Polish underground. There was no place to run any more. The Poles are ethnically pure. A semitic face could be spotted easily in a crowd. My mother could not ever make it. She would stand out because her face differed so much from those around her. Father and I were the relatively few who looked Aryan enough, but we could never abandon Mother.

Besides, where would we sleep if we left the ghetto? Nobody would give us shelter. So let us just hope that it was Madagascar or some other simple explanation, like "resettlement," that they would let us live. . .

In the meantime, the list of silenced Ghettos grew longer. Our turn came nearer. A certain hush fell over the Ghetto like a shroud. People began to talk in whispers.

In the courtyard at Twenty Garibaldi Street, we children skipped rope. There was nothing else we could do. And I still went out on my escapades almost daily, propelled by the creature inside me, — a trapped, restless creature.

We discovered that Uncle Stecki and Aunt Mathilda were here in Czestochowa all along, lost in the multitude of refugees and we did not even know it! We went to see them immediately and brought food along. They were hungry and emaciated, barely hanging on, and so glad to see us! I hardly recognized the once beautiful Aunt Mathilda. We fell into each others arms tearfully and exchanged stories.

They told us that their sons were alive and living outside the Ghetto. Heniek, the physician, was in a prisoner of war camp pretending to be non-Jewish. He assumed an identity of the dead husband of his fiancee who was Polish. Stefan was somewhere also, in a prisoner of war camp. Isidor and his wife were hiding out among the Poles. The Stecki's were too cautious to tell us exactly where they were and we could well understand.

People with false papers were caught all the time, often because someone from the Ghetto, in desperation, sought them out, hoping for shelter. Aunt Mathilda, however, gave us the name of Heniek's fiancee. She wanted us to know it just in case we survived and they did not. The woman was Polish; she had nothing to fear. She could be our link to each other.

In our apartment at Twenty Garibaldi Street, we children now could no longer ignore it. There were two others; Jasio, my little cousin, age seven, and a girl of eight also named Zosia. I was the oldest and they turned to me.

"You were in a Labor Camp. You can tell us. Were there any children there? What was it like? Was there a place to play and food to eat? What if the children were too young to work? What will the Germans do with the children?"

Zosia had lived in Czestochowa all her life, in this very apartment. Now her parents were worried all the time.

Her mother cried at night. She sewed gold coins into Zosia's collar and told her to wear the blouse all the time. She might need to use the gold coins to buy food if they became separated.

Separated? What could she do if this happened? How could she buy food with gold coins in a Labor Camp? Who would sell it to her?

Jasio looked at me with his large blue eyes shaded by long eyelashes in an angel-like face. Did I think that maybe he could also work? Maybe they would let him sweep the floors. He had practiced with a broom in the apartment. He was big for his age, maybe there was hope. Would I stick nearby, since I was older and more experienced in the matter of Labor Camps?

They looked at me respectfully. I had been "there" and was very much alive. Jasio made me promise that I would stay close to him on the train. His mother was acting strangely lately. She exchanged a diamond ring for some vodka. . . she never did it before. And this veil of mourning for herself. . . At night she held him so close he could hardly breathe. She hugged him and cried. He had to calm her down. His father hugged his mother and stroked her hair as if she were a little girl. They hardly slept at night any longer. Jasio was terrified. Was his mother going to die?

I went to visit Moishe to get away from these questions. He was in the alcove but the Latin books were put away. Instead, Moishe had his Hebrew prayer books there now. His hazel eyes were cloudy and serious. All the Latin declinations we studied, all this practice; what good will Latin do us in Labor Camp? Prayer was more what we needed; a Hebrew prayer. But did God understand Hebrew?

I put my arm around Moishe. I told him that he was young and strong, that he should snap out of it. The world will need good teachers after the war is over. We all missed so much education. He had a job waiting for him and I was going to be his very first pupil. I would not let anyone else teach me Latin!

The summer had drawn to an end. A cold breath of wind was in the air. Brisk Polish fall with leaves fluttering down from the trees, yellow and gold. There were no trees in the Ghetto. The narrow winding streets were more bleak and gloomy than ever. People milled around, collars buttoned up against the first chill.

God, how I needed to see a tree that was yellow and gold! I needed to get out of here. It was like entering a whole different world just a street away. The wide street which led to *Jasna Gora* Cloister had trees on both sides. People walked with a purpose, the faces were different. Occasionally, I heard the sound of laughter, so strange to my ears. If I were shot getting in or out, so what! It did not matter. I knew all about Labor Camps, only too well. They could do nothing to me!

I treated myself to my favorite lunch at the little restaurant. The waitress knew me by now. Winter was just around the corner, she remarked, as she served me the hot tea. It was sure to be a bad one.

Four SS were sitting at the next table. High gutteral German voices. They were drinking beer and laughing. Spiffy black boots. The "rat poison" insignia on their black caps. A swastika, *Totenkopfverbaende.* Were they the very ones who will come to get us, maybe tomorrow? Damn all of them! Their heads were not made of steel. They could be cracked with an iron basket. . . I knew. . .

My parents and Uncle and Aunt Stecki had a plan. Father had the keys to the SS owned factory inside the Ghetto. There was a wooden platform on one side with a hollow space under the boards. Father examined it very thoroughly and loosened a few boards on the sides so one could crawl under it. If deportation came, we could hide there. It was in a way a German territory. An oasis, within the Ghetto. The SS might not even bother to enter the factory. There was enough space there for the five of us. It was going to be tight but we were not planning to take up a permanent residence under these boards. We would stay there during the deportation and after the Germans left we could crawl out again. They could not deport everybody, after all. Fifty thousand people was a mammoth task, even for them. They surely needed to leave some of us to work in the factories. But no one could be sure exactly what they planned to do.

Father began to stash some food into the crawl space; enough for a few days if necessary. Also some water. We would tell no one else because the space was limited, hardly enough for the five of us.

The Jewish holidays were almost here. "Yom Kippur," the Day of Atonement and "Roshhashana" the Jewish New Year. The *Judenrat,* Ghetto militia, seemed to be very agitated lately, as if something was brewing. They would be the first to know and it was a bad sign. We knew that they took their orders from the Gestapo. Starting on Yom Kippur, we would sneak into the factory every night and stay there until morning. The factory was empty at night and Father had a set of keys in his possession. It was not safe to sleep at home any longer. It must be done, it was decided. It was our only option, there was nothing else we could do.

On Yom Kippur, Jews fast from sundown until sunset. Prayers are said for the dead. It is a somber holiday. A day of atonement. It was an especially somber occasion for the frightened Jews of the Ghetto. At least those religious enough had their faith to lean upon. They could simply place their fate in God's hands. I knew it was this way for Moishe, and I almost envied him. Hungry as the faithful were, they fasted and prayed more fervently than ever.

Mother and I shared a small cot in the kitchen. Father slept near by. Darkness came and enveloped the restless, waiting Ghetto. The night before Yom Kippur. . . I curled up in my space on the narrow cot and Mother put her arms around me. Somehow we knew that our time was up. It was hard to sleep; the clock was ticking loudly, relentlessly on the table. The Ghetto was very quiet, a stillness before a storm.

We clung to each other.

"We might not be able to talk to each other like this again," she whispered in the darkness. "They might come for us any time now." I snuggled close to her. If only time would stop, if we could stay like this. But the clock kept on ticking.

"Mother, we might be separated. . . " I whispered.

"I know," she answered, "but this might not be the worst of it. They cannot hurt me. I am not afraid of them for myself. The only way they can get at me is to have me watch you being killed. You are only a child and I want so much for you to be able to live your life. . . I just do not want to see you die!" It is strange how both of us thought the same thoughts. We remembered the camp in Silesia.

"They can hurt us most through the ones we love. This is the control they have over us," she said.

"Mother," I whispered. "You know I could run away if I wanted to. . . I know how!" I told her about my recent trips to the outside and that I knew my way around. I told her I hadn't wanted her to know before because it might have worried her. I told her how much I loved her and Father.

"Tomorrow," she said, "we will not be sleeping here. We will be in the crawl space at the factory. It will not be possible for me to hold you like this or for us to talk. . . If they get us, I would just like to have the chance to get one of them before I go. . .

but there may not be the chance. They can kill you slowly or fast and no one wants to die slowly."

I knew what she meant. Death was not the worst by far. The flesh cringes from pain. We knew that all over the Ghetto, mothers held their children close, thinking that it might very well be the last time.

Mother decided that we shall not fast. We have known enough hunger. "God would want us to be strong. There will be many days we will not eat if we are deported, the Germans will see to that. They will starve us every day we are in their power. We must commune with God by having courage. We have nothing to atone for. We have done nothing wrong. . . "

Mother made lots of food for us to eat. Maybe it would be the last meal she could ever prepare for her family, for a very long time. She made it with so much love. There was chicken and spaghetti, all cooked and ready. Of course the Germans knew it was Yom Kippur. They would want us to fast, feel guilty and grow weaker. God surely did not want to be used by them to defeat us.

We held onto each other in the darkness. It was growing late and we were very tired but out of the walls the bed bugs came and fed on our blood. We could feel them all over our bodies. We put on the light and they scurried away, round and fat, gorged with blood. Our skin burned where they bit us. We turned out the lights again and slowly sleep came, troubled and restless.

It was partially cloudy next day and I went out of the apartment. In the daylight the terror seemed almost unreal. I walked around all day but did not want to leave the Ghetto. Mother would worry, now that she knew.

The afternoon dragged on slowly. We were to pick up Aunt and Uncle Stecki since they lived close to the factory on our way there. We packed some more provisions. I felt oppressed. Maybe I could walk over to the Altmans and talk to Moishe. But I could see Mother looking out of the window and again decided to stay in the courtyard where she could see me, so she should have at least this small measure of peace of mind. I decided to skip rope with the other children playing on the cobblestones. Shadows began to fall, the sun was going down.

Suddenly there was the sound of a motorcycle. We froze, what now? It must be the Germans! Watchful eyes turned fearfully towards the entrance. They were coming! The motorcycle drove into the courtyard and came to a stop. It had a side car, but there was only one German; an SS no doubt. He dismounted and went up the stairs to our apartment! I folded my rope in alarm; what should I do? What does he want from us? I was very worried. I waited a few minutes but there was no shouting, so I ran up the steps two at a time and walked in.

The German sat peacefully in a chair just talking and everybody was standing around him. He was of medium build, blue eyed with sparse blond hair. His hat was on his lap. He was here on business, he told us, to see if we had some gold to sell to him. We might as well take the opportunity and arrive at a price. The Jewish Deportation Commando, the *Einsatzgruppe*, was already here in the suburbs of Grosz. They were ready to go into action in a matter of hours. We would need money more than jewelry where we were going and he was willing to buy it. Everybody watched him wide eyed. There he sat with his gun in the holster. What if he took whatever we had and shot us? He could if he wanted to.

I came in and sat down on a sofa. The German looked at me and a look of surprise came over his face. "Who is she?" he asked my mother. "She cannot possibly be Jewish! She looks just like my kid. Is she adopted?"

Mother reassured him that I was not, but he looked skeptical. Mother told him that we had no gold and the German got up.

"All right, suit yourselves, but believe me, the truth is that in a few hours the deportation will start!" He walked over to me and looked at me thoughtfully.

"She should not stay here tonight. You ought to let her go," he said to my mother. "In a few hours it will be too late. . . I will take her out of here, if she will come. It is getting dark and the guards have seen me drive through the check point with my daughter many times. If you put a scarf on her head they will just wave us by."

Mother looked at him in amazement, then turned to me. "Zosia, what do you want to do?" she asked helplessly. I took the white band with the Star of David off my arm. It was my answer and she understood. "Smart girl!" said the German.

Now Mother and Father began to scurry around. Mother put another dress on top of the one I already wore, then gave me a sweater and a scarf. The German was impatient. She called me into a corner and whispered quickly.

"There is a parish in the suburb of Grosz. The priest is an old friend of mine from Praszka. Maybe he will be willing to help. In a few days get in touch with us somehow." She pressed a gold coin into my hand, a five Ruble piece. "It is all I have to give you. . . "

I walked over to Jasio who sat in a corner wide eyed. "I wish I could take you with me. . . " I whispered. There were tears in his eyes.

"I am too young. . . " he whispered back. "I couldn't make it. . . " Father stood by the door and Mother reminded me to kiss him goodbye. "I know you will be all right Zosia", he reassured Mother and me. "You are very intelligent. You can do it."

The door closed behind me and we went down the steps. The German helped me up into the side car of the motorcycle, to the amazement of my little friends. I did not dare to look up into the kitchen window. I could not bear to do it knowing that Mother was watching me. The motor started and soon the Ghetto streets streaked by. It all had happened so fast! The first evening shadows fell upon the old buildings. The setting sun caught in the window panes.

The motorcycle barely slowed at the Ghetto gate. The guards waved to us and waved us on. We rode for a while longer, then the motorcycle came to a stop at the curb and I climbed out.

"You must realize that I cannot take you home with me. . . " said the German. "I live in a German community. But I really wish that you will make it." He stuck his hand in his pocket and gave me a few crumpled bills. He told me that he was a *Volksdeutsche* and a member of the SS, but never gave me his name. He did not want me to know it, of course, and he did not want to know where I was going. I was too confused even to thank him. He told me that the Ghetto will be sealed and surrounded any time now and I must stay as far away as possible from its borders. When the deportation was finished, no children would be left alive. "Good luck. . . " he said and drove away.

Now the reality hit me like a stone. It made me stagger. Two hours ago, I was skipping rope at Twenty Garibaldi Street. Now I was standing on a street corner in the falling evening shadows. Lights began to go on in windows where people lived and slept. Where was I going to sleep tonight?

I hoped anxiously that my parents had already made it to the hiding place in the factory. I prayed that they hurried; they were forewarned and I knew that the German told us the truth. My fingers curled around the small gold coin Mother had given me and held in her own hand just a short time ago. I was too frightened to take the trolley. I wanted to melt into the darkness and stay within it. I had about two hours until curfew time and started to walk briskly toward the suburb of Grosz where I would have to find the parish. I hoped I had enough time to get there on foot, but knew that I could not be close to people for awhile. I was certain that the sadness of my face would give me away.

I wondered how it was that the German came up to our apartment! Did he choose it at random, or had he done business with someone there before? Nobody seemed to know him or even trust him. He did not buy any gold or jewelry. Maybe he just picked any place along the way that seemed promising. He seemed to know a lot about the deportation. Who was he, and what was his name? It was all so very strange. Just a twist of fate. I was afraid for my parents. It was just as well that I had to walk all the way to Grosz. It will help me to calm down and stop shaking. My heart pounded in my chest like a hammer. A wave of pain spilled over me. The pain of sorrow.

# 10

# YOU CANNOT STAY

It took almost two hours of walking but at last I approached the suburb of Grosz. I was tired and dazed. What sort of welcome would I receive from that priest when I knocked on his door? Was he even there? Mother had no time to give me his name. I only knew that he was from Praszka and a friend of hers. I had some of my own money earned by smuggling butter in my pocket, in addition to what the German gave me. But I knew that no one would permit me to stay the night even if I paid well for it. I had no papers and nobody under German occupation could be without papers at any time. This was how they maintained their iron stranglehold upon the population. It was their control, vital to their purpose and they enforced it ruthlessly. Every one, young or old, had to have an identification with a picture and a fingerprint on it.

We in the Ghetto knew about it only too well. It was this airtight system that made it impossible for Jews to survive on the outside. It was not the cordon around the Ghetto, the barbed wire or even a wall. This could somehow be managed. It did not take a very large hole for a human being to crawl through. It was the elaborate system of registrations that was insurmountable.

For example, in order to leave the precinct area where one lived, in addition to papers, a person had to have the so called *Aussmeldung,* an Out-Registration. This Out-Registration was needed to stay in another precinct area however briefly, in order to get a permit to stay there called an *Inmeldung,* or In-Registration.

In addition, every apartment house or private home was collectively responsible for its inhabitants. It was a system specifically designed to keep track of all occupied Poles, but it especially affected any Jew trying to survive on the outside. We have discussed this system in the Ghetto in small detail. This was why if the Poles ever hid a Jew, it had to be in a hole, a boarded up hiding place or something similar. It was very hard.

Now I was out, but the hardest thing was to survive on the outside. When I had slipped out of the Ghetto in the past I mainly needed to worry about being stopped and asked to show my "papers." I had a place to sleep in the Ghetto and only had to get back in. It was all but impossible to remain on the outside without papers. Then there was the curfew. Once it was in effect everyone was stopped who was not in their home, and those who had no home to go to had not a chance. After the curfew, the streets were empty and hollow. Only the Germans and the patrols were about, and now it was almost that time.

I asked directions, found the parish and nervously knocked on the door. The housekeeper opened the door and we stared at each other. She was a large, blond woman of middle age. She was from Praszka also but I did not recognize her, it had been too long.

I told her, trying to appear calm, that I was looking for a priest from Praszka. She immediately ushered me in and asked my name. I told her and her hand flew to her mouth "Zofia Sieradzki!" she exclaimed in alarm and hurried off to get the priest. He came in looking very grim.

"My God, child, you could not have come here at a worse time! We are under surveillance at this very moment. We are being watched by the Gestapo!"

My heart sank. The priest introduced himself as Father Krzeminski and anxiously asked about my parents and what had happened. He seemed to be frightened and spoke in hurried whispers, looking around nervously. It was dim inside and I could hardly distinguish his features or how old he was. Later, I found out he was about my brother's age and knew him well. I told him about what happened dispiritedly, expecting no help under the circumstances.

There was a furtive knock on the door and the housekeeper answered it, then came running back to us.

"They are coming," she stuttered frantically. "Gestapo!"

They both grabbed me by my arms and opened a floor trap door leading into the basement. The housekeeper and I descended down the ladder into the musty interior. Like most Polish basements, it was full of food, provisions, sacks of potatoes, beans, barrels of sour cabbage and pickles in brine.

The housekeeper pulled me toward an empty barrel and made we crawl in. It smelled of pickles. Then she poured cucumbers over me until my head was covered and loosely placed a round wooden top over it. We could already hear the pounding at the door upstairs. Then the housekeeper ran up the ladder and I vaguely heard the trap door being shut. I sat in my cramped position, my mind a blank. I banished all thought out of my consciousness, it was too frightening. I experienced a strange feeling as if all this was not happening to me at all. It felt as if my real person detached itself from my body and became a separate entity. It withdrew into myself like a hermit crab into a shell. My body became only my shell.

From above came the sound of boots stamping and loud voices. I heard the trap door being lifted and someone coming down the ladder. I held my very breath. Footsteps again very near to me, noises of movement, banging. . . Then I heard the trap door again. Were they leaving? Again stomping upstairs reverberated dimly in my ears. Voices I could not make out and after a considerable while silence again.

They came and left! I felt a powerful surge of relief and waited. The cucumbers were lifted from my head and the housekeeper whispered loudly "It's allright Zosia." I wiggled out of the barrel and wearily followed her upstairs again. Father Krzeminski was sitting at a wooden table by a kerosene lamp.

"This was close. . . " he said, "very close. You see we were tipped off that they were coming. We knew it." Now he needed to decide what to do with me and immediately told me that I could not stay the night, it was too dangerous. They could always come back.

But it was after curfew already! I was instructed to follow a country road to the next town and take a train from there back to Czestochowa. At the Czestochowa depot, I could switch to a train going to Warsaw. When I arrived there, I was to go to my father's sister, Aunt Hela, who was living with her daughter on Ulica Zielona and whose address I remembered well. Father made me memorize it just in case. I was to stay with Aunt Hela for two weeks and then I was to return to Father Krzeminski's.

He had no way of providing me with proper papers but would make out a false christening and birth certificate which would be better than having nothing at all. But I must not come back any sooner because Father Krzeminski was having problems with the Gestapo. They had nothing on him but suspicions thus far but if they found me here it would be the end for all of us. The housekeeper gave me a piece of bread but I could not even stay long enough to eat it. I had to leave immediately regardless of the curfew. The country road should be empty and I should sleep in the fields.

It was cold and foggy, but there was no other choice.  The door of the parish closed behind me and I was again on the street. I was on the very outskirts of Czestochowa but had to be very careful until I was on the open road where it was, hopefully, a little safer. I crept ahead staying close to the walls of houses to be less visible. Soon the houses grew sparser and I was out in the country.

Only yesterday I had slept with my mother on the small cot in the kitchen of our apartment. Where were she and Father now? What was happening in the Ghetto? I was a dog out in the cold, — a homeless dog. . .  I was less than that.  People could give shelter to a dog without being killed for having done so. Most dogs had a shelter. Dogs were permitted to be alive but I was not. I had no right to live. . .  It was only a few hours since I had left the Ghetto, but already I had almost lost my life. The war would not end in a day, but I would hardly survive that long. How long could it last? Was there any hope?

The Germans already had won as far as I was concerned. Unknown to me, the  *Wehrmacht* was now battling its way into the heart of Stalingrad, where on the first of November 1942, they would be halted. And on the sixth of that month, their advance would be halted in the Caucasus. It would not help the Jews of Czestochowa, or my parents, but I would have felt better if I had known. All I felt was bleak despair.

## RECOLLECTION

*There is nothing I can do now but keep on walking. The empty road is almost invisible in the thick, clammy September fog which swirls all around me. It softens the blackness of the night, it envelopes and mercifully hides me. I have been walking for hours, now, and the outskirts of Czestochowa must be far behind me.*

*There must be fields on both sides and I can smell the pungent damp earth but can see nothing at all. Just darkness and mist. My footsteps echo in the stillness. The sound carries and is magnified, as if captured in the stagnant air. I must keep going, although I don't even know exactly the name of the town where I am to get on the Czestochowa- bound train. I must now put distance between me and the Ghetto. I am certain that during deportations, the Germans must be more vigilant than ever and it is doubly dangerous because of the curfew. To be apprehended means death, and I almost sense it stalking me.*

*There are now other sounds traveling upon the fog, sometimes very clearly, sometimes faintly. My God! I now can tell what they are! They are coming from the train depot which cannot be very far, maybe just across this field. The sounds seem to invade the stillness around me. I can clearly distinguish gunfire, shouts, cries and the barking of dogs.*

*The Jews of Czestochowa Ghetto are being loaded upon the trains. I can clearly hear the deportation in progress. I can hear a train whistle, more voices, shots and commands but around me all is eerily still as if I were the only one left, suspended in another dimension.*

*Well, not exactly. Ahead, I hear footsteps coming towards me. Hobnail boots! Two figures appear as if from nowhere. I can hear their voices, can even distinguish separate words as they talk to each other, gutteral German words.*

*Well, I think, I didn't get very far. It is the end. My attempt at escape ended before it had even started. I almost feel relief, almost don't care. No need to veer off the road any longer. They can surely hear and see me clearly enough. I could not out run them anyway if they decided to apprehend me. I keep my footsteps steady, try to control my fear. They are now only meters away, I can see their uniforms, the contour of their faces. Wehrmacht soldiers. They are talking about girls and laughing. They glance at me in passing and continue on indifferently, their footsteps recede again. Just two young soldiers walking home from a date, who did not want to be bothered, couldn't care less.*

*I am alone again on the empty road and can hear another train pulling up to a stop in the distance. I can hear shouting again and it seems to be even closer. Am I walking towards the depot? What if I am. . . I get off the road and walk into the field. The earth is soft under my feet. It must have been plowed recently. I lie down between the furrows and curl up to protect myself from the chill of the night. I feel suddenly terribly tired and close my eyes but I cannot sleep. I can hear the loading of the trains too clearly, can almost exactly imagine it happening.*

*Suddenly and for the first time in my life, I feel completely alone. And as the haunting whistle of a departing train wails again, followed by clatter of wheels upon the track, I sense all I ever knew receding along with it forever. I still don't want to believe it, but I instinctively know that nothing in my life will ever be the same. Yesterday was the Day of Atonement "Yom Kippur". I was with my parents yesterday. In five months I will be thirteen years old and for the rest of my life I will always remember the sounds and the chill of this night. The very smell of this damp earth, the wailing shrill of the train, the screams and the shouting. It will be an*

*image frozen in time. And tomorrow, where will I go?. . . Eventually
fatigue takes over and I sleep.*


I must have been very tired to have fallen asleep almost instantly in a burrow like a rabbit. It was hard to estimate time
when I opened my eyes again shivering from the penetrating
dampness. The fog was dense and low, almost no visibility at all
and of course I did not have a watch. The sounds from the loading ramps of the depot continued unabated. I was overwhelmed
by a sense of guilt; how could I sleep against the background
sounds of my people suffering? I imagined their faces as clearly
as if they stood before me. My parents, my cousins, my friends, a
long procession of figures in the mist. I had never realized how
mournful and heart-rending the whistle of a train could be. I imagined the cattle cars being bolted shut. The trapped helplessness of unfortunates transported into the unknown.

Were my mother and father among them? The two children
Jasio and Zosia, were they frightened? Of course they were, like
young flowers torn out of a garden. Will they wilt and perish?
What was Moishe thinking now? I felt I knew. He was reciting
prayers in his mind. Maybe he was glancing around to see if he
could spot me in the crowd. Did I ever tell him how much I
loved him? Maybe he did not know. Now I will never have the
chance to touch his hand and let him know. I saw his face before
me. Hazel eyes behind horn rimmed glasses. Shoulders slightly
bent, his familiar voice. "Deus-Dei" Latin declination of the word
God rang in my ears in his voice.

Why were the Germans shooting at that ramp? Where did the
bullets fly? In whose direction? There was such a pain in my
chest, a real physical pain and I could not stand it any longer. I
had to escape these sounds; had to get back to the road. I
stumbled ahead in that direction. If I were caught, let it be! It
will happen anyway sooner or later. I had no right to live if they
could not! But then I could not give the "Rat Poison" gang the
satisfaction of willingly bending to their will! I kept on walking to
that nameless town. I too will board a train but I will buy my own
ticket. I was lucky to have escaped.

The fog began to lift and daylight moved in together with a
sense of reality. It was late in the day by the time I arrived at the
small railroad station, but decided to wait a day before returning
to Czestochowa, where I could catch the train for Warsaw. I spent

the night at the station on a bench in a corner. Time really did not matter any more. No one was waiting for me. I needed to regain my composure before going anywhere.

I arrived in Czestochowa just before the curfew and bought my ticket. The Warsaw train was not leaving for many hours but all the passengers were already at the station because of the curfew. Everybody had a suitcase or a bundle but I. It was conspicuous to be different. I had had nothing to eat all day because my throat was too tight to swallow anything. It was drafty and people sat around patiently on the wooden benches. I hoped that no one would talk to me, — I was in no mood for conversation.

But people do get bored. . . After a while a man sat down next to me. He carried a new brown suitcase. I gave him a furtive glance. He was nice looking and well dressed, but he kept fidgeting with his gloves. He smiled at me. "Where is *Panienka* going?" he asked very politely. I told him that I had a ticket for Warsaw.

"So do I," he said a little too eagerly. "We have a very long wait." I did not answer hoping he would go away, but the man continued. "Can I buy you a sandwich at the restaurant? Please come along and let's see what they have."

I declined politely and looked at him again. He had dark hair and brown eyes. I felt a vague stirring of uneasiness. He acted too eager. "If you are not hungry, then perhaps we could just sit and talk together to break the boredom."

Suddenly, I knew in a flash. The man was a Jew on the run. He was nervous, too chatty and eager. He must think that I am a Polish girl and would feel safer sitting next to one. Poor fellow, I thought with sympathy. Maybe he thought that being with a bona-fide Pole would seem less suspicious than traveling alone. He couldn't have made a worse choice. I needed to get rid of him somehow and began to get up from my seat and move away.

Then I froze and sat down again. In the entrance stood a black clad SS man with a dog on a leash flanked by two others in the same uniforms. I had to stay put. They obviously were not travelers. It was an inspection. I watched them from the corner of my eye as they moved from person to person. The SS with the dog stopped in front of each traveler and stared for a few minutes. If satisfied, he just moved on. If not he requested identification papers and checked their luggage. He simply opened whatever people carried, spilled the contents on the floor and the other two men examined it. The dog, a shepherd, followed an inch from his boot.

I carefully edged away from the man next to me so it would not appear as if we were together. Then I simply leaned back closed my eyes and pretended to be dozing. Again I experienced this weird sensation of detachment. My other personality was again in control. A creature without fear but only a sense of self preservation. It was by far stronger than I. The SS man stopped in front of me and my eyes opened. I looked straight ahead of me. Then I glanced at him with an expression of blank boredom. I did not smile, but I let our eyes meet indifferently. After a moment, I lowered my eyes glanced, at the dog, then leaned back against the bench.

The SS man moved on and faced the man sitting next to me and repeated the procedure. The man jumped up and asked in German, again too eagerly, "Sir would you like to see my papers?" His hand whipped out his wallet and out came his *Ausweiss*. My heart sank. The man was much too jumpy. The Poles never spoke German unless they needed to and most did not know the language at all. The man just lost whatever chance he had.

A big smile lit up the face of the SS man. He pushed the *Ausweiss* away and addressed his helpers. "Take him to the men's room and examine his *Shwantz* (tail)," he ordered. Now the poor man was shaking all over. They prodded him forward with their guns while the one with the dog continued with the inspection. After a while, they brought him back. They spilled the contents of his suitcase on the floor. It contained only clothes. They ordered him to repack grinning all the time. The hunting had been successful tonight. They had caught their prey — the Jew. The inspection was completed and they marched the man out of the door, a gun in his ribs. The Poles watched the spectacle indifferently. The poor Jew had papers, he must have obtained somehow, but he was circumcised and a Pole never was. In Poland it was not the custom.

After a while, I went to the entrance. I could not go out because of the curfew but I could see the street ahead and watched the man being led away until they were out of sight. I felt absolutely nothing. The Creature was not afflicted with the emotion of sadness. Anger was all she felt.

The train to Warsaw was very crowded usually. It ran only once every twenty-four hours. There were many *Wehrmacht* traveling on it and some SS. The Creature now knew the importance of who one should sit next to. The lesson at the station was not lost on her. I found myself sitting next to a German soldier by choice. All I felt was fatigue. The monotonous clatter of the wheels put me right to sleep for most of the way.

I arrived in Warsaw in the rain. It was frigid, but I was rested and found my way to Ulica Zielona by asking directions. It was a very long walk. Aunt Hela was my father's younger sister. She was married to a Catholic Pole who had died several years before. She had accepted his religion as did Franka, her daughter by a previous marriage. They never advertised their Jewish origins and, in fact, were devout Christians. They both, like my father, were blue-eyed and pug-nosed Aryan types. Oh, how I hoped for a welcome! The bitter sense of loneliness already cut into me like a knife. It was the most painful feeling I ever experienced, worse than hunger or fear.

I knocked on the door and an elderly woman let me in. She looked me over indifferently and asked what I wanted. I told her that I came from Czestochowa to see Hela and Franka. She informed me that they were both at work. They rented a room in her apartment, but since the weather was so bad, I could wait there until they returned.

It was a large, well furnished room with two beds and a sofa. I made a mental note that I will probably sleep on it then sat down in a corner and waited. Again the ticking of the clock. At last they came home, and were already told that I was waiting for them. I was instantly aware of the expressions of annoyance in their faces and all the things I wanted to say froze on my lips. Instead, I just answered their questions. Hela was neither upset or surprised by what I told her. She knew all about the deportations. Warsaw also had a Ghetto of almost half a million. It was happening here also.

At first she told me flatly that I *could not stay*. I was putting everybody in danger by my presence. I had no papers at all and they were only subletting. I explained that Father Krzeminski will have a birth certificate stating that I was a Catholic in less than two weeks now. It has already been three days since I saw him. Could I just stay for a few days?

Aunt Hela shook her head. "You cannot even be seen entering the apartment. People will be alarmed, will ask questions. You have no *Out-Registration* and obviously cannot obtain an *In-Registration* permit. You would have to completely stay out of sight. Besides our landlady will object."

I told her I only needed a few days. . .    Franka took her
mother aside and they consulted in whispers. Finally Franka went
out to talk to the landlady while I sat stiffly in a corner of the
sofa. She came back and smiled for the first time. She asked if I
could visit for one week and the permission was granted. The
landlady did not know that I was Jewish, and took it for granted
that my papers were in order, but if I stayed longer, she would
probably double check.

We had dinner and afterwards a long talk. It was most unpleasant. Aunt Hela was bitter towards her family, including my
father. She complained, her voice rising with anger. First her
family had forced her to marry the husband of her sister who
had died in a terrible accident. She was warming up formula for
her infant son when she accidentally overturned an alcohol
stove. Her gown caught on fire and she died of burns. Someone
had to care for the motherless child and the family prevailed
upon Hela to marry the father. He turned out to be a despicable
man, a fraud, and she hated him. Her life was ruined, but fortunately he died fifteen years later. Franka was only fourteen
then and Hela was left with two children to care for. Her second
husband was a saint of a man who loved her dearly, but he died
soon after they were married.

Hela was a bitter woman. My father had been no help at all.
In fact, when he went to Paris on business, he only brought her
back a purse but gave Pani Szczepanska, the doctor's wife, an
elegant hat! Aunt Hela's voice rose to a high pitch. She could
never — but never!— forgive him for that.    I sat there and
cringed. Father could well be going to his death now and she
blubbered about presents from Paris. The oldest brother, Ludwig, was in America now, and she thought he was much nicer,
even if he did marry a German. . .

It occurred to me that I did not know Uncle Ludwig's address
or even what city he lived in. I asked her about that. She looked
at me with suspicion. No, she would not give me such information. After the war she intended to get in touch with him and he
would have to help her and Franka get out of Poland. If I contacted him also, it would complicate matters. She and Franka
deserved his undivided attention. Besides, she said coldly, it was
most unlikely that I would make it. The birth certificate from
Father Krzeminski was not a sufficient identification. I most likely
did not have a chance. I looked at Franka while her mother
talked. She looked straight ahead impassively. At last I was per-

mitted to retire for the night on the sofa and Aunt Hela went to the bathroom.

"I am sorry about your parents, Zosia. . . " said Franka to me from her bed. It was all the sympathy I got but I was strangely touched by this, and I thanked her for it.

That night I had a very vivid dream. I was on the shore of a vast ocean. Upon it sailed a lonely ship. Its sails were full from a fierce wind, like a hurricane. The sky was slashed with lightning. The waves heaved and they were red. It was an ocean of blood. I stood on the shore helplessly watching it drift away. My parents were on that ship.

I stayed with Aunt Hela for a week and it felt as if I were in a cage. I burned with restlessness. I could hardly wait to go back to Czestochowa. My parents were hiding in that crawl space in the SS owned factory. I held frantically on to hope. Maybe the deportation was over. Maybe they were back in the Ghetto waiting for a word from me and worrying if I was allright. Didn't Father think that the SS would need to leave behind some workers in the War Effort Industries? I was bursting with impatience to see them again. I listened to the ticking of the clock and counted the hours.

Before I left, Aunt Hela looked me over. Yes, I did look very Aryan, except for the reddish tinge in my hair. She bought a bottle of peroxide and washed my hair in it. It got lighter but even redder than before. She did hope, after all, that Arnold, my father, was alive. If so I should give him best regards from her. She would really want to know and made me promise that I will get a word to her as soon as possible. I could see how relieved she was when I said goodbye.

I walked back to the railroad station as the first snow of winter began to fall gently upon the streets of Warsaw. I still wore both my dresses, one on top of the other and a sweater, but I wished I had a coat. I still had some money in my pocket. I intended to buy some butter with it on the black market, to take back with me to the Ghetto for my parents. I had so much to tell them! So much had happened! They will be so proud of me! I imagined them and the Steckis being back in the Ghetto, maybe even back at Twenty Garibaldi Street.

I got off the train, whiplashed by strong emotions, fear and joy. I was back. Now I would be able to find out for myself what happened in the Ghetto. While I waited in Warsaw, in Aunt Hela's oppressive apartment, I gave in to fantasies of hope, that my parents were waiting for me, and were allright. They had to be — there was a very good chance of that! I burned with longing to see them. The uncertainty was a torture. Now I was so very close, only a few minutes walk from the familiar gate to the Ghetto.

I made a mental plan of how I would get back in. I would have to be very, very careful, will have to circle around the area to make sure my old routes of re-entry were not changed by the deportation action. There had to be changes, I thought, but I will find a way. . . I will make it! But in the back of my mind was a cold fear. What if they did not make it, if their plan did not work! I walked impatiently down the now familiar street. It was snowing and cold but I found myself sweating. My stomach was queasy and I shook inside. "Steady, now," I told myself. I would need calm nerves; one wrong move, one bad decision and I will never find out what happened to my parents. They would be waiting, frantic with worry, and I will be caught. I must not disappoint them.

The gate to the Ghetto was boarded up at the nearest check point. No guards. There it was mute and impenetrable. Steady now, there were other streets leading into the Ghetto. They were blocked off with barbed wire but I could at least see the street. I could look in. I walked through the falling snow circling the Ghetto like a moth circling light. Before me was the narrow corridor of a long street. It was blocked off with barbed wire and patrolled by a guard with a gun. I had to get closer to see. . . The street which only a week ago would have been jam-packed with people was completely empty behind densely crisscrossed barbed wire attached to tall posts.

It was desolately empty of all life. Nothing stirred. . . . A white undisturbed carpet of snow covered the cobble stones. No sign of footsteps anywhere. The houses stood mutely vacant and lifeless on both sides as far as I could see. Sidewalks, empty like long, white ribbons, ringed the buildings. Most doors were ajar as if the inhabitants had in a hurry. A ghost town not a soul in sight, so very still.

I walked over to the barbed wire and gripped its coldness. I wanted to shake it. I could see many windows left wide open, curtains fluttering like sails in the blowing wind. As if a plague wiped the street clean of all life. The plague deathhead and cross bones, poison! I couldn't let go of the wire. Someone was standing behind me — it was the guard.

"You cannot go in there," he said in accented Polish. It jolted me back to reality. "It's empty," I said dazedly. "Nobody there. . . "

"Spooky," said the guard, not at all unfriendly. "It gives you the creeps. . . " I could tell by his accent that he was neither German nor Polish. He was a Ukrainian conscript.

"What happened to everybody there?" I asked.

He smiled, "Don't you know? It's Jew Quarter. *Yewrey.* (Jew in Ukrainian)."

"But where did they all go?" I asked cautiously.

"Deported, all of them taken away," he informed me.

"Are there any left at all?" I pressed on. Now the guard stopped smiling and regarded me with suspicion.

"Why do you want to know?"

"It is very strange, that's all," I answered in Russian, remembering what Mother had taught me. The smile was back again.

*"Gaworish po Rusky?"* (You speak Russian?). He was now happy to chat, but not about the Jews. The snow reminded him of Ukraine, he told me. I took my hands off the barbed wire and told him I was cold. I hoped he would have a good day and that I was going home to warm up. "Boring duty. . . " he remarked as I walked away.

Home to warm up, did I say that? There was no more home! It was too risky to continue talking to the guard. Not good even to have him notice my face. I was not being careful. He could have requested to see my papers. I walked as quickly as I could and continued to circle the Ghetto. It was the same everywhere. Empty streets and complete desolation. Maybe nobody was left there any longer. The desolation seeped into every part of my being. The snow was getting thicker.

I went back to the railroad station and bought a hot drink. I had absolutely no where to go. Father Krzeminski told me definitely not to come back for two weeks. If he discovered that I had no place to stay, not even with my Aunt Hela, he would hesitate to give me the birth certificate. It would be too risky for him. Without shelter, my chances of being caught were too high and it could implicate him also. I had to wait three days longer; but where? There was only the railroad station. I was a dog left out in the cold to die.

## RECOLLECTION

*The snow is falling steadily from a slate colored sky. It accumulates on the scarf I wear, on my head and on my shoulders. I keep brushing it off from time to time, otherwise I will look like a snowman. My leotards are wet and so are my feet. But I cannot stop walking. The Ghetto which once housed around fifty thousand people is a large impenetrable island within the city of Czestochowa. I circle it compulsively, stubbornly looking for a sign of life within any of the visible streets but there is none.*

*The wind drives its chill right through my two dresses and sweater. I was able to wash everything when I was at Aunt Hela's but now I am wet to the skin. It is getting darker. The railroad station is my only hope for shelter tonight, but I will have to buy a ticket to somewhere to have an excuse to stay there after curfew. They are very careful about this, otherwise it would become a gathering place for homeless people. If you have no ticket you cannot stay.*

*And what if tonight the SS comes again? What if the SS man with the dog and the penetrating stare sees me again sitting upon the wooden bench. He might remember my face. . . I must be very conspicuous without a suitcase! Lights glow in windows, people hurry home from work and the sidewalks are full of pedestrians. I must ration my money. A railroad ticket is more important than food, even if I don't need to buy one all the way to Warsaw.*

*The station is not very busy tonight and most people arrive just before curfew time. Some are seen off by friends and relatives. Hugs and goodbyes. I have to make myself as presentable as I can. I am grateful for the small comb cousin Franka gave me. I have nothing else. I wash my face in the ladies washroom. There is no soap or paper towels, it is war time, after all. I allow myself another hot drink for today and find the darkest corner of the station. I am too tired to worry about inspections or the SS. There are times when nothing else matters but sleep.*

*I am awakened by a feeling of dread, must have had a nightmare. The night curfew is over at 6 a.m. and a group of night arrivals is clustered at the door, eager to leave. Today I will circle the Ghetto again from the other side. It is colder and the snow is dry and slippery. The restaurant at the station was still closed when I left but I feel no hunger. I am obsessed with finding out what happened to my parents, nothing else matters. My mind is racing.*

*I remember Father mentioning Herr Buhler's address and I am electrified by an idea. He is a high ranking SS and in charge of a factory inside the Ghetto. He surely has a free access to there. I know where he lives. It is the most prestigious address in Czestochowa, a wide street with a neutral ground in the center, well landscaped with shrubs and trees. I will go to see Herr Buhler. Father believed him to be a reasonable man. . . All he can do is kill me. At this point it does not matter to me, and probably he will not. I hear Father's voice in my mind, "a reasonable man this Buhler."*

*It must be close to noontime and a family man will come home for his lunch. I am almost out of breath when I arrive at his door. Now I will know! I knock without hesitation and a woman answers the door. She seems pleasant. I tell her that I came to see Herr Buhler.*

*"What do you want of him?" she wants to know. I frantically search for an answer to this but cannot come up with anything. "I cannot tell you," I say honestly. "Well," she hesitates, "allright, come on in." She can see me shivering and thinks it is only from the cold. She leads me in to the kitchen and pours me some hot milk. Her son, a boy about ten years old, is sitting at the table eating lunch. "Herr Buhler should be in any minute. . . " she says and hands me a slice of bread. The boy smiles at me. There are school books on the table and the kitchen is cozy and warm.*

*I can hear the front door being opened and Herr Buhler comes into the kitchen. His wife tells him about me immediately and we look at each other. He is a stout man, about forty years old with blue eyes and ruddy complexion, dressed in civilian clothes, which makes it clear that he is Gestapo. They are the only SS who wear no uniforms.*

*He gives me a questioning look. "Who are you and what do you want?"*

*"I am Zofia Sieradzki. . . " I introduce myself and do not need to say any more. Herr Buhler's expression undergoes an instant change and he sends his wife and son into the living room without giving them any explanation. He takes a gun out of his pocket and gestures with it towards the door. "Let's go!" he says curtly. I put the half eaten piece of bread back on the table and walk ahead of him out the door and on to the side walk, then across to the divider. It is obvious that Herr Buhler wants me away form his front steps and his family as if I were a bomb ready to explode.*

*"Why did you come here?" he asks me, the gun pressing against my rib cage. It makes me very angry. I am absolutely certain that he is not about to shoot me in front of his kitchen window.*

*"I came here to find out what happened to my father," I say calmly.*

*Herr Buhler looks at me with incredulity. "I did not know that Sieradzki had a child. . . " he says, perhaps because Father was a grey haired, sixty year old gentleman.*

*"And why not? You have a kid yourself." I say indignantly. "And you can put away that gun, Herr Buhler, I only want to know about my father."*

*"Do you realize," he tells me, "that I am an officer of the Gestapo? It is my duty to take you to the authorities in charge of the Ghetto immediately."*

*"I am not going!" I tell him. "You can shoot me right here if you wish in front of your family."*

*Herr Buhler knows that I mean exactly what I say and he changes his approach. "Look girl, nothing bad will happen to you. The deportation is over and now nobody will hurt you. I will simply deliver you back to the Ghetto and let you lose among your people. No one is being killed there any more."*

*"But the Ghetto is empty" I tell him. "I looked in and saw no one in the streets."*

*"You are wrong," he says persuasively. "Some Jews are still left inside there. Let me take you there and you will see for yourself." It is an impasse between us and my frustration is boiling over.*

*"What kind of a person are you anyway?" I lash out. "You are murdering women and children, killing helpless people! Do you really think that I will just walk with you to the police station so they can kill me also? My father thought that you were a decent man, but you are not! You are a murderer like the rest of you. Are you not ashamed of yourself?"*

*Herr Buhler is completely taken back by my outburst. "It is my duty, as an officer of the SS, to take you in," he tells me almost apologetically.*

*"I want to thank you for the kind offer," I tell him, "but I will not go with you. If you force me I will scream and you will have to kill me here in front of your very nice family." I can see that Herr Buhler has made a decision.*

*"But where else can you go? You will not survive on the outside. I promise you that there are still Jews in that Ghetto and you will be better off there. No harm will come to you. You really have no where else to go." I am beginning to feel defeated by now.*

*"Thank you Herr Buhler, but I will take my chances." He turns toward his window looking very uncomfortable now. Here he is standing in the middle of a divider pointing a gun at a little girl. How must it look to his wife and son?*

*"Allright, tell me, did your parents hide in my factory?"*

*My God, what did I do, I think to myself. What if they are still there and I have stupidly given them away. I will be responsible for their death. . . It will be my fault! "I don't know Herr Buhler, I have no idea," I stutter.*

*"Well, I was there after the deportation," he said slowly. "The factory is closed for the time being; nobody is there. In the courtyard there was a hat lying on the ground, a maroon color, felt hat. Didn't your father have a hat like this?"*

*Is he trying to lead me on? What is this man trying to tell me? Have I inadvertently given away my parents' hiding place? It is now two weeks after the deportation. They would be out of food and water by now. . . My mind can not absorb it all. It is splitting and splintering. It is reeling. I am losing my mind!*

*"I am leaving now Herr Buhler," I say quietly. "Thank you for telling me what you know. I will start walking and you can shoot me, but you cannot follow me. If you do I will scream as loud as I can." I begin to walk without looking back, certain that he is very much relieved to be rid of me, and certain that he would not shoot.*

There was no need to circle the Ghetto any longer. I was drowning in sadness. I needed a place where I could think. My legs were weak as if made of jelly, but they still carried me, up the hill, and up the steps to the ancient, medieval cloister of Jasna Gora. It was shady and peaceful in the baroque, ornate chapel.

I knelt in a pew and began to pray for my parents, wherever they were. In front of me, above the altar hung the picture of the Black Madonna, as it had for hundreds of years. It looked down at me with oblique, strange, almost oriental eyes. I abandoned myself to sadness. I knew that my parents could never survive in a Labor Camp for very long. No one ever came back from there. Not even a word, a message or a letter, as if they had entered the realm of the dead.

# 11

## THE PLASTER SAINT

I woke up feeling disoriented and confused. Where was I? My whole body was stiff and ached. I was in a corner under the pew wedged against the old unyielding wood of the bench, practically rolled into a ball to preserve some body warmth. It was an effort to straighten out. When had I fallen asleep? I did not remember crawling under here, or waking during the night. My teeth were chattering with cold and my clothes smelled of dampness. It was almost morning. I have made it for another day.

The cavernous chapel was still dark. Nothing moved and nothing creaked. What time could it be? As if it mattered! I tried to congratulate myself. This was a lot cheaper than the railroad station. I did not need to have a ticket to any destination. Well, maybe to heaven; the place was other-worldly. What did time matter in a chapel that had been built in the sixteen hundreds to replace the monastery's original wooden church?

Here, what was happening to me seemed in a way minimized; my own lifespan an insignificant moment in the flow of centuries. Time hung heavy upon this place, layers upon layers of happenings, of winters, summers and springs. Somewhere within the stillness had to be old echoes or old ghosts. And I should be right at home with them. Was I not a ghost myself?

People certainly reacted to my presence as if they had just run into an apparition. I remembered having arrived at Doctor Szczepanski's last winter, unexpectedly in the middle of the night, and how upsetting it was to them to see my face appear at the door. Certainly they were not happy to see me and not through any fault of mine. I carried the plague, I was death arriving right at their doorstep. How very relieved they had seemed as I left. Their house would be safe again. It was the same with Aunt Hela. My sudden appearance even frightened an officer of the Gestapo into frantically reaching for his gun. And Father Krzeminski? I still had a picture clearly lodged in my mind of his housekeeper clamping a shaking hand over her mouth as if in a gesture of horror.

Once in its history, Poland was decimated by the Black Cholera Plague. A third of its population was lost to it and to this day each Pole probably utters the word "cholera" every day. It is one of the most often used words of the Polish language, because, especially at the time of war, people tend to curse a lot. People say it in anger, out of frustration, to express contempt or even disappointment. Most do not even connect it with the plague of long ago. It is just the most ritual curse word in Poland. I am as welcome as "cholera" wherever I go, I thought. People stare at me with horror and dismay which perhaps is mixed with a sense of guilt. People want me not to be. . . Not to exist.

### RECOLLECTION

*There are still a couple of crumpled bills left in my pocket, all that stands between me and starvation. It is not much, just enough for a trip to Warsaw or for two nights "lodging" on a bench at the rail station. That is if I do not use the ticket and pretend that I overslept if questioned as to why I am there after the curfew. The ticket is my only excuse, my right to sit on that bench. That is provided I avoid being apprehended for having no identification.*

*But then, congratulations to myself, I have just discovered another place to where I can escape the cold and spend the night. How could there be a more extravagant lodging than the Gothic Chapel of the famous Jasna Gora Cloister! If only the Jews in the Ghetto knew that there was such an opportunity. There would be poor, hunted human wretches hiding under every pew; but only until they were discovered. I have to be careful not to be noticed by anyone. Am I as welcome as the "cholera" even here?*

*Outside, it is winter in earnest, and I am blinded by the glare of sunlight upon the snow. Maybe Father Krzeminsky will help me. If he is under surveillance by the Gestapo, he must be involved with the partisans, the underground. Are we not fighting and fearing the same enemy, the Nazi Poison? It is time now for me to see him again. I will tell him how desperate I am, at the end of my rope with no place to go! Maybe he will think of something, he is now my only hope. Again, I walk past the Ghetto and all the way to Grosz. Along the way I rehearse in my mind what to say when I get to the Parish, how to present my desperate need without begging.*

*It is a great relief that Father Krzeminski is still there. Anyone who is on the list of the Gestapo has an uncertain future.*

*Today he is not nearly as nervous, and true to his word, he has a typed out certificate of Birth and Christening waiting for me. It is made out on yellowing, aged paper to give it a genuine appearance. He has made me three years older than I really am. People would be less suspicious if I am a little older, especially if I need to find work. Being a young orphaned girl will invite questions. Even a suggestion that I might be Jewish could be fatal. Fortunately I am developed enough to appear older.*

*The place of my birth on this counterfeit certificate is a small town near the city of Krakow named Bochnia. The spelling of my mother's maiden name has been altered to sound more Polish, otherwise the other information is the same. I am given a small prayer book and Father Krzeminski instructs me to learn everything in it by heart. It is well worn but has a lovely mother of pearl binding. He also gives me a silver crucifix on a chain.*

*I explain that I have attended catechism classes as a child, but he actually knows this part of my history already. Father Krzeminski seems to know my family very well. I am extremely touched by this and ask him if he would wish to christen me. But even there he surprises me. He remembers my mother's wishes. It is to be done when I am sixteen, and he will give it due respect. I am under stress now, and this is a very serious decision to make.*

*We sit and talk seriously about what I shall do years from now, while tonight I have no place to stay. But then he is under the happy impression that I have just arrived from Warsaw, from Aunt Hela's house, and will be returning there tonight. He thinks that I have a safe home to live in until the end of the war. I have to tell him otherwise if he is to help me and I have rehearsed every word of it in my mind, but somehow it is very hard. Maybe I just dread another rejection.*

*"Will you be taking the night train to Warsaw?" he wants to know. A perfect opening for me. I open my mouth but the words that come out of it shock me to the core. I am telling him calmly and in a steady voice that I will, indeed, be taking the night train. Words and sentences strange and unbidden come out of my mouth as if a record was played against my will. I have no control over them. They glibly escape from my very own lips. My face smiles pleasantly. I thank him and tell him how my parents would appreciate all he did for me if they knew. My legs straighten up and carry me to the door. At the door, Father Krzeminski pats my face. He does not know how hungry I am or the desperation within me, does not even suspect anything wrong. He knows nothing.*

*"If you are ever caught," he tells me, "the Gestapo will trace these papers to me, you know. You will not be able to withhold the information*

*from them. . . They have a way. . . They torture people. They will get it out of you in the end. If this happens and you should suffer guilt, — do not on account of me. I have done for others what I am doing for you. Those are the chances I have to take. Zosia, I want to give you absolution now in advance and my full forgiveness. Save yourself from torture with my blessing. Nobody can withstand it anyway. . . "*

I stand rooted to the floor. If this is being a Christian, then it is beautiful. He places his life with me like a gift and I leave carrying it wherever I go. He had placed it on the line. The meaning of his words seeps into me. I want to tell him so many things. . . but all I do is thank him again. My legs carry me out of the Parish and into the street. I walk like a wind-up toy upon the snow towards Czestochowa, past the Ghetto, up the wide boulevard leading to Jasna Gora, up the steps towards the cloister and into the Basilica.

There is a sign on the iron gate leading inside Krolowa Polski Modl sie za nami. (Queen of Poland, Pray for Us). The ancient inscrutable face of the Madonna seems to gaze at me. I kneel in the pew, my face in my hands. I cry but no tears come out of my eyes. I cry inside my stomach. My eyes hurt and burn as if they needed to burst and let out a flood of tears, but they remain completely dry. I am certain that I have lost my sanity. I do not have control over what I do or say. I don't understand, do not comprehend at all what had happened at the Parish.

There is a creature within me, and it is stronger than I. It is oblivious to all consequences, even death. It has no feelings other than anger and fear of rejection. It is almost indifferent to what will happen to me. Father Krzeminski was my only chance, and now I have none. My greatest enemy is within. It has condemned me to die, almost capriciously. I cannot fight it.

This, I am certain, will be my last night. Yesterday I stood in front of a bakery store. People went in and out and bought bread. I could smell it. My stomach was cramping with hunger, but if I were to beg, someone would have been suspicious and called the police. I thought of grabbing the bread and running but the pedestrians would have stopped me for sure. A dog out in the rain, or out in the falling snow! Today I do not even feel hunger; just weakness. Surely Father Krzeminski would have fed me, but I could not even ask.

Now I own several things. I have the gold coin from my mother. I have exactly the price of a one way ticket to Warsaw, a silver crucifix and a prayer book with old, worn, mother of pearl covers. I have a false Birth and Christening certificate, and the responsibility for Father Krzeminski's life if I am caught. And I have an implacable enemy within myself. What I no longer have is hope. All is for naught.

*I used to pray to Jesus when I was very young. Those were the only prayers I was ever taught. How nice it would be if there was a heaven waiting somewhere beyond. If there was justice. My parents would benevolently gaze at me from that other dimension where they would exist forever in a state of complete peace. How desperately I wish it were true. All these people I knew and loved would be there waiting for me.*

*Deep down I instinctively know that they are dead. Moishe, my friend and teacher, the girls I skipped rope with, everybody. If only, instead of a filthy, crowded, locked cattle car, I could imagine them floating in the silvery mist of heaven. Instead, I see in front of me a crowd of people in the morning fog, dimly visible, stark, staring faces, all somehow familiar. If only religion was the truth! I want it to be, I want to believe it!*

*I start with the Lord's Prayer and say it over and over again. It is hypnotic. Our Father. . . Above me hangs the gilded, ornate ceiling of the Basilica. The baroque gothic lief. Every inch of it is intricately carved. Before me is the altar with the tall candle holders. An other worldly light illuminates the Black Madonna as if upon a heavenly stage. All the props are perfectly in place.*

*I tightly grasp the white, pearly, prayer book and hypnotize myself into a trance with fervent repetitious prayers. I try to reach my parents with my mind, I almost feel that I can. I feel elated. My mind reels and spins and floats. There is a scent all around me like incense and I drink it in. Then a great tiredness overcomes me, a peaceful drowsiness. I can hardly wait for sleep to come. I want it and it is a comfortable feeling, like a baby in a crib. The corner under the pew is so inviting, even the floor feels soft. I give myself permission to relax completely. Not a bad thought in my mind; all is peaceful for the first time. I feel no hunger at all, no cold. I wedge myself under the pew and fall asleep instantly.*

*Towards morning I crawl out and stretch, feeling actually rested. I am the only one here now and I wonder if people came by and went while I slept. There are statues of saints and angels. Yesterday seeps into my mind with a sense of unreality. A statue catches my eye in the semi darkness. I don't know who or what it represents, it is still too dark to tell but I see its face. It is chipped. A statue of a saint with a cracked face. Just like my mind. It disturbs me. I was praying to a plaster saint with a cracked face! I have not only lost my sanity but also my intelligence. How could I do it? Did they manage to strip me of everything?*

*"Damn you, plaster saint!" I yell and my voice echoes eerily and bounces off the high ceilings. It is frightening and I finish in a whisper: "They can take my parents from me, and everything else. They can take my life away, but not my reason!" I stand defiantly in the Basilica, facing all of*

it. *"I will not pray to plaster saints and I am not afraid; not any more! Not of anything!"*

I sit quietly on the bench and prepare myself to accept reality. Reason tells me that I will not make it. Nobody will give me shelter and I will not beg! Even if I did, it would be useless. I am as welcome as the plague. I will wait here until the restaurants will open for breakfast, then I will spend my money on food. I feel regret that Father Krzeminski went into all this trouble for me. Wasted effort. I am at peace; do not care at all about anything, have come to terms with death. I will join my parents, my cousins, Moishe, everybody. I am contented.

Outside, it is calm and grey. There is an accumulation of snow on the steps leading up to the cloister. On both sides vendors have set up shop and are eagerly competing for customers. They sell souvenirs, small pictures and now also already Christmas decorations, many of which are hand carvings. Visitors and tourists are beginning to arrive, including Germans. Jasna Gora is a famous attraction, and here, for the last couple of nights I had this place all to myself! Christmas will be here before long. The melody of Christmas carols resound in my mind like a background music. *"Slumber baby Jesus. . . "*

I am in no hurry, nobody is waiting for me anywhere, except in eternity. Only there am I wanted. And eternity is for ever. . . Christmas decorations fill me with nostalgia. I always loved it so much. So many memories.

I stop at the display tables and examine everything. I feel apologetic because I am not here to buy but just to look. Out of a small framed picture, Jesus looks at me with unbelievably blue eyes, hair like it just came out of beautician's hands, wavy and blond, a small red Valentine shaped heart on his chest, radiant and cherry pink. I wonder what he really looked like. . . If he were here now, he would probably have been deported, he would have been on the cattle train on the way to a labor camp. On one table there are small replicas of the Black Madonna and sculptures of a creche. They are beautiful and intricately made. Each figure and the animals can be removed and inserted again, Mary and Joseph in the stable at Bethlehem. Each figure is expertly chiseled out of whitish wood.

There is a man and wife behind the display table. They smile at me when they notice my admiration of their work. The woman tells me that her husband has been making these for years and they put them out about this time of the Christmas season. But people are not buying these days; nobody has money but the Germans. Lots of them come around, but they expect you to speak their language. . .

*Oh well, speaking of the devil. . . . A* Wehrmacht *officer and a woman approach our table and browse around. They think I am with the couple and address their questions to me. I tell them all I know about the Cloister, then show them the way the little figures fit precisely in. Children could take them out and snap them right back in. A wonderful toy for Christmas, or a present for friends, a souvenir from Jasna Gora. The woman is very interested but they want to do some sight seeing today and the carvings are bulky to carry around.*

*Well, no problem, we could deliver if she told us where they are staying. In that case she will take three. I ask the vendors about the price and increase it a little bit. The German couple is staying in a hotel near by and gives me their room number. I set up a time in the evening and consult again with the vendors. Everybody is pleased, but I feel very weak. I had almost nothing to eat in days.*

*The vendors do not want me to leave. They tell me their names which are Antek and Stasia Mikula. They have sandwiches in their basket and I could have one if I am hungry. It was a big item sale for them, it made their day. The sandwich tastes very good and I eat it very slowly.*

*I tell them that I am from Silesia, have no parents and only a grandmother in Warsaw, with whom I hope to stay. They accept it readily and I soon notice why. The silver crucifix hangs reassuringly from its chain against my sweater. Besides, they are very simple people and I soon find out that Antek Mikula can neither read or write, and his wife only a little. They tell me that they have a grown son at home who is severely retarded and has to be fed and changed. It is very sad, but it is God's will!*

*I stay with them for the day and business is very good. In the evening we have the sculptures to deliver and they practically beg me to stay in their apartment for a while. Stasia Mikula usually frames the pictures while her husband does his carving. The caring for the son takes a lot of her time, so maybe I could help with the framing.*

*We fold shop in the afternoon because it again began to snow and push everything in a little cart down a couple of streets to their apartment. I look over my shoulder at the ancient cloister as we leave. I have an eerie feeling about that plaster saint. He surely did not hold a grudge! The Mikulas are happy to have found me. They hope I can stay for a while, if it is allright with my grandmother.*

*The Black Madonna painting is famous for having caused miracles to happen. It is the most holy shrine in Poland and today it extended its magic to me. "Hail Mary," I thought. She was, after all, a Jewish mother.*

*Mrs. Mikula sets out to cook dinner and Antek and I trudge through the snow to the hotel. The German couple is having some friends over and* meet us drinks in hand. Before we leave, we get two more orders to be delivered first thing in the morning. Antek, who is a very shy man, is overcome with wonder at such success. These are very big items, he tells me. "It is like a miracle to sell so much in one day." Yes, if only he knew how great a miracle.

The Mikula's have a comfortable, clean apartment. Antek has a pedal- operated, old-fashioned machine on which he grinds and polishes his wooden figurines. But the bulk of his work is done by hand. He works expertly with his chisel with total absorption. It does not matter that he is illiterate. He is an artist in his own right. Their kitchen table is heaped with pictures and frames, ready to assemble. There are bottles and jars of paint and glue. There is lots of work to do, especially at Christmas time. But they work in silence, hardly exchange a word all evening.

The source of their unhappiness is their son. He appears to be in his late twenties. He needs to be fed and the saliva dribbles from his lips as he eats. He can do nothing for himself at all. Stasia cares for him with great devotion. Their entire lives revolve around the care of their son and the wares they produce for their little stand at the Jasna Gora.

Antek takes hours with each small carving. Even the lips have to form an expression, the eyelids have to be just so. Then, of course, the final touches of the paint brush.

The atmosphere in their apartment is bleak and depressed. They talk bitterly about their son. Who will take care of him after they are gone? It is very much on their minds. Their worry goes beyond the grave, it is endless. At night Stasia expertly fastens a large diaper on him. She seems to have a way of communicating with him.

The Mikula's are compulsive about cleanliness. They scrub and iron. It seems as if their hands never cease to work devotedly, and in silence. They get up at dawn, say their prayers and begin all over again. Their money is kept in a jar in a locked cupboard. They get their food on the black market and scrape out a living. Still it is a hand to mouth existence. People have no money these days. Five special carvings are now a season's sale. I sleep on the floor but my pillow cases are immaculately clean and the quilt is very thick, made of goose down.

Each morning now we set up shop by the entrance to the Jasna Gora, each day exactly identical to the one that past. The Mikula's are not concerned with "in registration" or "out registration." They have no suspicions about my being Jewish. They are happy to have me. They need me. Now Stasia can stay with her son and work at home. Antek and I do pretty well, and she can mount the souvenir pictures also during the day. It is a dreary life, but it is safe. I could survive the war here easily, in the shadow of the cloister, compliments of the Plaster Saint. But is my life *really worth the effort? I am beginning to chafe with impatience. I am bothered.*

*While talking to some of the other vendors, I hear electrifying news. I hear that there are still Jews in the Ghetto! I feign indifference, cannot afford to show interest, but I mention that I have looked into the street and there is no sign of life; they must be mistaken. But the vendors are certain. Jews are marched out of there daily, early in the morning in a long column under guard. Yes, there are Jews in the Ghetto, they are certain. The Germans have left some behind, probably needed still to work somewhere.*

*"They are as hard to kill as bed bugs," one of the vendors tells me. "You'd think the Germans got them all, but here they are again, tough to stamp out. But their time has come!" I also hear that now if a Jew is discovered hiding on the outside, a reward can be collected from the Germans for turning the fugitive in. There is money in it, including a bonus of sugar and vodka, I am told.*

*"It would come in handy, especially now that it is Christmas." The friendly vendor, who tells me the story, is also keeping his eyes open. "You never know, it is like getting a bonus, easier than selling this stuff nowadays," he says pointing to his wares. On his table, the pictures of the blond Jesus sit under an overhanging to protect them from the snow. The replicas of the Black Madonna with Child are stacked in a row.*

*Antek brags about the popularity of his carvings with the Germans. Thank the Lord, Zosia can talk business to them, it's been a blessing. The other vendor regards me with open hostility. He surely does not like all this competition one bit.*

*"Soo, Zosia speaks German ehh?" Most Poles do not, and I can see a hint of expectant suspicion flicker across the vendor's face. Maybe he can smell a bonus. I tell him that I used to help clean house for a German couple in Silesia. Cannot be too defensive now, it would only make him more suspicious. I stop at that.*

*Christmas. It is in the air along with the sounds of carols. People walk faster; a decoration in a window here and there. Stasia and Antek dressed up the apartment, and baked spiced cookies.*

*Within me a storm is raging. I am wracked by restlessness. I am propelled by it a terrible need to get away, to get free. The apartment stifles me. I cannot stand the sight of the Mikula's retarded son. It enrages me. Why is this drooling, diapered creature living on, when young beautiful Jewish boys are dying in those Labor Camps? Why must Moishe die and he live!*

*I have a terrible need to know what is happening in the Ghetto, cannot rest until I do. From time to time, the Mikula's son smiles at me, his vacant smile. What does he perceive? Does he have feelings? I feel guilty for begrudging him being alive, and it makes me even more impatient. I want to leave here even more than I care to stay alive myself. The restlessness is not unlike this which I felt in Aunt Hela's when I had to stay in her cramped apartment for a week. It is a churning at the pit of my stomach, it is a torture. I am a little bit relieved when Antek and I are out with the stand, but even there I am restless.*

*I had Antek fashion me a tray held by a strap from my neck. This way I can place a few smaller items on it and roam on the steps. I approach Germans going in or out of the cloister, smile at them and say "Gruss Got" (God Greetings) which is a greeting popular in some parts of Germany, like Bavaria for example. It usually elicits a friendly response. I have learned a lot from my German customers. The religious respond to my greeting and if they do not, I waste no time. I usually single out the "chest eagle" which identifies the simple* Wehrmacht. *I stay clear of the "arm eagle" which means SS.*

*Sometimes they come over curiously as I talk to the soldiers, listen and occasionally buy something. The older they are, the better the chance of a sale. The ones going home on a furlough from the Russian front are the best customers. The other vendors hate me, especially the one pining away to get himself a bonus by catching and delivering to the authorities a fugitive Jew. I intercept customers from right under his nose, and he and Antek almost jostled each other over it. But then I come home and the restlessness starts again, and I cannot even sleep.*

*I succumb to it one day, it is beyond my power to resist. I stuff my few things in my pocket and simply leave without explanations. Antek chases down the stairs after me and implores to know if I will be back. I tell him that I will.*

*I feel relieved to be free again and embark upon my search for the Ghetto entrance where I might catch a glimpse of the Jews being led to work. But the first day is fruitless and I return home to the Mikulas. Stasia is happy to see me. I helped her fill their cupboard jar full of German marks. They try to induce me to stay by giving me some money, and wonder if I miss seeing my grandmother in Warsaw.*

*I leave again very early the next day. There are many streets leading into a Ghetto. It might take me a while. I stand next to a traffic signal looking into the depths of a Ghetto street. It has not changed, it is empty and lifeless. The vehicles drive very slowly past me over the heavy snow down the cross street. From time to time pedestrians pass by indifferently. A vehicle stops for the traffic along side. It is driven by German guards.*

*Suddenly, I feel myself being grabbed from behind. "Zosia!" an insistent voice whispers urgently into my ear. "For God's sake be very still! It is I, Koplowicz!" I feel myself being lifted bodily and other hands pull me up swiftly into the truck. Tattered snow covered figures loom above me in the open back of the truck and push me down.*

*Jews! "Don't make a sound," they whisper and I feel myself being covered by empty burlap sacks. "Be very quiet!" The truck rumbles ahead slowly for a long time, then comes to a stop. I am lifted up again and deposited on the ground and covered with a heap of the empty burlap sacks so the Germans will not see me. Several men wearing white arm bands bearing the Jewish star hover over me. The truck backs up and drives away again, empty. I look around and know immediately that I am back in the Ghetto again.*

*Before me stands Koplowicz. I remember him very well. He is a young man from Praszka, a little older than my brother and a good friend of his. He is a tall, blond, blue eyed man who used to be known for his wit. He used to write humorous songs, some of which I knew by heart. He married very young and was the father of five girls, the oldest, Helenka, was a friend of mine. Like her father, she was blond, blue-eyed and extremely pretty. She adored him and was his favorite. His wife was a tiny, chubby woman, pregnant most of the time and busy with her children. They never had much, but were a devoted family, laughing no matter how broke they were, always full of affection and love. Helenka, because of her Aryan features, had been very successful at smuggling during the Praszka Ghetto days. I had no idea that they had somehow made it to Czestochowa or were also in that Ghetto at the same time we were.*

Koplowicz looked at me with intensity. There was something about this fixed stare that made me uneasy. There was such desperation reflected in his face.

"I recognized you right away," he said. "Every time we were outside the Ghetto, I kept looking. I was sure that eventually someone out of that transport would come back and try to make it back in. But nobody would believe me. They said it could not happen. Now!" he said approaching me closer as if afraid I would disappear, "Tell us now, where are they?"

"I don't know," I said helplessly.

"What do you mean you don't know! You came back, didn't you? You are the only one. Tell me where they took them, my wife, my children, Helenka. . . " His voice broke. "All of them!" Koplowicz grabbed my shoulders and began to shake me violently until I heard my teeth rattle. "You've got to tell me where they are!"

By now the others tried to restrain him and calm him. "Let her talk, Koplowicz. . . "

I told them that I have never been deported on that transport. That I had no idea where the others were, — that I wished I knew.

Koplowicz fixed me with a bitter stare. There was madness in his eyes. He grabbed my shoulders again and shouted. "Why are you alive! Why do you live if the others do not; if my Helenka is gone! Why are you here!" Tears began to roll down his cheeks. "What right do you have to live?" There was no way to reach him.

"He is cursed with hope," said one of the men. "He keeps believing that any day now somebody will come back and bring him news that his family is allright. He refuses to give up wishful thinking." Koplowicz turned around and left without another word.

Now I looked around. We were on the sidewalk of a street in front of a row of dilapidated old buildings. The other side of the street was cordoned off by densely tangled barbed wire. On the other side of the wire, the houses were abandoned and empty just the way I saw the Ghetto street from the outside.

Now the other men explained to me what I saw. The Germans had deported everybody from the large sprawling area. Out of the some fifty thousand people, there were just a couple of thousand left, hand picked to do the work the Germans wanted done. They were young people between the ages of eighteen and perhaps thirty, women and men. Those left were all strong and healthy appearing specimens. Nobody older or younger was permitted to stay, and only a total of a couple of thousand were permitted at that.

In the center of what used to be the old Ghetto a small area of houses was blocked off and encompassed by barbed wire fence. It now housed the remaining few. Now there was an inhabited Ghetto *hidden within* the old vacated one like a small island within a dead, empty "no man's land."

The vacant part of the Ghetto was off limits to everybody. Nobody could enter it because these vacant houses contained the belongings of those deported. These "dead" streets were being cleared building by building, apartment by apartment. Out of the present, so called little Ghetto, a crew of women workers left each morning under SS guard. They sorted and crated the contents of these abandoned apartments. Then, when only naked furniture was left, a crew of men loaded it on trucks and it was all deposited in SS warehouses for disposition.

It was a trip like this Koplowicz and the others were on when he grabbed me, hoping that I had returned from wherever his family had been taken.

In addition to those sorting and packing the contents of the apartments, there was also a work detachment of several hundred who were marched off daily to a munitions factory a few miles outside the Ghetto. Otherwise, the new "small Ghetto" was surrounded by the empty area called "no man's land" as if by an impenetrable moat.

Anyone caught in the vacant part was shot, and this applied to Jews and non Jews alike. The SS guarded jealously what they now considered their possessions. The new, small island Ghetto, was impossible to escape from, because the "no man's land" was patrolled by guards with dogs. All this dangerous territory had to be crossed and it was many streets, and miles wide. Those attempting it were unfailingly brought back and shot on the assembly place where roll call was held each morning to form the working detail parties.

My first question was whether any of the factories which the SS operated within the old Ghetto were still active. The men told me definitely that they were not. This meant that Herr Buhler had told me the truth. I wanted to find out for myself and now I knew.

No one under the age of eighteen was supposed to be here, which meant that now I was in the Ghetto illegally. I was told that some "too old and too young" people were still here, however. They had managed to hide in the basements or in hiding places during the deportation and crawled like worms out of holes when they could. Now they were constantly scared of being picked up for deportation.

A small hope flickered within me. Maybe my parents were among them. But the men did not know. There were not many people left here now, I would find out very soon.

There was a man and his son here from Praszka, both working at the munitions factory. Their name was Markowicz.

My heart leapt with hope. The Markowicz family had shared an apartment with us in the Praszka Ghetto. They would know about my parents. We walked down the snowy, grimy, bleak street of the "little Ghetto." It was getting dark and long shadows of evening were falling. I was back in a trap, after all I had been through. But I had to find out for sure. There was no other way.

My knees were weak with apprehension as I followed the men to the room where the Markowicz's now lived. We stopped in front of a door. The windows were boarded up on both sides of the building. We knocked and waited. A voice came from the inside, "Come in."

# 12

# RUSSIAN ROULETTE

Zenek Markowicz and his father occupied a narrow room on the main floor of an old building. It was dimly lit, damp and chilly. At first, I was so overcome with emotion that my voice seemed to stick in my throat. Zenek came forward and I could tell how happy he was to see me. I would have cried if it were possible, but I could no longer cry. Two very dear familiar faces I remembered so well from Praszka, as if from another life. I remembered Zenek's little sister Celina singing a song about the Sahara desert and the three of us playing outside in the sun.

How glad I was that Zenek and his father were alive and well! Strange, but those days in the Praszka Ghetto seemed so wonderful to me now; rats and all. I had my parents then, I was not alone. I had a terrible urge to hug Zenek, to kiss him, but first of all I needed to ask about my parents. In a way I already knew the answer, was just reluctant to accept the truth; still hanging on to an illusion of hope.

Now I had to face it. I was told that my parents were not here. They had been deported. Zenek told me that there were only three young men from Praszka still left behind in the small Ghetto, who were strong enough to suit the Germans, and no women at all. He was only fifteen years old and very concerned that at the next selection he would be deported. They welcomed me to stay with them.

Mrs. Markowicz and Celina were also alive and being hidden from the Germans by a Polish family. I envied their good fortune. It was a miracle, a very rare occurrence. They did not tell me any details, and I knew better than to ask any questions. This was a secret not to be entrusted to anyone, even to best of friends.

I was very impressed that they managed to arrange it. Mr. Markowicz was a very resourceful man, very smart. I couldn't help being jealous, even though it filled me with guilt. I should have been happy for them, but all I could think was how much I wished that I, too, still had my parents. Was I as bitter as Koplowicz?

It was so very hard to give up all hope, but now it flickered dimly within me. We still did not know where the deported people were taken. We have never heard of Auschwitz or Treblinka, or any of the death camps the Nazis had set up in Poland. Nobody ever came back to tell us, it was a very well-guarded secret. We had our suspicions, but could never imagine the awful truth. It was inconceivable. But we feared, knowing the Germans, that the deportations had a terrible meaning.

I was confronted by the likelihood that I was now an orphan. The very word had a strange and ominous sound to it; a dreadful meaning. Mother had once taught me a Russian song about a little orphan walking alone on a cold winter night in the Russian snow. It used to make me feel so sad to sing it. It had a mournful, haunting melody, but a very touching ending. A lonely old lady finds the lost orphan, tucks him into bed and takes care of him forever after. The last refrain was about how God feeds the little birds on the frozen plains and sustains the flowers, and how surely, Almighty God, would never abandon a lonely orphan. The melancholy song played like a record of my mother's singing in my mind over and over again.

Zenek and I sat and talked until late and I found myself singing the song for him. Then I sang another haunting Russian song about two roses, one of them white and pure and the other red and vivacious. One day, a cold wind came and they wilted. Now nothing could touch them again, neither joy nor sorrow and with them together passed springtime and love.

The song was like a premonition, though I never knew it then when Mother taught it to me, of a cold wind that was to come. A wind that would sweep away all dreams, hope and love which like the roses, would wilt away for me. I sang and my voice rang so strangely in the narrow, dim little room in the Ghetto. But Zenek understood. It was the only way I could express my sadness because I was not able to cry. It made me realize how heavy was the loneliness on the outside, where to show my feelings would give me away, where there was not one person to whom I could open up, who could understand.

Now that I was here, what could I do? Would I have to wait until another selection when the "illegals" were weeded out and sent to this ominous, shadowy "Labor Camp?" Maybe this would be for the best. I had no reason to hang onto life and loneliness. The words were synonymous to me. Except for one thing. I did not want to give in to the Germans and couldn't stand the thought of being confined, restricted or restrained. This would be worse than death!

It was quite unreal, being inside the ghetto again. It was eerily quiet. There were no sounds of traffic or voices drifting from the street. The room was cramped and smelled musty. What would tomorrow be like?

Zenek and I spoke in whispers as we sat in a corner and discussed my options. He explained that tomorrow I would have to attend the roll call, — it was dangerous not to do it. Everybody here was supposed to work. I will have to line up with the women's detail which was assigned to do the crating and packing of all the contents left inside the apartments by the thousands who were no longer here. All their belongings were systematically sorted and shipped away. There would be SS guards present who would personally oversee the work.

The factory workers were all assigned their individual work stations at the munitions factory. If I joined that detail, I would have no number or station to report to. I would be exposed as an illegal, too young, and consequently deported.

I felt terrified. It was a trap. How could I get out of here if I had to? We discussed the possibilities. It was not as easy to escape from the Ghetto as before the deportation, when the Ghetto bordered the outside streets. Now I had to cross the "no-man's land" which was like a moat full of crocodiles surrounding a prison. It was patrolled very thoroughly and watched carefully by the Germans. After all, each building within that area was full of loot, which they jealously guarded. The streets which connected with the outside were solidly blocked off. It was impossible to get out that way.

The only way to escape, according to Zenek, was to line up with the workers who were daily marched out to the factory. They were guarded by Ukrainian conscripts spaced out along the length of the column.

The way to do it was to position myself behind a guard so that when the column turned a corner, I could be a few meters behind him. Then for a short while, the guard behind me would be still around the corner and I would not be in the field of his vision.

This was like a window. It only lasted a very short time but at that moment I could make a break for it.

The column was not permitted on the sidewalk. It had to march in the middle of the street. If I made a break, I would have to get onto the sidewalk quickly, mingle with and get lost among the pedestrians.

The pedestrians, of course, might want to alert the guards and give me away; there was always that danger. The Poles were often hostile and anti-Semitic. But if they shouted or attracted the attention of the guards, they would also be taking a chance. The guards marched with their guns pointed and fingers on the triggers. They might very likely shoot to stop me and this would put the pedestrians in line of fire.

There was another problem. I *had* to make the break somewhere between the Ghetto's outer wall and the factory. If I arrived at the factory, I would be quickly spotted as not one of the designated workers. This would be fatal.

Of course, anyone caught trying to escape was shot on the spot. There were no exceptions to this rule. I had one important plus on my side. It was winter time. The column started for its destination just before the night curfew was over, very early in the morning while it was still dark. The sidewalks were crowded with pedestrians hurrying to get to work and in the darkness they might not even notice if I suddenly joined their ranks.

The same applied on the way back into the Ghetto. I had to intercept the column close to where it turned a corner, jump in among the returning Jews, mix in, and march back as if I belonged. It was very dangerous. It was like the *Russian Roulette*. It had been done successfully before. It has also been known to fail, but that person did not live to talk about it.

I went to sleep emotionally exhausted and frightened. I was not ready to break out yet. It seemed very complicated. It boggled my mind. My nerves were shot and there was no margin for error. I had to function well to pull it off. And if I did where would I go? The Mikula's now would be suspicious about my sudden disappearance. I did not want to go back there anyway. My restlessness did not permit it. I did not want to live with them. The sight of their son disturbed me.

Why did I have such a terrible restlessness within me? What was driving me like that? I could not help myself, could not fight it. Why was I unable to ask Father Krzeminski to help me? Fate, or was it the Plaster Saint, gave me a golden opportunity for shelter and survival. Why was I unable to accept it?

The Creature within me surfaced, — and when it did, I was helpless. The Creature did not permit me to have a chance. It was destructive and restless. It was an enemy within me and it was dominant. Had my mind broken in two? Was I insane? I had no defense against it. Did it want me to perish? It surely did not care very much, it had no other feelings but restlessness and anger. It even had a different voice from mine and it did not tolerate humiliation or rejection. It was unreasonable and it did not permit me to accept a helping hand when it was offered. It denied me and it pushed me.

What would my mother say about it if she knew? What would anybody say? Besides what did it matter! I was not very likely to survive anyway. Still, I was ashamed about how I was. I hated myself. I was in the Ghetto again and I was glad in a way because I was with my own people. It was so much easier than the loneliness and isolation outside.

Zenek gave me the white arm band with the blue Star of David. I put it on my sleeve and presto-changeo I was Jewish again. I fell asleep thinking gloomily that if the Nazis did not get me, the Creature within me would.

We lined up for roll call right in front of the building where I stayed with the Markowicz's. How familiar! The SS were back. I stood with a group of women of the crating detail. It was a clear night just at the edge of a morning. There were stars in the sky. The sky was untouched by all of this; it represented freedom. The universe was majestic and reassuring. We marched, the snow crackling under our feet, into the empty, ghostly street of the "no man's land."

The daylight was breaking as we entered the first building to be cleared. Now in the light I could see the faces of my companions. Young and strong women between the ages of eighteen and thirty. Sad faces, eyes full of confusion. Almost every one had lost her family. Some of the very fortunate had a sister.

There was a young woman in charge of us, our overseer. She was strikingly beautiful, blue eyed with flaming red hair, easily the prettiest girl I have ever seen. She noticed me immediately because I was clearly too young to be here, and walked over to me. She asked me my name and advised me to stay out of sight. "Be very careful!" she whispered. "We have two SS with us at all times." She touched me lightly on the shoulder with a gesture of concern and sympathy. I felt such a feeling of warmth sweep over me, of not being so completely alone. It almost made it worth being back in the trap of a Ghetto and made me realize how much I had missed this sense of belonging and caring.

Around me the girls were working steadily, emptying drawer after drawer, closet after closet, cupboards and kitchen. Dishes were carefully packed away, clothes sorted out. In the center of the room stood a refuse bin. Into it went papers, books, family albums, and photographs. Mementos of the past of those departed. The symbols of a lifetime. Portraits of mothers with babies, diaries, wedding pictures and prayer books. It was all now rubbish and refuse. The girls discarded it indifferently, they were very much used to it by now.

The two SS stood around very bored smoking endlessly. Our red haired overseer chatted with them constantly. They seemed to like her, lit her cigarettes and laughed at what she said from time to time. She seemed to be entertaining them. They paid almost no attention to the rest of us or to what we were doing as long as we worked and appeared busy.

"She is distracting them so we can steal," one of the girls whispered in my ear. She pushed me toward a closet. "Go in and see if you can find a decent jacket or a skirt in there. Maybe also some shoes you like. . . I will cover for you." By the end of the day, I had a new outfit, including a fleece lined woolen jacket. I also found some jewelry in a purse on the floor and slipped it into my pocket.

The two SS were still courting the red-haired overseer. They were completely taken with her, not that it could do them any good. The Nazis had, after all, the *Rassenschande* (Racial Shame) law to abide by. If they ever broke it, the penalty was very steep. It meant that no member of the "master race" could, at any time, have intimate contact with us, the "nonpeople." It made the beautiful, charming redhead completely unobtainable to them, and therefore, maybe even more tempting. She certainly had both these men quite under her spell much to our advantage. The girls found some flour in one of the kitchens and some sugar which they hid under their coats. I, too, ended the day loaded up with a small share of the spoils.

The small Ghetto was a very strange place. It was unreal. Those left behind were numb, shell shocked, the only survivors of the deportation. There was this stillness of isolation. Doors were closed. People were mostly preoccupied with the devastation of being the only members of their families left behind. Around this tragic island, beyond the barbed wire fence, were miles of ghostly, empty streets. Within it were people in mourning, all of them, with few exceptions like Zenek Markowicz and his father.

The food supply was supplemented by staples brought in by the women of the packing crew. By now, these were only the foodstuffs which did not spoil. There was no electricity in the empty buildings, or refrigeration.

The Germans were temporarily quiescent, like a python that has to digest the prey it swallowed before it kills again. Living beings have a need to hope, and so we did. Maybe this was it, no more deportations. They needed us now to do the work, months of it, just to do the crating. Once this was done, and the buildings were stripped of all their contents, when all this loot had been sent away to SS warehouses, the women workers might be needed in the munitions factories. They were all young and strong. But in spite of these hopes, fear permeated the Ghetto. The Yom Kippur deportation was fresh in everyone's memory.

I went along with the same work detail for several days. I did not find any more jewelry anywhere. Something very violent must have happened in that apartment during the deportation to make someone drop a purse full of jewelry. Surely everyone took along whatever they could that did not weigh very much and was worth a lot. I looked over what I had. There was a diamond-encrusted platinum watch and four diamond rings. It was beginner's luck to find it on my first day of work.

I had a chance to speak to our overseer. She seemed so vivacious, so carefree when she chatted with the Germans, as if nothing here touched her at all. But it had. She told me that she was the only one left of her family. Her eyes were very sad as she spoke. She kept up a facade.

The two SS were young men who did not seem vicious at all. In fact, they promised to warn her if another selection was to take place. There was a number of illegals here who would then be deported and it included myself. Maybe if we had a warning, we would have a chance to hide. She also told me that the Germans authorized only a certain number of people to be left behind. They already had an idea that this number was exceeded now by the illegals and she fully expected they would do something soon. I did not look like an eighteen year old, and sooner or later they would get me.

I told her my story briefly and about the factory where my parents took shelter. She sensed how I felt. I had a need to see this shelter for myself. It was completely illogical; they could no longer be there. The action had taken place months ago. But she knew that I could not leave until I did what I came here to do, and she made it possible.

Only two days later we were working in houses adjacent to the factory. I walked over to it and approached the porch. It was covered with snow but it was intact. No hole was visible, or loose boards to indicate an entry or an exit. It seemed undisturbed and quiet. I walked over to the spot where the Gestapo man, Buhler, said he saw my father's maroon hat lying on the ground. The place was empty and clean. No signs of anything violent having taken place here anywhere, just a smooth carpet of snow. I went around to that porch again. I was not supposed to be here, near a locked-up factory which was the property of the SS.

I called to my mother as if I expected her to be there, under that porch and able to answer me. "Mama!" I called stubbornly over and over again. I stood there as long as I could. Then slowly I turned around and returned to work.

All those days of circling the Ghetto as a moth circles the flame, of wanting to somehow get inside on the irrational hope that I will call and Mother will answer. I felt a wrenching pain of guilt. Maybe, when I went to see Buhler, my questioning gave them away. Maybe they were here for a long time without food or water. But maybe Buhler told me the truth! How could I ever believe a Gestapo man? The guilt tore at me. I should have stayed with them. Maybe I could have saved them somehow, — done something.

A woman came to see me unexpectedly. I did not remember her, but she knew my mother. She wanted me to know that she had seen *Pani Sieradzki* on her way to the train. Mother was crying and she was alone. Father was not with her.

"Why was your mother alone?" the woman asked, as if I could possibly know the answer. "And why was she crying?"

"She was being deported and sent away from me!" I said almost defensively. The woman repeated these questions several times, as if it was important for her to know. She said that she knew my mother well, had heard that I was searching for information and wanted to tell me what she knew. I thanked her and walked away, dazed, afraid to imagine what could have happened to my parents.

The next day during roll call I stood next to the bodies of two men who had been shot for attempting to escape. They lay there, crumpled in the snow, which was splattered with blood. The restlessness rose like nausea within my stomach. It was a terrible feeling, I could not bear it at all. It was worse than death. I needed to get out of this Ghetto. I did not care if I were caught, or shot. It did not matter at all. I no longer had a reason to stay here.

After work I was approached by a man who had heard about me from one of the men who smuggled me into the Ghetto on that truck with Koplowicz. His name was Bursztyn and he was a physician. He had a wife and a son who were hiding out with a Polish family on the outskirts of Czestochowa.

He has been sending payments to these Poles through someone from the munitions factory. But now he had lost his contact. He was frantic with worry.

If I could somehow get out and check for him whether his wife was still allright and safe, he would pay me anything I wanted. He made me swear that I would not mention it to anybody. It was amazing how secretive and cautious people were about relatives in hiding.

It was this way with Uncle Stecki and with the Marckowiczes. It was always a jealously kept secret. But this man could not help it. He was typically Semitic, would be stopped very quickly if he were on the outside. He came to me in desperation. The Poles would want their payment if all was well and he was also concerned that his family might have been discovered and executed. No effort had been made to contact him for quite a while.

I agreed to do it at first opportunity, preferably when the weather was bad and it would be easier for me to disappear into the crowd after I made my break.

He gave me a roll of money to give to his wife and heaved a sigh of relief, then asked suspiciously if I intended to come back to the Ghetto and report to him what I discovered. The poor man did not trust me very much. I gave him a promise that I would. I rehearsed thoroughly in my mind the instructions Zenek gave me.

On the first cloudy day, I lined up at roll call with the munitions factory workers. I would have done it anyway, my terrible restlessness would have forced me to. Now I had a reason and a destination. I had spent the evening making myself presentable. Hair had to be washed and shoes rubbed clean. I now had a warm jacket lined with red fleece and an adjustable hood. I had to look clean not to attract suspicion.

My heart pounded as we began to march, more with excitement than fear. Strange, but the whole thing was becoming a

game to me. Since I accomplished my mission of seeing my
parents shelter at the factory, a change came over me. Now if I
got killed it would matter to no one. It would be like a tree falling in the woods unseen by human eyes. A non- event.

It was snowing and I positioned myself a few meters behind
the *Ostdeutsche* guard. As soon as we arrived on the outside, I was
poised and tense, like a cat. We turned the first corner but the
guard behind me had not yet done so and could not see me.

Now! A quick leap onto the sidewalk and into the crowd of
pedestrians. I moved close to the shadows of the buildings and
continued walking. How easy it was! I experienced a sense of ex-
hilaration at how clever I was. Then, after a while, I noticed in
horror that I had forgotten to simultaneously tear off and hide
my white arm band with the Star of David. I ducked into a
hallway and did it, thanking God for the driving wind and snow.
Otherwise, I would have been noticed. It was dangerous to lose
my humility.

Free again! I indulged myself with a nice breakfast in my little
restaurant. I sat at my favorite table by the window and drank hot
tea, watching the snow flakes drift outside. It felt cozy. The
waitress remembered me and said hello. After a while, I started
on my way to find the address Doctor Bursztin gave me. To my
left I could see the steps leading toward the Cloister of Jasna
Gora where the Mikula's had their stand. Czestochowa was now a
very familiar place.

It took me a couple of hours to find the house I was looking
for. It was partially damaged by a recent fire but still looked quite
intact. The door was locked. I observed it for a while from across
the street but saw nothing, no smoke coming out of the chimney,
no movement. Eventually, I knocked on the door and when there
was no answer turned the knob. It swung open. The house was
empty. Part of the ceiling was down and there was water damage
to the walls.

I stood there in confusion; what now? Two little boys appeared in the door and asked me what I wanted. I told them I
was looking for a Pani Walewska. Where was she? They looked at
each other meaningfully and told me to wait. They would get
someone to help me and disappeared again.

I stood in the middle of the smoke-blackened empty room
and waited. Was it a trap? I began to feel uncomfortable. After
what seemed like much too long a time, a man dressed in black
appeared at the door. A priest. . .

I introduced myself but he did not give me his name. However, he asked me to walk with him a little way. We talked in circles, each suspicious of the other. Finally, he asked me if I came from the Ghetto and I admitted the truth. We began to communicate very quickly and found a place to sit on a deserted bench next to a trolley stop.

Pani Walewska was allright and so were the Jews, but he was not free to tell me where they were or give me his name. There has been trouble here lately, a real blood-letting. Partisans were arrested in the neighborhood and tortured by the Gestapo. Everybody was in hiding and scared. Somewhere there was a leak; a traitor. They had a suspicion who he was but could not act on it until they were certain. No names could be mentioned; no addresses given. I had to take his word for everything.

These particular Jews were also a problem. The boy was unstable. He had fantasies of killing Germans; entertained ambitions of fighting with the Partisans. There was not a chance of that. The Partisans were the *Armja Krajowa* (Country Army). They operated on a shoe string. Unlike the Partisans in France and other countries, they received no help from abroad absolutely zero. Ammunition and explosives were hard to come by; had to be bought from turncoats or stolen. The Germans were their only source of supply and it was expensive. The "cell" had little money. Couriers lasted no longer than a few months and when they were caught they talked. The Germans had a fail safe method of extracting information. Torture! In Warsaw guns were needed desperately, but delivery was hampered. The Partisans had to use strictly "blind contacts."

Now I was curious. What was a blind contact? A blind contact, the priest explained, was someone known to the right people, but who, in turn, did not know much about any of them. This way if a blind contact was caught by the Gestapo no information could be extracted from him or her, because a blind contact only received instructions to carry and deliver, but knew nothing about those who gave them.

The priest wanted to know if I had brought money for Pani Walewska. He could get a note from Pani Bursztyn to reassure her husband but I would have to come back for it some other time.

I guessed that it meant that they were not close by. I gave the priest the money and told him that I would return for the letter if he told me where to find him. But he could not do that. If I were at the railroad station at 10:00 on Tuesday or Wednesday, I would be contacted, now that they knew my description and what I wore. In effect, he smiled sadly, I was now a blind contact of sorts, myself. He was sorry it was this way, but there was no other choice. Lately there had been a massacre within their ranks; too many good people had died a terrible death.

I took a diamond ring out of my pocket and told him I wanted to sell it. Yes, he would buy it from me. He told me honestly that I would not get the whole price, or anywhere near it. The Partisans would use it for bribes or sell it for more. They were strapped for money. It was the best he could do. He gave me a roll of bills for the diamond ring, and I did not even bother to count them. At least he would not hit me on the head and take the ring for free. I was not even convinced that the man was really a priest, but I liked his face. He seemed honest. We parted with the understanding that I would seek contact at the railroad station and that I would bring more jewelry to sell.

On the way back I skirted the ghostly, empty, blocked-off streets of the Ghetto. Only now, I knew exactly what lay beyond. I managed to buy a sausage on the black market and stuck it under my coat, then I positioned myself on the sidewalk, strategically near a corner and waited for the column of Jews to appear at dusk. It was easier to get in than to get out. Inexplicably, I found myself enjoying the adventure. It was a balm for my restlessness and I managed to make a contact, nebulous as it was.

It was already January of 1943 and I was still alive. It was a bitterly cold winter and heavy with snow. My parents were gone and the small Ghetto was a place of gloom and misery. Yet, during the evenings I found myself singing poignant Russian songs Mother had taught me. This way I could still feel her closeness. A part of her lived on in those melodies she left in my memory.

And to the North, in Russia, snow was also falling. Out there on the nineteenth of November, 1942, the Soviets launched a massive counteroffensive at Stalingrad. The frozen and mauled German Sixth Army under General Von Paulus was encircled. The *Luftwaffe* was unable to supply it from the air. German soldiers died like flies in the clutches of the merciless frost. Now it was their turn to hide in rat- infested holes while armies of lice fed on their emaciated bodies. On the twenty-fourth, the Soviets launched a counter-offensive on the Central Front and on the twenty-ninth, in the Caucasus. From there the Germans began to withdraw on the second of January, 1943.

On the tenth of that month, the Soviets attacked the Stalingrad pocket and on the nineteenth opened a narrow supply route to there from Leningrad, which became their lifeline. On the twenty-seventh, the U.S. Eighth Air Force raided Wilhelmshaven in its first major attack on Germany.

The tide of the war really turned decisively in February of 1943 when, on the first, German withdrawal was completed as far as the Don River at Rostov and Kuban-Novorossisk. On February second, General Von Paulus and what was left of the German Sixth Army surrendered at Stalingrad. Three hundred and sixty-five thousand Germans disappeared into that black hole. Only five thousand ever came back. Somewhere out there the fierce Russian winter dug in its icy claws into helpless human and this time German, flesh.

And in the Czestochowa Ghetto, I lived to see another birthday.

# 13

# THE ACTION

## RECOLLECTION

*It feels very unreal lining up with the munition factory workers again, but it is not very hard. We are not counted before leaving, probably because the Ukrainian conscript guards are lazy. It is still dark, the stars are out and it is very cold. I feel uneasy because the weather is clear, which makes it more dangerous.*

*As we leave, I watch the guard ahead of me adjust his rifle. He carries it slung under his arm with the barrel pointing down and fingers curled around the trigger. He has a wide, peasant face. It occurs to me that perhaps this nameless man will today become my executioner. My pockets are bulging with things. I have some jewelry to sell and letters to be mailed on the outside. Hopeful messages to Polish acquaintances to let them know that the sender is still alive in case someone should ask. People still hope that members of their families will come back somehow, someday to seek loved ones. There are hopeful letters seeking help, a place to hide perhaps. But how can they ever be answered? No mail ever comes to the Ghetto. The letters are nothing more than hopeless attempts to establish contact.*

*I have a few addresses of people who might offer salvation to an illegal on borrowed time. Money had been pushed into my hand to run such errands. I carry in my mind messages to be delivered to friends. Pleas for help, short, fervent speeches rehearsed carefully. As if the right sentence would touch the special heartstring and open a door to a shelter. I find myself being a messenger, a delivery person and a diamond merchant. If I am caught it will be a disaster for so many.*

*I am very careful and stop short of making my move when the guard unexpectedly glances back. When I do, I almost collide with a German on the sidewalk among the Polish pedestrians. He looks at me slightly annoyed about having been bumped into and goes on. The contact at the railroad station does not materialize and I have to take the jewelry back in that night. I could try to sell it elsewhere, but it is too dangerous. There must have been an inspection at the station that day an instant before I arrived.*

*I deliver my fervent messages and meet with blank stares; "Do not know such a person, beat it!"  Or, with a sympathetic smile and a regretful decline. Sometimes there is a polite message in response: "Wish them well in their endeavors from me." I think to myself, how ironic it is.  As if to say "Best wishes on the way to your funeral." But in this madness, even funerals are a peacetime luxury.*

*I find it hard to enter the marching column during my re-entry, dodging Germans on the sidewalk or someone particularly looking at me. I try to walk alongside the column until I have a "window.". I have to be watchful and alert. No room for error.*

*Back in the Ghetto, I have to disappoint those waiting hopefully, for an answer. I sell the food I brought in. It is already spoken for while I am still trying to blend in with the marchers. "Co Panienka ma?" (What dose the Miss have?). Urgently whispered inquiries are directed at me from all sides.*

*The next trip is more successful. I am intercepted at the station by a woman. She nods surreptitiously for me to follow her. I meet with the priest and another man who comes to observe and to see me. I sell the jewelry and the priest makes me an offer. It is possible for them to forge a birth or a christening certificate. Of course they are not able to provide a proper identification like a* Kenkarte *(an Ausweiss) which is a stamped identification with a fingerprint and a photograph. But even a birth certificate is better than nothing at all.*

*It is all I have for myself. Its value is perhaps mostly psychological and since I am still a child, I might even get by with it if stopped but this is doubtful. Still, there are many buyers of the birth certificates and prices are steep.*

*The priest is obsessed with one theme: "They need everything in Warsaw! They need explosives and guns. . .  and it all is expensive, — it costs money. Those bribed to sell take a chance with their lives and expect to be paid very well."*

*His companion mentions that the Jews in the Warsaw Ghetto are just begging to purchase guns of any kind; defective, homemade, or antiquated outmoded ones. And they will pay any price! His eyes gleam as he talks about it. A big smile slashes his face, teeth from ear to ear, a face of greed, beaming with anticipation of riches.*

*"But is it not for a good cause?" After all the heroic and patriotic, the very noble* Armja Krajowa *needs money! Jewish money; the more the better. The* Armja Krajowa *needs explosives very badly. the plastic explosives called* Plastelina *by the partisans, in particular, if it could be obtained.*

*"Maybe some could be used to blow up the tracks in front of the deportation trains carrying the Jews," I suggest. The woman giggles. The man*

with all those teeth dismisses such a silly notion. *Cannot afford good explosives on such frivolities. It is the military trains they are after. "We cannot waste it on the Jews."*

The priest looks apologetic. It comes to me in a flash that he did not tell his compatriots exactly who I am. Just a blind contact, that's all. A blind contact "sees no evil, speaks no evil, and hears no evil."

I have now made it in and out of the Ghetto ten times. I am very superstitious about the number "ten" and more nervous than usual, but it goes without a hitch. I am unnerved when I see the dead bodies of those like me who have tried, but failed. I manage to close my eyes when someone is shot but afterwards I must see. It is an irresistible reflex; I must bear witness.

There are occasions when I just cannot re-enter the marching column safely and have to spend the night at the Jasna Gora. I have to make a choice and it is either there or the railroad station. It is very lonely under a pew. Memories crowd my mind like a movie picture. I almost cannot stand it and barely lasted the night. The place casts a strange, spell-like influence over me. It is the heaviness of the ages and its utter loneliness in the dark. I promise myself that next time I have to sleep on the outside it will be on a train going to anywhere. I must also keep my sanity!

February. I realize that one of these past days was my first birthday alone in the world. Nobody knew or remembered, not even I as it came and went.

I have found a small store front with a sign above it; Pralnia (a laundry). It is run by a couple. I went in and inquired if I could also take a bath there.

"For a price, why not?" The woman fills a tin bath tub with hot water next to her washing tubs. I undress while she works and she notices my crucifix on the silver chain. She looks very relieved and hints obliquely that I am a courier for the partisans. I pay her another visit at a first opportunity. It is an unimaginable delight, a great luxury. I wash my hair and dry it with a towel. My clothes are cleaned and I spend the day at the "Pralnia." I am charged a reasonable price, which makes me think that they do not suspect me of being Jewish.

I am again straddling two radically different worlds. One, a world within the realm of the dead. The hidden little pocket of humanity surrounded by empty desolation of the old Ghetto. A place where an egg or a little butter costs a fortune. The other, a place where one can walk for miles, go anywhere at all and where money can easily buy enough food to eat pretty well. At times I hesitate to return, even though on the outside I have no possibility of finding a place to spend the night in a bed.

*When I am not on the outside, I go out to work with the crating detail. They have already cleared all the apartments where I used to live at Twenty Garibaldi Street. Our meager possessions have already been sorted out; my mother's pots and the few dishes she had, my long romantic poem had been discarded into a refuse bin. The pearl embroidered sweater my aunt had given me was in a crate on its way somewhere. My notebooks and Latin textbook were now in the trash heap. The lilac dress with a princess skirt I was so proud of. . . Memories are now like dry leaves in the wind, all that is left of a summer past, of another life. During the crating detail, sometimes we find a piece of new cloth or some leather, which we also conceal on our bodies and smuggle back. The war has been going on for so long that there is a shortage of everything.*

*Our red-haired overseer has a message, a warning for us. The two SS hinted that something is about to happen soon; another selection to deport illegals like me is about to take place. It could happen any day now.*

*I have to complete my errands and remain on the outside. It must be done! But I have to pick up those birth certificates and bring them back in first. They might be especially precious to have if an action is brewing, and all have been paid for up front. This is the only way the priest conducts business.*

*There is a girl I work with who is a little older than myself. I offer to teach her how to get out. If only I had a companion, I would not be so completely lonely. She looks too young and might easily be deported. But she declines. She is more frightened of being on the outside even than deportation. There is a false sense of safety in staying with the herd. It is an instinctive response. Maybe once long ago our primitive ancestors traveled in groups to be safe from predators. There is a sense of security stemming from staying with the tribe; the idea of safety in numbers. I can understand how she feels.*

*"My happiness," she said, "is gone with the wind." She was completely depressed. All she now had was the warmth of the herd to turn to and could not abandon its sheltering presence.*

*It is my eighteenth trip and it is uneventful. By now I feel like a pro. The priest marvels at how I do make it over and over again. He tells me that I have made a great contribution to the "AK" partisans. However, to me it is a doubtful complement because actually the Polish partisans are also my enemy. I hear that no young Jewish persons are helped or accepted among them. Quite to the contrary. Those who try to join are found dead by the side of the road, killed by the partisans themselves.*

*Still, I have no quarrel with the priest. He is a dedicated patriot and a fairly decent man. Also, the partisans are my only contact. I have been dealing with them for months now. The priest has a lot of questions about*

what is now happening in the Ghetto and tells me that the forged birth
certificates he sold to the Jews are actually backed up by altered records. I
have a feeling that he likes me. Still, I know nothing about him, not even
his name. He is a very cautious man and protective of his "cell," very
much a man with a sacred mission. Someday, he tells me, the partisans
will strike hard at the oppressor but it is very difficult.

Then he gives me some electrifying news. He thinks that the Warsaw
Jews are getting ready to revolt. Why else would they pay such exorbitant
prices for any guns or ammunition they can obtain? He also tells me that
in Warsaw, because of its size, the Ghetto is very different. There the
deportations have been an ongoing process, unlike Czestochowa where it
was done all at once in a short period of time. But even in Warsaw, there
are not many left out of the original population.

He shakes his head sadly; "It will be a suicide mission if the Jews
strike back." And also we both know very well that there will be very little
help from the Poles. The Poles are not ready to make a big move and the
Jews have no choice. It is now or never. We also know that many Poles are
just as anti-Semitic as the Germans. We do not even have to put this into
words, it is for him an unpleasant subject. It is too bad, but his role is
strictly limited to Polish Resistance. The Jews will make a desperate stand
but they do not have a chance. He wishes them well but there is not much
he can do. I personally do not confide in him, not even about the warning of impending action. I trust no one, not even him.

I hesitate to return back on my eighteenth trip out of the Ghetto. I
have no doubt about the warning. The small Ghetto's population is now
increased by many who have been trying to hide on the outside and found
it impossible. They have survived the Yom Kippur deportation, but had
to return. Most of the illegals, however, are those who hid within the Ghetto itself, inside basements or hiding places inside the walls and attics.

I go through a personal tug of war. I have a responsibility to deliver
the forged papers in my possession. But I know I am cutting it close. At
last I make a decision and enter the column almost at the last possible opportunity. It is a self destructive decision but in a way I cannot help it at
all. I feel that I owe it to my fellow Jews in the Ghetto. I promise myself
that the next day I will leave again and stay out at least for a while. It is
a matter of only one more day. Maybe I will have enough time to do it.

But it is too late. Early next morning the Ghetto is sealed. All work
parties are canceled. Mr. Markowicz is frantic. Zenek and I must hide;
but where? The SS will be here within minutes and they will search the
whole place.

We live in an old building with a steep, sloping roof. It has an attic
which is only accessible by climbing a ladder. Under its pointed roof is an

*open entrance without a door. We have no other choice, there is no time to even think about it.*

*Mr. Markowicz places the ladder against the wall but it is too short. It does not quite reach the entrance and it is caked with ice. But fear propels us. Zenek climbs first with his father behind him. He then stands upon his father's shoulders and pulls himself up into the attic.*

*Then I go up the icy, slippery ladder and am pushed up by Mr. Markowicz. Zenek gives me his hand and I jump in. It is just in time. As Mr. Markowicz pulls the ladder away from the wall, the trucks full of the SS come to a stop on the street below. He has no time to conceal it and it is left on the ground below, by the side of the building.*

*There are shouts and commands. People are assembled in the street right below the building we are in. Then the SS with their dogs fan out and search every house in the small cramped Ghetto. We can hear screams and shooting. People are herded out and made to assemble together. There are trucks lined up to take away those selected for deportation.*

*We can see right through the cracks in the wooden wall of the old house. And then we hear the SS searching our building. "Heraus!" They screech, "Heraus" (all out). The ladder is propped up against the wall again and an SS man climbs upward. "Everybody out of there!" he yells. "Or I will shoot!"*

*Zenek and I flatten ourselves between the beams, afraid to breathe. The SS man cannot quite make it in but his face and shoulders appear in the opening. We know how slippery it is, everything covered with ice.*

*He lets go a volley with his machine pistol. It is much like a machine gun. The bullets fly everywhere. They zing through the air and ricochet around us. Splinters and small pieces of wood scatter about. We lie very still until it is over and the SS man climbs down. We can hardly believe that we are still alive. After a while, we both sit up. I lost my shoe when I threw myself between the beams and when I retrieve it, there is a bullet inside.*

*We edge up to the front wall of the attic from where we can see the street below. We can see all the inhabitants of the Ghetto lined up for an inspection. The SS and their dogs swarm all around on the snow covered street. There is constant shouting. Those Jews who work at the munition factory are separated from the rest one by one and lined up on the side. After this is done, they are marched away under guard. The rest are left standing in the snow.*

*Now, like a stage show, the selection for deportation takes place right before our eyes. Each person has to step forward and is examined by the SS. Those selected for deportation are assembled by the waiting trucks; the others stand aside. A poignant drama of separation is enacted before us.*

*A mother is being sent to the trucks and her weeping daughter clings to her. The SS separate them with rifle butts. It is a life and death drama.*

*The trucks are loaded with those to be deported. They are beaten and prodded to make haste. There are screams and blood on the snow. The motors start up and some of the trucks move forward. Dogs are barking and growling at those who dare to hesitate. It is a heart-rending scene. My face is flattened against the boards of the attic wall so I can see it all. There is only one thought in my mind; if only I had a gun, I would give my soul for it! I can see why the remaining few of the Warsaw Ghetto are trying to buy guns at any price. They have nothing to lose.*

*At last, the trucks leave, and those left behind are marched off to work. The street below is quiet again with only the bloody snow as a reminder of what has taken place here today. The stage is empty.*

*Zenek and I wait patiently until his father comes back and helps us down the ladder. The shadows of evening fall oppressively over the few square blocks encircled by barbed wire fence. People are back from work again and take stock of what happened. Who was deported and who is left behind? People are mourning those taken away but still are secretly happy somewhere within their hearts that they were spared. They have another chance to survive. Now the small Ghetto is suddenly less crowded. There are fewer people left to compete for sleeping space. It is a very sad evening. Tomorrow, I, too, will be gone. I say goodbye to Zenek and his father. I am certain that I have used up my luck. Tomorrow I will be leaving for good. I tried so hard to deliver the forged papers, and almost paid for it with my life! There must be people being deported now with these papers in their pockets, useless to them anyway. Too late and too little.*

*We line up again at five in the morning. It is a clear starry night. The snow beneath my feet is hard and crunchy. I look up at the morning stars with a silent prayer. "One more time — Lady Luck please smile at me one more time!" One look back at the Ghetto of Czestochowa. There are a couple of bodies in the snow. It must have happened during the night when we heard shots. Still, lifeless, dark bundles; we do not even know who they are.*

*We march forward. I have all my possessions in my pockets including a thick roll of bills tucked in against my chest. We march through the "no man's land" and out into the outside. I do not escape at first opportunity, but march a little longer with my people. Then I make my break and am again among the stream of pedestrians. I discard the white band with the blue Star of David in a convenient hallway. I know that I will not be needing it again.*

*It is a brittle, bright and very cold day. I go to my favorite restaurant to have breakfast. It is hard to believe sitting here and sipping hot tea that only yesterday I almost was shot in the Ghetto. And now, I think to myself, where next? Where will I go?*

# 14

## A TRAIN PERSON

### RECOLLECTION

*I spend a nervous night at the railroad station again, hardly able to doze on the hard wooden bench. From time to time I find myself glancing apprehensively at the entrance expecting any time the SS man with the dog and his entourage to arrive for another inspection. I have heard all about him while in the Ghetto. He prides himself on being able to spot a Jew by just looking at a person for an instant. His fame had even reached there.*

*I have ample time to consider well my very few options. I hear that the Germans are now regularly rounding up Poles to be sent as laborers to Germany. Sometimes they simply close off a street and collect all able-bodied people for this purpose and let the others go. I know it would be risky for me if I were caught in such a roundup because my faded paper birth certificate might not pass muster. It has no impressive stamps upon it whatever.*

*Also I might not look strong enough to be conscripted for the heavy labor they want the Poles to do. In fact, I might need to volunteer. Poles often do so simply because they are starving, so it would not seem unusual. However, again I would have to face the same danger. Well, it is an option. At least in Germany I would have a place to sleep and they would hardly look for a Jew among the volunteers to work there.*

*My other option is to meet my contact again and talk to the Priest, but this does not look promising either. I know the Partisans would be twice as suspicious of me than they are the Germans. Their sentiments are well known to me already, but the Priest might have a suggestion about what I can do.*

*I see him again the very next day. We sit on a bench and talk. He is very disappointed when I tell him that I will not be going back to the Ghetto again. The birth certificates were a very lucrative business and he also hoped they might do some good for the recipients. He seems to have great faith in my abilities; had even considered my entering the Krakow or the Warsaw Ghetto to sell a few. He must imagine that I get there by* flying on a magic carpet and for the first time I describe to him in detail how difficult and dangerous it really is. "Well," he tells me, "you still have a potential."

I am a fine blind contact; a natural. In fact, his "cell" sometimes has a delivery to make to Krakow or Warsaw and he thinks I can be trusted to do a good job. This is also dangerous because all too often trains are searched and everybody is frisked. Luggage is often examined for contraband. If I am caught, however, only my life will be at stake. My only knowledge about the underground "cell" the priest belongs to, is our contact place and they have a way to be cautious about that.

I have no family they could trace or interrogate. I can be met by someone I have never seen before but who would have a good description of me. In fact, the more the priest talks about it, the better he likes the idea. And who knows, we might even find a possible way to infiltrate the Krakow Ghetto to everyone's benefit.

He thinks he has a job involving a delivery for me right now. It will be a suitcase to be taken by train to Warsaw. It should make no difference to me what exactly it contains because if I got caught with it, the end would be the same. We both know what he means but I am certain it will be explosives or guns.

Sometimes even such mundane things as underground news has to be delivered from town to town. The Germans would kill me just as surely whether it is illegal publications or guns. The death penalty applies for having either in one's possession. The priest warns me that if caught, I would undergo an interrogation by the Gestapo and he feels obligated to describe to me in brutal detail how this is sometimes done, just so I can make an informed decision.

We part with the understanding that I will arrive the next day at the appointed time for contact and most probably my delivery suitcase will be brought to me with instructions. Of course, he tells me that I will be paid. The AK is neither rich nor generous but then I, too, have to live.

I told him about my having discovered a place where I can bathe and it met with his hearty approval. It is imperative for me to look well kept and clean. I must appear like a young school girl on her way to grandma's house. If I look shabby, it would cast suspicion upon my person. The Pralnia was an excellent idea. In fact he might have some clothes dropped off there for me so I will have a change. "You must groom yourself like a cat," he advises me.

Within a couple of days I embark upon a new career. The suitcase that is brought to me is not very large. But it is so heavy, I can hardly pick it up, as if it were filled up with rocks. I am instructed to sit in the last car of the train so that if there is an inspection and they are about to *search my baggage, I have at least a small chance to jump off and try to escape. Of course, I am told as if I did not realize it already, this might not be possible at all. If I am caught with whatever is inside that suitcase, I do not have a chance.*

*Still, I am strangely experiencing a sensation of pleasure. I am very glad to be doing something against the Germans. It is a privilege to have such an opportunity. I literally sit on pins and needles until it is time to board.*

*It is crowded and chilly. There are many Germans boarding the train. A locomotive hisses steam. The first car, of course, will become the last car because of the way the train is pointed. I struggle up the steep steps dragging the suitcase with me. It is too heavy to manage and it makes me nervous to bump it. What if it explodes? God only knows what is inside it! The car is crowded already but there are two empty seats in the middle. I leave the suitcase on the floor next to my feet. It is not possible for me to heave it up on the rack above. Across the aisle from me are two nuns and an older couple. Behind them are four Wehrmacht soldiers probably on their way to join their outfit after a furlough because the train is headed east.*

*Every seat is already taken but the one next to me. I hope it remains empty. The train jolts forward and I give a sigh of relief; oh, how I wish to stay alone on this trip. But it is too soon.*

*There is a last minute arrival, a German carrying a duffel bag over his shoulder. He almost loses his balance as the train lurches forward and he stops by my seat. "Move over!" he growls. I see that he wears his eagle on the sleeve of his uniform. I shudder; an "arm eagle" means he is the SS, and a breast eagle is the Wehrmacht. What rotten luck to wind up sitting next to an "arm eagle" on this particular trip. Now my suitcase is in his way.*

*"Hoist it up!" he orders me. I reach for it but in vain; it is too heavy. The Arm Eagle curses, reaches out for it and almost falls forward under its weight. He throws it on the rack.*

*"What you got in it Polak, stones?" I move towards the window and try not to answer. The SS man shoves his duffelbag on top of my suitcase and sits down next to me. He reeks of schnapps.*

*The train chugs on. So far so good. I figure out that the Arm Eagle is in a panzer outfit because he is not wearing a black uniform but I am not certain about it. I only hope so, because if he is with the police I am in trouble. I sit wedged between him and the window, feeling completely trapped. I try to pretend that I am asleep, but it does not work.*

*Suddenly I feel his hand entwine itself in my hair and my face is jerked toward him roughly until our eyes are centimeters apart. I am overcome by the smell of his breath. It is pure alcohol.*

*"Now let's see what we got here," he sneers at me. I feel as if my hair is being torn out by the roots. "A doll," he laughs. "Damn, it's a doll! All you need is a good bath; a scrubbing. . .    all the Polaks need a good scrubbing. When we get to Warsaw, I'll attend to it myself.  How old are you, Doll?"*

*I feel myself cringing away from this man. I am terrified. Then something happens in my mind. I feel as if I, Zosia, withdraw and recede into a corner of my consciousness where it is safe. All of a sudden I am not afraid any longer. The Creature takes over and even my voice is different when I speak. My German is effortless and excellent rather than halting as usual. "I am seventeen," I tell him.*

*"Well, you don't look it," he growls. "Fourteen is more like it."*

*"I am seventeen," I insist. "And you are not so bad looking yourself. . . "*

*The SS man relaxes his grip on my hair and laughs.  "Where are you going, Doll?"*

*"To Warsaw."*

*"Well, that's a nice coincidence! I will have a whole week in Warsaw. . . If you stick with me, Doll, I will let you tag along and will give you a bath personally, back scrub and all!"*

*"I'll bet you could use one yourself," I say.*

*"We will take one together," he bellows an inch from my face. His breath is sickening. It makes me feel nauseous.*

*The train shakes and rattles, but his voice is loud enough to be heard by others in the car. The* Wehrmacht *soldiers snicker. The two nuns try very hard to pretend that nothing is happening. Their eyes are cast down demurely under their headdresses.*

*The SS man tells me that I can call him "Fritz" and produces a flask out of his pocket. He takes a swig and hands it to me. I hope that soon he might pass out; surely he is drunk enough already. I pretend to take a sip and hand the flask back to him.*

*He is getting louder as time progresses and begins to paw at me. I try to push his hands away to no avail. It is very embarrassing and I am very angry. We continue to struggle with each other until he entwines his fingers again in my hair and immobilizes me. He plants a revolting long kiss on my lips. My face is wet with his saliva and I practically throw up. It is my first kiss; what a way for it to happen! At long last he gets up and staggers towards the men's room. I try to dry my face with my sleeve* and hope that I am invisible. I feel humiliated, but it is necessary to humor the beast.

He stops by the Wehrmacht on his way back and they have a conversation. I can hear them laughing. I wish I could leave but there is no place to go and my contraband, heavy suitcase sits immovably on the rack under his duffel bag. He comes back and sprawls himself in the seat. I am almost squashed against the window. His arm is around my shoulders now and he yawns. I thank my lucky stars; he is getting sleepy. He leans against me and falls asleep practically crushing me with his weight. I am very uncomfortable, cannot move at all, but anything is better than another kiss.

Suddenly from the corner of my eye I see a black uniform in the center of the aisle. Inspection! I can see the nuns produce their identification papers and being searched. Even the nuns! They have to open their suitcases, also. I cannot move an inch with Fritz's arm hooked around my neck and close my eyes in horror. I sense the SS standing above us for what seems like a very long time but is not. They do not want to disturb one of their brothers fast asleep against my shoulder. They move on and I give a sigh of relief. I can see them search everybody but the Germans in the car and they are very thorough. Suddenly I feel exhausted. The tension leaves a queasy sensation in my stomach and I feel myself sweating. This was very close! I try not to imagine what would have happened if they searched me; it is too awful.

The SS man is snoring, his mouth half-open. He has a lean, taut face and a sharp nose. It reminds me of the death head and cross bones insignia he wears. I boil over with hate. A girl dreams about her first kiss, but for me it was a nightmare. But then someone like me cannot even ponder normal things; a kiss means nothing in the face of death and it is again stalking me. The train comes to a halt and lurches forward. Some travelers are getting off. Warsaw will be next.

The SS man wakes up looking disoriented. "Where are we?" I tell him and he sits up and gives me a leering smile. "When we get to Warsaw, you can come with me Polak." I nod; I'll worry about this later.

I am correct about his being Waffen SS (a fighting unit of the SS) and he is with the panzer. He fumbles with his wallet and shows me a picture of himself next to a tank. Then he remembers his flask again and takes another long swig, telling me that it is to settle his stomach. He is still so drunk that his wallet misses his pocket as he tries to put it away and lands on the floor. He will be no trouble to get rid of in Warsaw in this condition, I hope.

However, the drink seems to give him new energy and he kisses me again. I suffer through it in resignation. It cannot be much longer any more. He rattles on about how filthy all the Polaks are and rasps lewd things in my ear. But the schnapps does eventually take an effect. He gives a huge belch and tells me that he is not feeling so good; he needs some fresh air.

I reminded him that we are in the last car. On the end of it there is a small open platform encircled by a railing. It is cool and windy there and would be very refreshing. All he needs to do is go through the folding door and stand in the wind for a spell. It will clear his head. I am hoping that he will go away at least for a little while. He agrees that it is a good idea. He looks sick, as if he were about to vomit.

But then he gets an idea. "Come along Polak," he tells me as he unsteadily gets to his feet. "You can use some fresh air also." He pulls me up by my hair again and pushes me ahead of him as he staggers down the aisle, past the nuns and the four Wehrmacht who are dozing. We enter the small platform and close the folding door behind us.

It is very noisy and windy there. The car is very old fashioned. The open platform is very small and rounded. The railing is very low and it almost feels scary. There is a roof above but all sides are open with just the railing and poles on both sides to hold on to.

"Shit!" yells Fritz holding on to one of the poles for support. "I am going to be sick!" He leans over the railing and retches. How lucky he did not vomit all over me. I am thinking that we got here just in time. He straightens up for a minute unsteadily and fumbles in his pocket for a handkerchief. He wipes his mouth with it and for a moment lets go of the pole and staggers as the platform shakes. If only he would fall over; I wish fervently.

He doubles over again as another wave of nausea comes over him. The Germans have excellent toilet training, I think. He'd rather take a chance of falling off the train than dirty the floor. It is ingrained in them.

The train lurches changing its track and Fritz titters almost losing his balance. It happens very suddenly without any premeditation on my part, without a single thought. I crouch behind him and grab his ankles then pull them up with all my strength.

Where did my strength come from? I pull and then shove forward. His scream is muted by the sound of the wind and the rattle of the train. It takes only a second and his feet are high in the air. He still has a hold on the railing with one hand, but it is slippery. One good shove and he disappears almost taking me with him.

I hold on to the pole as I am thrown forward and steady myself. I am gasping in the frigid wind but I am now alone on the platform. My mind is reeling. Why did I do it? Why did I take the chance? We are almost in Warsaw. What if it did not come off? This man would have killed me! I took a chance with my very life and it was not even necessary. I should be grateful that I was not searched! The Creature within me wants to destroy me! Or maybe it simply did not care, it does not tolerate humiliation of any sort.

I sit on the floor afraid to stand up, afraid to fall off the train because I came so close to it. I am chocked up with fear. Above me the night is fading as darkness becomes daylight. I can almost see in the distance outlines of trees against the grayness. The train changes track again; we must be very close to Warsaw.

The door opens and the conductor walks on to the platform and almost steps on me. I get up hastily mumbling vague apologies then go back into the car. Everybody is asleep but the nuns. I ignore them. On the floor is Fritz's wallet which I hastily stick into my large pocket next to the prayer book and my forged birth certificate. I can see buildings on both sides now and the train pulls into the station. I beg the conductor to help me with my suitcase. He pushes Fritz's duffel back to the side and takes it down for me, then goes on his way. I wait impatiently by the door and am the first one off, almost falling as I drag the suitcase hastily down the steps. I wonder vaguely where Fritz is now.

I have to walk for blocks and blocks to the trolley stop where I make my delivery. My arm feels numb by the time I get there and I am out of breath. There is a group of people waiting for the trolley on the bench. When it arrives, everybody gets aboard but myself and two ladies. They smile at me and give me a password for the priest. I give them my suitcase and they leave in a hurry. They appear extremely nervous.

I feel relieved but feel empty inside. Now I have the whole day to kill. I am in no shape to speak with Aunt Helena or anybody else. I am walking around Warsaw with an SS man's wallet in my pocket, a reminder of what happened last night. Still I instinctively seek out the Ghetto.

There it is, impenetrable, behind a wall and barbed wire. I hang around a street that seems to be an entrance. Please God, I want to see another Jew! Just once. It is very cold and I am grateful for my fleece lined jacket.

Eventually I see guards accompanying some ragged figures pushing loaded carts. They are walking in the middle of the street looking neither to right or to the left. How terribly thin they are! They must be so hungry. I have a fantasy of being able to throw bread to them. Their feet are wrapped with rags. They wear the white bands with the Star of David on their arms.

I follow the carts as I walk on the sidewalk. They are straining to push them. Their faces are drawn and impassive, almost dead looking. This Ghetto must be a living hell, I just know it.

*I remember the grinning faces of the Partisan and almost hear him speak "The Jews will pay almost anything for guns." Squeeze it out of the Jews, I think bitterly. Always that! But these wretched men have nothing but tatters on their backs. They look starved. How could they fight?*

*I feel very guilty later when I eat. The food chokes me. The priest has an idea that I might be able to penetrate this Ghetto. Next he will want me to enter hell to sell his forged birth certificates. Straws in the wind. . . These desperate people will clutch at the straws. I circle the Ghetto until it is almost curfew and go back to the station.*

*There are not many Germans going back to Czestochowa. I sleep all the way back, my head against the window pane. I wake from time to time staring into the darkness outside. Somewhere out there must be those labor camps. Where are they? Maybe I will catch a glimpse of something, but what?*

*I don't know why, but I am searching for flames. Why flames? Somewhere out there, there must be a belching fire. . . Why a fire? I look and look. . .*

*Czestochowa almost feels like home to me after Warsaw which is so big and complicated. I go straight to the Pralnia (laundry) and am welcomed like and old friend. The reason is that a package is waiting there for me. It was left there by a priest and it contains a clean change of clothes. Now they are convinced that I work for the underground and the best part is that they no longer ask me any questions. I get a nice hot bath and some soup for which they do not want to charge me. But I pay them anyway. Fritz's wallet was stuffed with marks. He probably just got paid.*

*I could probably ask them to let me stay the night but do not take such a chance. To be able to come here and bathe is the most important thing of all. I do not want to jeopardize it in any way. They would become too suspicious. Besides, I am now like an alley cat; it does not matter if I must sleep at the Jasna Gora. I actually feel safer that way. A person can get used to anything eventually. I never had any problems there, it is an excellent place to hide, even if it almost seems haunted. But then I should be comfortable with ghosts. They include everybody I know.*

*I meet again with the priest and the partisan with all those teeth. They are both very agitated and practically pounce on me.*

*"How did you do it?"*

*"Do what?"*

*They know that the train was completely searched and cannot imagine how I managed to deliver their suitcase. Why was I not caught? I craftily change the subject and let them wonder. They would probably find the truth hard to believe anyway. They are very impressed that I managed to deliver the goods in spite of the inspection; seem almost suspicious of me. I achieved the impossible.*

*I am paid a small sum of money and told that another job will be assigned to me soon. I have to continue showing up at the railroad station at designated days. What I do in between appears to be my problem. No offer is made to help me find a place to sleep. The contact remains very "blind."*

*Before we part I take out Fritz's wallet and show it to the priest. It contains various cards and identifications, including photographs and addresses. Could they use it?*

*They examine everything carefully and want to know how I got it. I tell them I found it. They seem suspicious but certainly are very interested. I name my price; no freebies for Armja Krajowa from me. It is strictly business!*

My next assignment took me to Krakow where I picked up a suitcase. I have never been there before and spent my free time walking around the city. The Vavel, a seat of the Polish Kings is very famous. Now it was occupied by the German *Gauleiter* (Governor) Frank. Within its walls is the tomb of Mickiewicz, the greatest Polish poet. It is an ancient and beautiful castle. The city itself, much larger than Czestochowa, was bustling with activity. There were Germans everywhere, some just sightseeing. It was also the center of the German Occupation Administration.

Of course, I instinctively drifted towards the Ghetto. It was walled off like a fortress and the wall was shaped like tombstones. German sense of grim humor, no doubt.

The birth certificate from Father Krzeminski gave my place of birth as the town of Bochnia. It was very close to Krakow and I was tempted to visit there but decided against it. I did not know it then but Bochnia was only a stones throw distance from Auschwitz, the infamous, huge, (forty acres) Death Camp.

Probably a pall of smoke from the crematoriums hung over Bochnia then.

I kept searching for flames and fire in the darkness as I traveled on the trains, thinking instinctively that this was what a labor camp might look like from a distance. I did not know it but I was very close to one. The ashes of millions were scattered around this green Polish country side, so very close to Krakow.

Auschwitz, the death place of *three million Jews!* Unknown to me at the time of my visit to Krakow, its gas chambers were disgorging the bodies of the Jews from the Bialystok Ghetto and the last remaining Jews from Berlin. The Greek Jews were arriving by the thousands. They were followed by those from Macedonia and Thrace.

The Priest did entertain the idea of having me penetrate the Krakow Ghetto, but it, too, was being liquidated about then. Yet, one could never have guessed it. Krakow throbbed with life.

I did not like my Krakow contact at all. He passed by me several times and I knew who he was long before he approached me. He did not have my suitcase ready, but walked with me to a park bench where a woman sat holding it. I then had to return with it to the station, which was a pretty long walk.

It was a very eventful trip for me. As usual I entered the last car and looked around. It was very crowded and I immediately spotted a young German in a uniform sitting alone. He was SS but by then I decided that if I carried contraband, sitting next to one was actually to my advantage.

This young man was a far cry from Fritz. He was sober, clean cut, very polite and friendly. He appeared to be no more than twenty years old. He immediately put up my suitcase on the rack and gave me a choice of where I wanted to sit. We chatted pleasantly enough and after a few hours, he shared his sandwich with me.

I seemed like such a nice girl, could he look me up when he was in Czestochowa? Who knows, maybe he could help me find German ancestors in my family tree and I could become a *Volksdeutsche.* He hoped I did not take offense to his invitation to let me rest my head on his shoulder. It was late and I could use some rest. He was nothing short of a perfect traveling companion.

After a while the conversation turned to his work. He did wear a Death Head insignia but appeared too young to be a policeman. Well, he told me that his was a rather unusual job. He was part of the *Judenfernichtung* (Jew-destruction) battalion and was very glad to tell me all about it.

In various towns, the entire Jewish population was rounded up and brought into wooded areas where there were open mass grave pits waiting to be filled. It was his job to sit on the edge and keep shooting. The *Judenfernichtung* battalions have been so busy that he had developed calluses and blisters on his trigger finger.

I tried to conceal the shock his graphic descriptions caused me. He went into details about the pits as I sat there and shared his ham sandwich. "How can anyone as nice as you hold such a job?" I asked. "Does it not bother you to kill?"

"Well," he explained, "at first it did. But then it is a job like any other job. A butcher does not worry about killing chickens; it just has to be done." This was the way he looked at it. It was a very necessary function he had to perform for his country. It was actually *high priority* in case I did not know it. They were actually not supposed to advertise it but it was surely no secret. Everybody knew about it, especially in the Ukraine and Eastern Poland.

The pleasant young man kept on chatting in a very friendly tone of voice. He would offer me a cigarette, but he did not smoke. However, if I wanted one, he would get it for me. I was very pretty and easy to talk to. He was so glad to have met me. . .

I kept thinking of Moishe and the time he told me he had heard of such mass killings in the city of *Wilno* and other places. So it was true! Now I knew for certain.

There was no labor taking place in labor camps; except when absolutely needed. They were *killing places!*

I did not know then about the gas chambers but thought that it was done on a huge scale by young men like this traveling companion sitting next to me. I looked sideways at the young, pink skinned face, the honest looking blue eyes and well shaped hands. He surely did not look like a killer but rather like a well brought up young man, the kind people would gladly invite home to dinner.

His voice droned on and on. He noticed that I seemed tired. "There," he prodded my head towards his shoulder. "Lean against me and close your eyes." I did at first to shut him up, but then my mind became very tired as if it needed to shut off the horror of what I just heard. The wheels clanged monotonously against the rails. The train had a hypnotic rocking motion. Finally my eyes closed and I slept all the way back to Czestochowa.

Just before we got there the young SS man woke me up. He told me that he did not dare to move his shoulder lest he disturb my sleep. I seemed to be so very tired. He carried my suitcase for me to the station and offered to wait with me until my family picked me up. I thanked him and gave him a fake address where he could look me up. It was becoming routine by now, the second time I have done this. The Germans were all alike, wanted to help me become a *Volksdeutsche,* wanted to visit and meet my family. This one might have already met them at the edge of a mass grave pit. He could possibly have shot my parents.

I kept wondering about it as I waited for my contact. I felt drained. My other option would have to wait. I intended to carry suitcases and anything else for the *Armja Krajowa.* It was a miniscule, tiny contribution. It probably would not save the life of a single Jew. But what was bad for the Germans was good for me.

My contact was late, and I felt a crushing sense of loneliness. Life now meant absolutely nothing to me. I actually wished desperately to die but something perverse and stubborn would not let me. I missed my parents more than I thought possible.

If only I knew exactly where they were, either dead or alive! I was going to be a train person, a hobo. How long would I be doing this? It did not matter. I was never going to be happy again in my life. I did not have the right.

# 15

# THE LAST TIME I SAW WARSAW

It was April of 1943, a pale, anemic spring, after a bitterly cold winter. It seemed as if nature also had unleashed its fury during the winter months and was retreating reluctantly. But time flows on as it must, and all that had happened was now a part of the past, like the melted snow. Living conditions in Poland have deteriorated further and there was less and less of everything. Food was scarcer and more expensive, when available.

There were many rumors about the progress of the war and I heard bits and pieces of information from the priest as well as from the Germans I met on the trains. There were more *Wehrmacht* and *Waffen SS* headed East than returning from the front. Gone was the arrogant bravado of past years, even though the trains still bore a slogan in bold white letters: "All wheels must roll to victory." Clearly they were not for the Germans. I ran into nervous, scared Wehrmacht, very young and middle aged, who were very unhappy about going to the front. The fortunes of the war were changing and many events were taking place.

On the 14th of February, the Soviets captured Rostov and Kharkov on the 16th. On the 21st the Germans counterattacked in the Donets Basin area, near Kharkov under the command of Manstein. But it was tough going in the unaccustomed cold of the Russian plains.

On the 25th the British Air Force and the U.S. Air Force began "round the clock" bombardment of Germany. On the 28th, the Norwegian Resistance fighters destroyed German heavy-water installations in their country which made it impossible for the Germans to complete research on atomic weapons. People did not realize until years later the monumental significance of this action.

On the 2nd of March, the Germans began their withdrawal from the Rzhev-Vyazma Salient. And on the 6th, in the Middle

East, General Rommel, so victorious up to now, was repulsed in an attack on the British Eighth Army near Medenine.

Still, the Germans had not lost all their teeth and on the 15th of March, Manstein completed the recapture of Kharkov. It was the last major German victory on the Russian front.

On the 19th of April, pitiful remnants of starving Jews in the Warsaw ghetto began their suicide attack against their Nazi oppressors. They had almost no guns but the inadequate discards that the Poles were willing to part with at exorbitant prices. Even those were laboriously smuggled against impossible odds by whoever was willing to put their life on the line. Crude explosives were made out of scarce petrol and rags inserted as fuses into bottles. There was no help from any quarter. There was no hope at all.

They fought this way against modern tanks and the might of the experienced German Army. And incredibly, it was not until May 16th, almost a month later, that the Germans wiped out all Jewish Resistance in the Warsaw ghetto. They did it by methodically blowing up and burning every building.

The ghetto fighters had no food or water left and nothing at all was brought in to help them. There was no help offered at any time by the Polish Resistance. At the end a few fighters were rescued as they crawled sick and filthy out of the sewers, but that was all. The sewers were the only escape route available to the Jews and most perished there, a horrible, pitiless death. And most who crawled out were immediately apprehended. They stank. Their clothes were wet with filthy refuse. The Germans picked them off very quickly.

After the 16th of May, 1943, there were no Jews at all left in Warsaw. The huge, almost half-a-million strong ghetto was only rubble, a page of history.

By the time April came, I had already travelled countless miles across Poland. I lived on the trains. It became routine for me. The names of towns became familiar and I learned to sleep on benches and railroad car seats. I had no watch or a calendar and time had no meaning other than the days of contact and time of departure.

It was a lonely life detached from any personal tie or contact. I could not avoid conversations with other travelers but they were guarded and defensive. I was afraid and distrustful of all Poles. They could figure out easily who I was and every question was a threat to my life.

It was much harder for the Germans to put two and two together. They were not sensitized to suspect me, I was just another *Polin* to them, one of their subjects of the occupied territory. They could never guess otherwise. But the Poles would have immediately wondered why a little girl my age was alone and traveling.

I carried suitcases and parcels from place to place and it did not matter to me what they contained. My only pleasure was the visits to the *Pralnia* (laundry) where I took a long, warm bath and dozed in an armchair afterwards for a couple of hours.

I could have gotten caught at any time, but luck was with me. I developed an instinct. Sometimes I walked the length of the train to see who was on it. If I felt uneasy, I just got off at the next station and took another train.   Especially worrisome were deliveries in small towns usually away from the train station. I felt much safer in busy crowded places. I learned to leave my suitcase on a rack above a seat and sit somewhere else so if there was an inspection I was not obviously connected to my baggage. I had to abandon my suitcase twice. There were a thousand ways I could slip up.

The priest became very fond of me, in his own way. I was never completely convinced that he really was a cleric, but there was no question about his dedication to the Resistance. He was a very disciplined person who never, even for an instant, let down his guard or caution. I never knew his real name and simply called him Father Jan. He coached me and I listened carefully to his advice.

When I asked him about the Jewish woman and her son from Czestochowa ghetto who were hiding out with a Polish family, he simply told me that even this was best for me *not* to know. If I were ever apprehended my knowledge had to be zero, or everybody I knew about would have to go into hiding.

I received a compliment once from him and his companion, the man with the toothy smile. "Zosia," they agreed, "was worth her weight in gold."

"Too bad that I do not weigh very much," I quipped, but my heart swelled with pride.

There were a couple of nights I stayed in a real bed in an apartment. A young mother came by the laundry one day and asked me to babysit her three small children. Her husband had been arrested and imprisoned, but she had a good job. I probably could have stayed with her safely enough.  She needed someone to watch over the children while she worked, but after only two days the terrible restlessness hit me.

I loved the children, but then I loved all children. I could not help thinking of all the Jewish children who had been deported. Babies who had not yet learned to talk, tiny girls with trusting eyes, little boys holding onto their parents hands. I thought of them when I fed the woman's baby and I would have cried if I could... I walked around the apartment like a caged animal, I felt driven. The restlessness tore at me, I could not stay.

I arrived in Warsaw sometime in April on a bright sunny day. As soon as the delivery was completed, I started out immediately towards the ghetto. That's how it was for me. I was irresistably drawn to circle it, to examine all entrances for signs of life or any activity in any large town I came to. In Warsaw, there was an air of festivity, springtime and Easter. The city had thawed out after a severe winter. People were glad for the sunshine and warmth, glad to take off their bulky winter coats. Young couples strolled arm in arm, laughing, in spite of the war. But above the ghetto, smoke drifted. There was the sound of gunfire and tanks rumbled towards the entrance street. Some of the pedestrians stopped to stare.

"What is happening there?" I asked.

"Don't you know? The Jews have declared war on Germany!" Everybody thought it was very funny; a joke. Imagine the Jews fighting back; fighting anybody. I looked in vain for any sign of compassion or sympathy; any expression of sadness. People gaped and laughed. "Imagine the Germans needing their tanks to fight the Jews! The chickens are fighting the butcher. Some revolution!"

I spent the whole day circling the ghetto listening to the sounds of violence within it; watching the drifting smoke. If only my eyes could penetrate those walls. If only I could see. If only it was possible that something I carried during the past months was in their hands!

I felt such crushing helplessness, it was like a physical pain. I knew exactly how weak they were, how hopeless and desperate and the revenge the Germans will extract from those they capture alive. I found it impossible to leave Warsaw and stayed another day. I spent the night on the bench at the railroad station feeling more lonely than ever. So few were left by now. If only they had fought back sooner! But I knew how it was. They still had hope then, did not know for sure what awaited them.

They had illusions, and their families to worry about. Now they knew better. And I could only bear witness to the drifting smoke.

The Poles who stood across the street and laughed did not know it then, but the same thing was awaiting them just around the corner in the future. Next August, they, too, were going to revolt. Not in order to survive, but to redeem their honor. To be able to have the glory of freeing Warsaw with their own hands. They were going to do it with help just around the corner as the Soviet army neared Warsaw.

But the Soviets were not about to let them have their glory. They were to halt at the Vistula River and from there watch the smoke raising over the city and perhaps also find it mildy amusing.

And the Poles also were to be like "chickens revolting against the butcher." And the Germans would tear the city apart block after block, house after house and bring them to their knees. History would repeat itself with spectacular irony but with a slightly different outcome. Almost nobody survived in the ghetto... But there was a definite parallel morally.

My next instructions were to bypass Czestochowa and go straight to Krakow for a pickup. I left Warsaw for the last time on a balmy spring day.

In Krakow, I stood calmly near the information desk. I had nothing with me to worry about. My pickup should be here, but the contact was a couple of hours late already.

At last a man wearing a beret began to observe me. He circled the station and sat down on a bench reading a book. From time to time he peered at me from above it and our eyes would meet. My instructions were to never make the first move. He was middle aged and very nondescript in his brown jacket.

After a while I went to the bathroom and afterwards made myself comfortable on one of the benches. I have been standing around for a long while. The man got up and slightly nodded his head. Well, at last...

I followed him out into the street and we caught up with each other. He smiled very pleasantly. "It's just a few blocks walk," he said. He continued chatting as we walked. He thought I must be tired and probably could use a little rest after traveling. How about some good homemade barley soup if I was hungry.

I felt a stirring of uneasiness. This was never part of the routine, these Krakow contacts were weird, they made me nervous. We kept on walking and I just smiled and nodded. He was right; I was very tired. The houses on the street were all identical and we stopped in front of one of them.

"Here we are at last," sighed the man. I followed him up the stone steps and my heart literally fluttered. *It is bad, oh, it is bad,* I heard a little voice within my mind. I was not supposed to know where anybody lived. This was unusual.

The man took a key out of his pocket and opened a door. It was a small, ground floor apartment. On one side of a tiny hallway was a bathroom and the kitchen on the other. The man helped me with my jacket, and hung it on a hook by the entrance along with his own.

"I guess I am hungry after all," I said trying to appear normal.

"All I need to do is warm it up," he said cheerfully. "Why don't you make yourself comfortable while I do it."

I felt a wave of sheer terror wash over me, I shook inside with it. "May I wash up first please, I really need to," I said. He pointed at the half open bathroom door. "The towels are on a shelf, *Panienka.* (Miss)."

The bathroom was very tiny with no bath tub, just a toilet and a sink. I let the water run but left the door opened and watched the man disappear in the kitchen. I quickly, opened the front door a bit and grabbed my jacket. I was now acting completely by instinct. I stood in the bathroom wearing my jacket with the water running. Through the slightly opened door I saw the man go into the living room. I flushed the toilet to make a noise and tiptoed out the door and out of the apartment. Once out, I broke into a run and did not stop until I was blocks away.

It was almost curfew time and if I was correct about the man, the railroad station was surely the worst place to go. The streets began to grow empty and I kept on running.

Was I being foolish? Nobody followed me when I left his house, nobody stopped me. There was no back up. If he were Gestapo, there would have been a back up outside on the street. Why would he go through this stupid "barley soup" routine?

Now that I thought back, he did not appear at all threatening. But I felt such stark terror in that apartment. Now the idea of a hot bowl of barley soup seemed very tempting. I was hungry.

Where could I sleep tonight? I thought. I did not have many choices. There was a park near by I had seen before. Some of the shrubs were very thick. So be it! I made sure that no one saw me and crawled in between the shrubbery. It was bristly, damp and scratchy, but there was a curfew out there and patrols were out in force.

I spent a miserable night curled up in a ball for warmth. There was a fine drizzle in the morning. Now I had to get back to Czestochowa, but had to take the train from another stop. I had to walk to the next town.

A farmer gave me a lift in a wagon. As soon as I sat next to him, the questions startd. Why was I walking alone in the rain? Where was I going? Where was I from? The ride was almost not worth the trouble.

I told him that I was from Bochnia. He had been there. Did I know this? Did I know that? By the time I got off the wagon the suspicion was almost palpable. Sly questions to trip me up. I was glad to be walking again and scared that the farmer might try to collect the prize the Germans offered for delivering a fugitive Jew. What happiness it was to be on the train again, how reassuring to hear the hum of the wheels.

I arrived on the day of contact feeling very embarrassed. I goofed, I over-reacted. No more compliments. They would laugh at me. But there *was* no contact. I went to the *Pralnia* to take a bath and this time I really needed it. I was also hoping that someone had dropped off a change of clothes for me; but nobody did. I made no contact.

I had no way to find out anything. The thin, flimsy connection was broken. Maybe they did not need me anymore. Maybe they were arrested! I would never know.

In Warsaw my contact days were Mondays and Thursdays, but only if they had wanted them to be. I could never go back to the ghetto! It was against my nature to retrace my steps especially if I had been burned ever so slightly. And the day of the selection-action was very sharp in my memory. It was a trap.

I had only one option left to me. I would volunteer to go to work in Germany. I knew how dangerous it was. If they found my papers to be inadequate and started checking, I was finished. I could not produce an address. The forged birth certificate was only a bluff. But it was all I had.

It was my only option and I had to sleep somewhere. My money would run out and what then?

I made up my mind to take this gamble with my life. Besides I desperately wanted to leave Poland. For me it was a cemetary of my people. I would have this restlessness as long as I stayed. I would circle these dead ghettos like a moth circles lights. It would kill me.

I considered going to the Germans immediately but then I remembered that I had one more obligation to fulfill.

I had to contact this woman who was engaged to Heniek Stecki, to report to her how and when Uncle and Aunt Stecki died. They had spent their last momemts with my parents and I owed them that. I took a last lonely walk around the Czestochowa ghetto; a last look at the Jasna Gora and then boarded a train back to Krakow. It was the last time I ever saw Czestochowa. I was going to be the bearer of bad news but I knew how children needed to know the fate of their parents. I had been through it myself. The three sons of the Stecki's had the right to be told the truth, however sad it was.

# 16

## MY COUSIN ISIDOR

Cousin Heniek Stecki's fiance lived in an outlying suburb of Krakow. I wondered about her as I rode the trolley through the beautiful city. She had to be very special for Henniek to have chosen her. He was a very special person himself; a young physician, handsome and gentle. He inherited Aunt Matilda's soft brown eyes and her sweet disposition. I felt that I knew him especially well because I read the books he loved. It was a shared intimacy for me.

I remembered the dreamy afternoons I had spent in the Stecki's dusty and quiet attic letting my fantasies roam in the ancient world of Cleopatra. I felt so glad that Heniek had a chance to survive, thanks to this woman. She must have suffered to have been widowed so early in life and I knew that by giving Heniek her husband's papers she was also taking a chance with her own life.

I was not disappointed when I finally met her. She lived alone and her apartment was very tiny. I told her immediately who I was and she simply took me in her arms. There were tears in her eyes. We spoke for a little while and I told her all I knew.

Afterwards, she picked up her purse. "Zosia, I have a surprise for you," she said. "We are both going to visit your cousin Isidor." I was almost weak with emotion at the thought. I did not expect to see someone I loved so dearly. I thought I was just going to leave a message with her to be delivered someday to the Stecki brothers.

Isidor lived with his wife and mother-in-law in a tall apartment building. With tears in his eys, he welcomed me like a sister. His wife, a physician, was a tall, beautiful blonde. They both led me to their bedroom where there was a crib. I was thunder struck... They had a year-old baby daughter. The baby opened her eyes and smiled at me.

What magnificent bravery it took for them to dare to have a child under such conditions! I picked up the little girl and rocked her in my arms. I felt very sad that Aunt Matilda never had the chance to do it. Heniek's fiance had to leave because of the curfew but I stayed. I basked in the warmth of their welcome. Tonight I would sleep so safely on clean pillows on their couch. They could hardly do enough for me, both of them.

"You will stay with us, of course," Isidor told me. "You are not alone any longer, you have us and you have a home." He marveled at how wise his parents were. They had set it up so that I could find them without telling me any more than was safe. We spoke about his parents, and about what had happened. We mourned our parents together, and I realized how much I needed this expression of mourning. How dammed up all these feelings were within my loneliness.

Isidor explained that his assumed name was now Paul and his wife's Josefina. They had very solid identification papers including food ration cards. These were not just forged papers, they belonged to persons who died and, of course, there were records in existance if anything needed to be verified by the authorities. Even the mother-in-law had papers.

In addition, Isidor had a very enviable job. He managed a shoe store and shoes at that time of the war were the scarcest of commodities. A pair of shoes was quite beyond the dreams of the average person. Most people wore wooden soled footwear with the top parts made of cloth. By today's standards, Isidor was actually very well off. And tomorrow, he told me beaming from ear to ear, he was going to bring me a pair of honest to goodness leather shoes!

After all, I was his little sister; it would make him happy to give me something of value.

We all tiptoed into the bedroom to have one more look at the sleeping baby. Isidor stood above the crib with his arm around his beautiful wife. I could almost sense the love between these two. It had to find an expression, and the baby was it. It was hope personified in that tiny bundle under a pink, knitted blanket. We remembered Aunt and Uncle Stecki once more before we went to sleep. They, too, continued on into the future through this little miracle, a living, peacefully sleeping, Jewish baby.

I experienced strange and strong emotions as I lay on the sofa in the dark. It had been so long. Somewhere out there trains were rolling through the night and trailing behind them was the haunting sound of a whistle. Gears ground as they came to a stop in obscure Polish towns. The countless faces of travelers indifferent and anonymous. Was it possible that this phase of my life was over now? Could it be?

I got my new shoes and a week went by. I felt unbelievably rested and clean. Isidor and his wife both went to work every day and I stayed home with the mother-in-law and the baby.

I had to be very careful, of course. I had no inregistration and had to stay completely out of sight. Nobody should ever see me. I could not leave the apartment and had to keep away from the windows. If there was a knock at the door and a neighbor stoped by for any reason, I frantically hid in a closet.

But it was 1943 and the war could not last forever. By late afternoon, the mother-in-law was always very nervous. I saw her unconsciously wringing her hands and glancing anxiously out of the windows as she waited for Isidor and his wife to come home. If a car came to a stop in front of the building she turned pale; could it be the Gestapo? I couldn't sing to the baby. The sound of my voice might have carried and be heard in the adjacent apartment. We mostly spoke in whispers. These were the normal logical precautions but her apprehension went way beyond it, I could sense it.

Yes, there was a problem. Isidor did not want to tell me about it because I had been through so much. He intended to anyway, because I had to know. Lately he had been blackmailed by one of the fellow employees where he worked. It was a subtle kind of blackmail. The man did not come out with outright accusations or threats. It consisted of hints and double talk. He mentioned Jews in passing conversation, then dropped a word of double meaning, sort of a cat and mouse game. Then he confided to Isidor that he happened to be strapped for money, was broke, and could use a few *zloty's*. If Isidor ignored it, the double talk intensified, the hints grew more direct, and became vaguely threatening. He mentioned the baby. . . Now Isidor would not want anything bad to happen to the baby. And Josefina, wasn't she beautiful? Isidor was very lucky to be married to such a stunning girl. . . should not be selfish about it. . .

I felt as if there was a rock in the pit of my stomach. This was terribly serious.

As soon as Isidor came home, I confronted him with questions. He confessed that lately he had been giving the man money. He had lost his nerve, even had to sell some of his mother-in-law's jewelry. He had been feeling cornered. But the

man was a Pole after all. He was taking advantage of something
he perhaps only guessed or suspected.

"But Isidor. . ." I said horrified. "Now that you have paid him
off it is no longer a guess. The man now knows the truth!" We sat
around the table and talked about it. Isidor was intelligent
enough to know it. He had been suppressing reality, denying it,
because he felt so helpless.

He had been trying to maintain faith in the humanity of a
Pole. But a blackmailer had no humanity. . . Isidor's papers were
very good, but he was circumcised. In Poland only Jews were circumcised. It was then like having been marked for death, all the
Germans needed to do was examine him. We sat around the
table, terrified. The baby cooed and smiled blissfully. The baby!
How can they be on the run with a small baby? Where would the
mother-in-law stay?

I felt a cold anger rising within me. "The man had to be
eliminated" I said. Their eyes bore into me horrified. But the
man had done nothing overt. Even his threats were just hints. He
probably would never do anything so terrible as to cause the
death of a whole family. My suggestion was unthinkable to them.

Then, I insisted, they must have another plan! They simply
could not take a chance just waiting and hoping. They couldn't
be at the mercy of a blackmailer. The baby could be given to the
nuns for the time being. Maybe the nuns would help! But Isidor
and Josefina must leave. . . But where? How could they separate
from their child? They had a home, an apartment. It was cozy
and comfortable. It was their nest.

I told them about my plan to volunteer for work in Germany.
Maybe Isidor and Josefina could do the same. Well, Josefina
could, but Isidor might have to undergo a physical examination
and his circumcision would give him away. He had already, in
desperation, considered it. I suggested that when I volunteered I
could find out for them if there was a physical examination involved. I could write and let them know. . .

Isidor suggested that all mail should go to Heniek's fiance for
my own safety. The implication of these words hit us and we fell
silent. The baby gurgled and made happy little noises. The pain
in her parents faces was indescribable. The mother-in-law wiped
off her tears. Oh, Josefina, why did you have to have a baby at a
time like this! It was pure madness. A magnificent madness at
such a price. . . I remembered my mother's words "they can only
really get you by hurting those you love. . ."

I left the next day for the *Arbeitsamt* (Labor Bureau). It was a little like entering a lions cage armed only with a faded little piece of paper, my phoney birth certificate. The door was draped with a German flag. Uniforms all around me. Pictures of Hitler on the wall. There was an information desk at the door and I was directed into the proper office. There, at a desk, sat an elderly *Volksdeutsche.* He spoke very good Polish. I told him why I was there and he hardly looked up at me.

"Papers, please." He took out a new file and wrote my name on it. Then he took out a form to fill out and used the information on my birth certificate.

"Your address. . ." I gave him a fictitious address in the town of Bochnia. "Precinct number, please." I gave him a number off the top of my head, hoping it was a lucky one and that it existed.

"Your picture identification, an *Ausweiss* now." I told him I did not bring it with me. He put down his pen and glowered at me angrily. "It is against the law to go anywhere without an *Ausweiss*, don't you know that!"

I told him a well rehearsed story. I had left in a hurry against my parents wishes. I wanted to go to Germany because there was not enough to eat at home. One less mouth to feed would be a blessing for my family, but still they did not want me to leave. But I was sixteen years old and I had the right to do what I wanted.

The *Volksdeutsche* listened with annoyance. It was a problem for him. But it was almost his lunchtime, he told me. I could stay in a cell while he gave it some thought.

"In a cell?" He gave me a disgusted look and I was escorted below by a guard. It was a cell alright, not very uncomfortable but the windows were barred. Well, what did I expect from the Germans? If someone volunteered for  *Aschwitz* or the Ghetto would they expect to get a better treatment when they got there because they did it voluntarily?

After lunch there was pandemonium. About a hundred people were brought in, and they certainly were not volunteers. They had been simply rounded up on the street and brought in forcefully. My cell was now very crowded with very upset Poles on their way to Germany to dig potatoes.

I did not see the *Volksdeutsche* official again. He had his hands full processing papers. It was a transport of farm laborers. This was what the Germans needed that day. I don't think anybody in this transport had ever worked on a farm; everbody was a city dweller from Krakow. Well, they would be farm hands from now on; it was decreed by our lords and masters.

I received a number and was loaded along with the others into a cattle car. It was not too uncomfortable and there were small windows for ventilation. The train pulled out of the station as the sun began to set. Out of the little windows I could see apartment buildings on both sides. The last rays of sunshine reflected a reddish glow against the window panes. The train rattled and shook. Darkness fell swiftly.

I looked at the Polish houses; places where people lived, maybe getting ready now to sit down for supper. I thought of Isidor. I would have to write him as soon as possible that there was no medical examination what ever. I was very happy about it! It was easy, — a breeze.

People were crying and wailing all around me. They were being taken to Germany against their will. Didn't they understand that the *Deutsches Reich* had its needs? Somebody had to dig potatoes and plant wheat if the war was to continue! I found it amusing and smiled in the darkness. I was going to survive the war right under Hitler's nose whether he liked it or not. I was glad to leave Poland for there was nothing there left for me. I would dig potatoes if I must.

I had a box of matches in my pocket which I bought early that morning. I always wished I had a gun to fight the Germans with, — to kill them. Well, in Germany I could do more damage with a box of matches than I could in Poland with a gun. If they would win the war and nobody was able to do them harm, I would be in Germany. . . And someday when they least expect it, I could take a small revenge. . . At least that. . . The matches were only symbolic now, but someday an opportunity would present itself. . . Some day!

We changed trains again in Berlin, and for the first time in my life I saw and rode on an escalator in the *Podstammer Bahnhof.* We were under escort and the place was very crowded. There was a huge crowd of people jammed into the plaza outside. Over the loudspeaker drifted an hysterical, rasping voice. It was Hitler's voice. There was a political rally taking place there. I was astounded; what timing.

"The pig must be somewhere near by." The Poles were very agitated. They whispered to each other as we were quickly herded into the next train. "Did you hear him? Was it really him?"

We were given some bread and water and our trip continued. We were unloaded in Magdeburg, Saxony and taken to the *Arbeit-samt* (Labor Bureau) holding center. We were herded into a large cavernous hall much like a warehouse where we waited. From time to time numbers were called and people were taken away to be loaded into trucks.

Finally it was my turn and the truck rolled upon German soil. I was delivered to the gate of a farm house and was told that the name of the town was *Shoenebeck-Elbe*. I had arrived; it was done and again there was this feeling of apprehension. What was I to expect in Germany, the land of the *Basiliscus?*

The driver opened the back of the truck. There was a tall SS officer waiting by the gate and he signed the delivery order sheet for the driver. I climbed off clumsily and stood before him. He was a very handsome man, darkhaired and brown-eyed. His uniform was pressed to perfection, all spit and polish. He looked me over from head to toe as if I was a new cow he had just purchased.

"You are very small," he told me with disappointment. "I expected a strong farm girl to be sent to me. I should have gone to Magdeburg personally to look you over first," he added regretfully and opened the gate.

Beyond it was a white farm house surrounded by a large yard, stables, barns and cow sheds. On the edge were long and narrow pig styes. He introduced himself as Herr Richard Muchow, the owner of the farm and led me to the workers quarters.

There were ten of us here, all Poles, women on one side of the yard and men on the other. The women were quartered in a small shed no bigger than one of the pigstys. It consisted of only one room with a dirt floor. In it were bunks for six of us. There was no bathroom or a washroom and no window. Hardly enough space to hang our clothes.

The women regarded me with curiosity and had a hundred questions to ask. I could tell by their dialect that they were all peasants. In Poland, the peasants speak with an altogether different accent.

I could immediately see why Herr Muchow was so disappointed. The women were all very much larger than I. They wanted to know all about me and were aghast when they heard that I was not an experienced farm hand. The work here was extremely hard, from dawn to dark, and they looked at me with pity. I would never make it. Willi, the foreman, drove people with a whip if they lagged behind and they were sure that I would. This was no country picnic. I was given a bunk and could immediately smell the dirty straw mattress I would be sleeping on.

I discovered that the only place to wash in was a trough by the water well and the girls held up a blanket to provide privacy. I was told that this was also where we did our laundry. They asked me anxiously about Poland, they missed very much being home.

Within an hour the hut was quiet and everybody was fast asleep. The women were plainly exhausted. I could hear the animals in their sheds as I washed up. The yard smelled of fertilizer.

Next morning, barely at daylight, I was assigned to help one of the men in the yard. He was a big, strong Pole and his name was Ignac. We had to feed the pigs and clean out the pig styes. It was heavy work and the pigs were actually dangerous.

Ignac showed me how to handle the pitch fork and how to fend off the pigs. "If you fall in, they might attack you," he warnd me. "The pigs are actually very fussy," he joked, "and unlike us, have to have their straw changed very often." Ignac did everything very swiftly and expertly giving me instructions while we worked. I was actually very clumsy and of little help to him. The work was very hard.

Before we cleaned the cow shed, Ignac told me to wait and disappeared for a few minutes. I practically collapsed of fatigue in the straw while waiting. He returned and sat down next to me.

"Now here is something else you will have to learn," he said. He took a couple of eggs out of his pocket and quickly made a small hole in each, then brought it to his lips and sucked it dry. Then I followed his example.

"Quickly!" he said looking furtively at the door of the barn. "You will catch hell if you get caught doing this, but you need the nourishment to keep up your strength. It's not exactly scrambled eggs, but as close to it as we can get under the circumstances." He crumbled the shells and stuck them into his pocket.

At noon time we were given a number of sandwiches to deliver to the field workers and rode there on a wagon.

As soon as we had a chance to talk Ignac clued me in on the facts of life on this farm. This one, in his opinion, could hardly be worse. "You should have heard how mad *Mucha* was when he saw you! He expected a "Polish slave" to be pretty hefty. The only thing he liked about you were your legs, which he noticed when you were getting off the truck.

Ignac called Herr Muchow, *Mucha* which in Polish means a fly and expressed a hearty dislike for the man. "The damned SS bastard struts around like a wind up doll and primps himself like a peacock." According to Ignac, *Mucha* never did any work whatsoever. In fact, his fingernails were manicured and polished. He spent his entire days in SS meetings and activities or chasing women. This was quite understandable because his wife was very ugly and waddled around like a duck. It was a known fact that "Mucha" married her for her farm and her money. His foreman, old Willi, ran the farm and he, Ignac, made the decisions about what to plant and where.

Ignac was an experienced Polish farmer and knew as much about animals as a veterinarian. *Mucha* valued him very much and give him a lot of authority. Ignac was about forty years old, had curly dark hair and dark eyes which was rather unusual for a Pole. He was also likeable. While we rode to the field, I remarked how easy it would be to run away from here. Nobody was watching us, we were completely on our own.

"Don't even think of it," he told me. "There are a couple of million Poles working in Germany and the Germans have an airtight system." Nobody had made it as far as he knew. Of course, it had been tried and those who did died or were sent to a concentration camp. Ignac himself was not about to be so stupid and intended to stick around until the war was over. At home, he told me with a laugh, he had a wife and nine daughters. "Nine, mind you!" If he had another one he would enter a monastery, would never forgive himself. Somebody up there had it in for him, nine was bad enough!

By the way, he told me, I would be wise to hold his hand when we arrived at the fields. I would be treated better if they thought we had something going between us, especially that sadistic Willi, the forman. He could be very mean. But if he got the idea that Ignac and I were "friends" he would go easier on me.

"Well, Ignac," I said, "you just got yourself another girl!"

"Don't even say such a thing!" he yelled.

I rode back from the fields very tired. It had been the most grueling day of my life. My muscles were stiff from work. I had spent the rest of the day bent double, weeding my row of sugar beets.

I did not have a prayer of catching up with the others and was left way behind.. Willi was behind me screeching and snapping his whip. *Mach Shnell!* (hurry up).

I had not straightened up once in hours, and at the end of the day I barely could.

I could hardly wait to write a letter to Isidor and tell him that he can safely volunteer for work in Germany. Nobody in the transport had a physical examination. He could make it. It was a horrible place to be but death was worse. Since letters were often censured, a post card had a better chance to get through faster.

I write only a few sentences:

> Dear Paul,
> My stomach is all better, and I did
> not even need to see a doctor. I am in
> excellent health. Wish you were here
> close to me.
>           Love,
>           Zofia.

The card did get through because within a month, I received a package from Isidor. It contained fresh, clean underwear, a cotton blouse and a skirt. I needed all those things very badly and my heart was filled with love and gratitude. I felt elated regardless of all hardships. If I were able to help to save even one person, especially Isidor, whom I loved like a brother, it would make everything worthwhile. My life then still had meant something. I waited hopefully for a letter and a week later Herr Muchow personally brought me a postcard. It was from Heniek's fiance.

I read:

> Dear Zofia,
>   Paul and his wife and daughter have
> joined his parents. Actually, the
> mother-in-law and the baby went first, —
> right away. Paul and his wife next followed.
> All this was thanks to his co-worker about
> whom you have heard so much.
>     Thank you for your post card.
>       Adela

I felt as if there was a stone inside my chest, a heavy, jagged stone, instead of a heart. I saw that smiling little baby before my eyes day and night. I raged at Isidor for having waited too long, for having had such foolish faith in the "humanity" of a "fellow

Pole." I found myself talking to Isidor, trying to reach him as if I could undo this which had happened. I fantasized that I was back in time and able to convince him not to wait. I was torn by guilt for not having succeeded, because I *knew*, I was certain, that this blackmailer was going to turn them in. I formed sentences and speeches that I should have made, within my mind. I was obsessed by it, went to sleep with it and woke up with it.

Isidor's face was ever-present in my mind. His voice reverberated as it repeated over and over again: "Now you will not be alone, Zosia, you have us. You are my little sister." The sun was so bright in the sky but it did not shine upon Isidor, his wife and his baby. It did not shine upon anyone I loved. They were no more...

# 17

# THE FARM

I could hardly believe that I had survived two whole months of the grueling toil and abominable living conditions at the *Muchow* farm. Now I really knew how it felt to be a beast of burden. I had developed a grudging admiration for my fellow sufferers, the Polish peasant women, who never before ranked very high in my affections. They have an unbelievable stamina, are very stoic and not given to complaining at all.

The sugar beets we were cultivating were planted in long uninterrupted rows. The field was flat and the rows stretched endlessly ahead. The women workers moved steadily forward each along her row, bent low, face close to the ground. One hand chopped at the earth removing the extra unwanted plants while the other hand weeded meticulously around the ones left to mature. We did not straighten up until it was time to break. By then, our backs felt frozen in that position and our leg muscles were stretched beyond endurance.

The row left behind each of us had to be done to perfection to satisfy the high standards of Willi, the foreman. He was always there behind us with his whip which he used without hesitation at the slightest infraction, such as standing up or leaving behind any unwanted growth. The only girl who could stretch occasionally had to be way ahead of all others. If he thought that we were too slow, the whip fell; if he thought we were too sloppy, we got it twice as hard. The pain was secondary only to the humiliation.

Later, he used the same system to "mound" the potatoes as we followed the grooving plow pulled by trudging, impassive oxen. At harvest time, a potato digging machine was pulled in a rectangle around the field by huge Belgian horses. Each girl had to pick clean her portion of the rectangle before the machine returned. The potatoes had to be in a bag by that time; all of them. Woe betide the girl who left a few behind, because there stood short, squat, old Willi with his horse whip in hand and he did not tolerate such a waste. Small wonder then that when lunch finally came, I ate my sandwich stretched out flat on my back. It was the only time I could rest. The food was adequate, but hardly sufficient to keep us going at this rate.

No words were exchanged between us until the evening and by then we were too tired to say much to each other. We often collapsed on our bunk mattresses as we were and only after a few hours did we have enough energy to go to the well and wash up a little. Our hands were calloused and our backs ached. We often returned from the field on foot; a very long walk. When I asked the girls how they managed, they just shrugged; farm work was all they have ever known, and they were used to it.

One of the women, Maria, was expecting a baby. Pregnancy did not faze her at all. In fact, she was the fastest and most productive worker of us all, and Willi held her up to us as a shining example. She was always in the lead row. She tried extra hard, hoping that her baby would be permitted to stay on the farm.

*Mucha* had promised her that: "Any child of Maria will grow up to be an exemplary worker." It appeared that they planned to have generations of Polish slaves. The father was also a Polish slave laborer on a farm near by and was permitted to visit her on Sundays.

Eventually Maria gave birth, one day in a potato furrow. We were all permitted to stop and observe the delivery. Four German women acted as "mid-wives."

Maria lay on the ground naked from the waist down and screamed the whole time. We were all clustered around straining our necks to have a better view of the spectacle. The German women held up her legs and yelled at the top of their voices for her to push. Finally, the baby popped out and the party was over. Maria and the baby were loaded on the wagon and the German women took her back to the farm. Before she left, a purple formless chunk of matter came out of her. I was terrified, convinced that Maria had lost her liver in the process of childbirth. People could not live without a liver and I was certain that she would die. But she did not. The baby was a boy and four days later, ecstatic Maria was back in the lead row. I discovered later that the chunk of tissue left behind in the potato patch was a placenta.

Another girl, nicknamed Black Maria because she was a brunette, was engaged to one of the men whose name was Josef. They had known each other back in Poland and hoped to get married as soon as the war was over. Both had great hopes and plans for the future.

Whenever possible, Josef joined her as we walked back from the fields and they held hands, but were usually too tired to talk to each other.

One night, Black Maria woke us all up from deep sleep in the middle of the night. She was thrashing in her bunk and uttering blood curdling screams. She had a nightmare. In her dream, she told us, something terrible descended from somewhere and sat upon her chest. It began to crush her. She tore at it with her hands but it had no substance or form and she could not get if off. Maria was covered with cold sweat.

"It is an omen of death," she told us. "I will have to tell Josef and it will hurt him very much that I will have to die.. "

From then on Maria was even more quiet than before. She continued to hold her own in the fields, but she prayed a lot. It soon became obvious that she had tuberculosis.

None of us had shoes any longer, they simply wore out, even mine which were quite new when Isidor gave them to me. We had been issued open wooden clogs. Earth and mud clung to them and stuck like cement. We had to scratch if off with our shovels because after a while it was like walking on stilts and they became too heavy.

On Sundays, we usually washed our things in the trough by the well, in cold water and without soap. Then we hung everything on a line to dry. It was better than nothing at all. One Sunday "Herr Muchow" decided that we needed some recreation and we were treated to a trip to a merry-go-round.

We purchased tickets for the rides and I found myself sitting on a wooden horse which went up and down and around.

The music was blaring loudly, playing a popular song *Mein Schatz soll ein Matrose sein, dann schmeckt ouch jader Kuss von ihm wie mer, wie mer...* (My sweetheart must be a sailor, then every kiss from him will taste of the sea, the sea...).

The scene appeared very bizarre to me. There I was in Saxony on a merry-go-round with German children accompanied by their mothers all around me. As I looked at their faces bathed in the sunlight, Isidor's and his wife's faces flashed across my mind. I saw the both of them with their baby girl on the merry-go-round. It was something they never lived to experience. The simple process of life.

The sirens woke us up in the middle of the night. We had no air raid shelter so we just sat outside and watched the fireworks. The air defense guns went into action and slashed the sky with sheets of light. The bombs exploded somewhere in Shoenebeck-Elbe and flames shot into the sky.

An aircraft was shot down in the fields nearby and Germans ran back and forth in agitation. Willi and *Mucha* grabbed pitchforks and ran out into the blackness of the night. They will get the English bastard and personally rip him to pieces on the spot, we were told. The next day, the damage was assessed in whispers. We were told that some Polish and Ukrainian slave workers were killed last night.

Mucha's daughter came around while I worked in the yard to tell me about it. She was a girl about my age who otherwise never spoke to me. She bragged that last night ten British aircraft were shot down!

"Ten?" I asked her if she knew how to count to ten in English. She didn't, but I could. I taught her how and returned to my chores. I couldn't imagine why I did it.

*Mucha* gave me a very fishy stare the next time he strutted past me, all dressed up in his SS finery. He also told Ignac that the *kleine Zofia* (little Zofia) was not only scrawny but also intelligent which was a miserable combination and that he would get rid of me before long.

Nothing could have suited me better. I had been having problems lately anyway. Our living conditions were so filthy that all of us had scabies. They were actually tiny, invisible mites, which burrowed beneath the skin and itched terribly. The welts became infected and burned like fire. We all suffered agonies and the mites could not be washed off or gotten rid of. Our hands and feet were raw from scratching. I lost a lot of weight, and felt weaker than ever.

One day I almost fainted while cleaning the pig styes and had to sit down. Just then, Willi, the German foreman, walked in on me and began to whip me with his horse whip. It caught me across the legs and ripped into my skin. I began to run blindly with old, bow legged Willi at my heels yelling for me to stop instantly. I darted out into the street through the open gate running for my life.

Less than about a block away, I collided head on with a stout German matron and almost knocked her over. She grabbed me by my hair very angrily just as Willi caught up with me, his whip high in the air ready to strike.

The German matron assessed the situation, let go of my hair and turned on Willi. How dare he strike a little girl like me and chase her down the road. She would not tolerate such an outrage. They were both about the same age and she knew him by name. Willi stood there sheepishly with downcast eyes. The German matron took away his whip and marched back with us. She would have a serious talk with Frau Muchow about it. It was giving all Germans a bad reputation. I was released again in the yard from where I could hear the German woman yelling at the top of her voice.

I told Ignac all about it as we rode back at noon to the fields. I will be in for it now, he prophesied grimly. Now old stupid Willi would certainly take it out on me. Of course, this would not be the case if Willi were convinced that Ignac was my boyfriend. But he was a crafty old guy and could easily tell that this was not the case. You cannot fool people forever.

Now, laughed Iganc, we should make it official. He turned towards me, closed his eyes and puckered up his lips like a fish. I should start by giving him a kiss.

A kiss? How a father of nine daughters could be so disgusting! Where were his morals! I expressed my opinion of Ignac in no uncertain terms. His lips soon assumed a normal shape again as I ranted on and on.

Now, he told me what a prude I was and with no sense of humor what ever. I was a seriously inhibited person and he did not appreciate my calling him names. Then he stopped the wagon to emphasize what he was about to say and glared at me.

It had occurred to him that I was Jewish; he lashed out at me. It was very threatening to me, but I retained my composure, I had to.

"Now what makes you think such a stupid thing?" I said icily. "You are insulting!"

"I can tell..." said Ignac, "because you are far more intelligent than the other girls..." He went on to explain that Jews are usually intelligent.

"What a thing for a good Pole to say!" I spat out. "Maybe you are Jewish yourself!" I continued derisively. "You have dark eyes and dark hair."

I am not!" he shouted. "And I can prove it to you right now. I am not circumcised." He began to unbotton his pants to prove the point. I could then see for myself.

I told him that he was a shameless person, that I could not tell the difference anyway, or cared one way or another. Furthermore, as of now, I would never speak to him again.

I climbed off the wagon and continued the rest of the way on foot. Ignac and I did not speak to each other for two days. I became very depressed remembering only too well what had happened to Isidor. Now this stupid Pole would surely give me away. He spoke daily to Herr Muchow, our boss, who was an SS man. I couldn't trust him. I had had it, and escape would be impossible.

A couple of days later, Ignac broke the silence. He had something important to tell me. He had a theory that Muchow was exempted from being drafted because he had paid off the local doctor and perhaps others to escape draft. Ignac had been flirting with one of the German women and obtained from her envelopes and stationary. He decided to write anonymous letters to the proper authorities, including the Gestapo. Ignac had proof that whole sides of smoked pork and wine had been delivered from the farm to various officials as bribes.

I thought the idea to be insane. Besides, if *Mucha* were drafted, Willi, our foreman, would become the final authority on this farm, and Willi was the worse of the two.

At least *Mucha* was never here. He carried no whip. All he wanted was to strut around in his fancy uniform. Willi would beat us to death.

But Ignac thought that he could deal with old Willi. Willi could meet with an accident. For example, the pigs were very dangerous. He could be pushed into the pig sty... Accidents can happen on a farm.

To my amazement, I realized that Ignac was absolutely serious. We meticulously printed the letters in gothic script and one day on the way to the field dropped them off at the post office. Ignac beamed all the way back. Our arguement was never mentioned again.

I was not equally optimistic. I had been sick lately and was growing weaker every day. My hands and feet were infected from the scabies. I had been coughing incessantly and became terribly thin. I had injured my heel which became swollen and purple. I actually did not care any longer about anything.

I was not the only one in such a dismal condition. Black Maria fainted twice and a girl by the name of Kazia was infected from head to toe. Ignac was concerned about my condition.

"You will have to somehow obtain a pair of shoes if you hope to live..." he told me. "Before long it will be colder. The sugar beets are harvested when there is frost. It is the worst chore and it is not very far off." Ignac was convinced that if I lost my spirit and had no shoes, I would never make it.

We discussed Maria's tuberculosis and how contagious it was, especially at such close quarters. The girls had skin infections. Everyone was sick.

Ignac was very upset thinking that we were being killed on this farm as surely as if we were shot. He actually had no problems. He was tough and *Mucha* took care of him because he needed him, but Ignac was concerned about me.

"If you become too sick to be of use," he told me, "you will disappear. They do not ever send you back to Poland, it is bad for their propaganda and they do not waste medical care on slave labor. They simply kill those who weaken or become ill as if they were sick horses. "Zosia," said Ignac, "if you have no shoes to wear in the fall, it is a death sentance!"

It was towards the end of the potato harvest that Ignac appeared for the morning chores in the best of moods. He performed a sort of war dance around the barn brandishing his pitchfork. "We did it!" he shouted like a maniac. "Mucha" has been drafted!" I was a bit skeptical that our letters had much to do with it but he was certain of it. But I was no longer able to appreciate these good tidings, it was too late. My foot was swollen and on my heel there was a large yellow bubble of pus.

A few days later, there was other news. This time for me. Black Maria, myself and Kazia were to be returned to the *Arbeitsamt* (Labor Bureau) in Magdeburg. We were obviously not able to keep up with the farm work any longer. We were told that perhaps we were still suitable for an armament factory where the work was less strenuous. We packed at once and were permitted to wash our clothes.

The evening before our departure, Josef came around to say farewell to Black Maria. They were to be separated like slaves by their masters. Josef, a very quiet man had very little to say. He just stood against the wall looking at Maria and tears silently ran down his face. Later, they stood by the door together holding hands. Maria's cheeks were flushed with fever. On my last night at the Muchow farm in Scoenebeck-Elbe, I felt no emotion whatever and slept soundly all night.

At dawn, just before we climbed aboard the truck, Iganc came running with a parcel. He pulled me aside so we could talk privately.

"Zosia, do not lose your spirit!" he implored me. He confided hastily, because we had very little time, something nobody else knew. He had been with the partisans back in Poland and had almost lost his life. It was pure dumb luck that he was still around. I was not surprised to hear this at all.

I asked him what was inside the parcel he gave me and he became very embarrassed.

"You will see when you open it..." I only had enough time to wish him luck and Herr *Mucha* in person gave each of us a loaf of bread. To our surprise he apologised for having to send us away.

The truck rolled ahead and only then did Black Maria lose her composure.

"Oh dear Jesus!" she wailed. "I will never see my Josef again... I cannot live without him..." I put my arm around her and tried to console her. She was burning with fever. I felt a great sorrow for Black Maria. I felt her pain.

The truck quickly covered the short distance to Magdeburg and we were led back into the cavernous hall which was much like a human warehouse. We were given numbers and our files were stacked among others already on the table. We found a place to sit on the cement floor and tried to find out from others what to expect. Everybody was confused, but they knew that our lives depended upon being accepted somewhere to work.

"Just sit, hope and wait..." they advised us. "If you are not chosen in three days, it is all over for you." Maria did not have to live without Josef — she might not have the chance to live at all.


In the meantime, elsewhere in the world, the summer of 1943 had arrived and passed again and the brisk wind heralded another approaching winter. Another layer of history had been added upon the ages, a saga of events big and small. The war continued. On the 16th of May, British parachutists joined the Yugoslav Partisans in the dense and inaccessible mountain forests. On the 5th of July, the Germans, trying to take advantage of the favorable summer weather, launched an offensive at Kurak which the Russians repulsed on the 9th.

Propelled by the victorious momentum, the Russians pushed ahead with an offensive against Orel on the 11th, and took Tagenrog by the 17th. It boded badly for the Germans. If they could not dominate the war during the summer, how would they manage when winter came?

On the first of August, the U.S. Air Force made a spectacular raid against Ploesti in Rumania to interrupt the oil supplies of the Germans. On the 3rd, the Soviets launched an offensive at Kharkov and on the 5th, captured Belogrod and Orel. On the 23rd, General Manstein reluctantly abandoned Kharkov and the slow German withdrawal had begun.

In September, the strategic bombing by the Americans and the British continued on, and on the 21st, British midget submarines attacked the "Tirpitz" in Norway. The battle of the Atlantic continued on.

On the 24th of September, the Soviets took Smolensk and on the first of October, the Germans began their withdrawal from the Kuban Penninsula.

On October 9th, the Americans bombed the ballbearing plants in Schweinfurt and the U.S. Eighth Air Force finished the destruction of this strategic industry on the 14th.

Each of these events was momentous and bloody. It was all bitterly contested every inch of the way and strewn with crashed aircraft and dead pilots. The earth was raked by explosives and irrigated with blood on both sides of the Russian Front.

In the Mediterranean, on July 10th, the Allied forces landed in Salerno, Sicily. On July 22nd, Palermo was taken. On August 5th the British took Catania, Sicily and completed its conquest on the 17th.

On the 3rd of September, the British Eighth Army landed in Southern Italy. The Italian fleet and aircraft surrendered on the 8th and the formalities took place at Malta on the 11th. In the meantime, on the 9th, the Germans seized Rome and on the 13th desperately counter-attacked the Salerno Beachhead.

Against this background we three girls sat, hoped and waited on a cold floor in Magdeburg, Saxony, but knew almost nothing about the progress of the war around us.

# 18

# THE DOG POUND

The Magdeburg *Arbeitsamt* was a busy place. Many groups of workers were seated on benches, or like the three of us, on the cement floor. Our files were stacked in a pile on a long table by the entrance door. From time to time farmers and representatives of various industries came in, examined the files and carefully chose a few workers. Those picked out were then taken to their new destinations along with their individual files.

Later in the day, since we were still left behind, I decided to open the parcel Ignac gave me in a farewell gesture. Inside it was a pair of short ankle-high boots! These were without any doubt the strangest boots anybody had ever seen. They were entirely hand made and the top parts were painstakingly hand sewn and fashioned out of various sized scraps of leather. The soles were meticulously shaped and included heels. Kazia and Maria peered over my shoulder in disbelief.

I could hardly get over the shock of what I saw. It must have taken a lot of imagination to design such a work of art. It must have taken a great effort to find and assemble the small pieces of leather which were put together like a jigsaw puzzle. It must have taken hours of tedious sewing, as I well knew at the end of a very hard day's work in the inadequate, dim light of a kerosene lamp.

These were no ordinary shoes. They represented affection, concern and the milk of human kindness. I held them up in the air for the girls to see, and they gasped and then laughed. They had never seen anything resembling these shoes. I had a funny feeling in the pit of my stomach and was too choked up to say a word.

The shoes attracted everybody's attention. The other workers came over to admire them and wanted to touch them. The guard walked over to see what the commotion was all about and shook his head in amazement. Unfortunately, however, I was unable to put them them on. My foot was throbing with pain. It was purple and swollen. But I felt warmer just looking at them.

Ignac did contend that it took spirit and warm shoes to survive a winter in Germany, and he must have truly wanted me to have a chance at survival. Now I felt very guilty remembering how I had spent a few miserable nights believing that this man was about to turn me over to the Germans! It must have taken him weeks to produce these shoes. How could I have been so wrong!

In addition, there were six hardboiled eggs inside the parcel, a piece of saussage, some stationary and a pencil. Even an envelope containing a few postage stamps was included. Ignac was obviously hoping that I would write him someday. That was if I ever had the chance. We broke the sausage into small pieces and distributed it around, then shared the eggs. I couldn't bear to keep such generosity all to myself!

A day passed and the big hall grew half empty. Most of the workers had been spoken for, but the three of us still sat forlornly in our corner. Nobody wanted us. Later, the guards brought us some bread with marmalade and some erzatz coffee and we settled down for the night. The hall was almost empty. We could see that those of us still left behind were a sorry lot. There was a pregnant woman sitting all by herself staring into space with a resigned expression in her eyes. Maria walked over to her and gave her an egg. They talked for a little while and Maria came back very depressed. It was the third day for the woman and she knew that tomorrow, if nobody accepted her, she would be removed from here. She was very frightened but these were the rules. She wondered what would happen to her.

Early next day new arrivals trickled in, men and women, alone and in small groups. A new group arrived straight from Poland and was almost immediately dispatched to a new destination. We had no chance to even talk to them. We marked our second day. Recruiters came, looked at our files, walked over and stared at us wordlessly for an instant then left. No takers. We did not appear very promising.

It was a little like a dog pound. Pets for adoption waiting helplessly sensing, that they will be soon put to sleep unless someone takes pity on them. But we were not pets, we were expected to earn our keep. Maria kept praying. She had a small snapshot of Josef and kept looking at it. She did not cry any longer.

Third day. I would have liked to walk around but my foot hurt too much. No sense advertising how miserable I was. The pregnant woman was now gone. By the afternoon, the hall was almost empty again. Kazia became very apprehensive. She was a blond, short girl of twenty, but somehow her face was creased with lines. She was not at all pretty and had a nervous harsh voice. Now her hands and arms itched and burned. They were full of welts from infections and scabies. She cursed Muchow and fretted that she might be taken to work in a factory. She had spent all her life on a farm. I tried to shut out her voice. She would have been lucky to be taken to a factory, but stupidly did not seem to realize it, or was just suppressing the truth. I again experienced this strange feeling of detachment and an urge to run. But how could I do so with a swollen foot.

At the door, a stout German woman was examining our files. She had two guards with her and they looked around the hall with disappointment. Slim pickings here at this late time of day. I hardly bothered to look up at their faces, and kept my eyes at the level of their boots as they walked towards us. They stopped and I forced myself to look up after all. The woman appeared matronly inspite of her impeccable uniform. She had a chubby round face and blue eyes; her blond hair was neatly arranged under her cap. She smiled. I mechanically returned the smile and said "Good afternoon. . ."

The woman asked my name and what was wrong with me. I wordlessly rolled up my sleeves and showed her my hands and arms.

"Oh, its just scabies. . ." she remarked to the guards after examining my hands. "Pretty far gone. . ." She went on to explain that scabies were lately an epidemic. She knew all about it because she used to be a nurse. I could see the woman weighing something in her mind, then she turned to the guard.

"Not many left here today," she speculated. Then she regarded me thoughtfully for a while. "A very young girl, aren't you?" I nodded. "I will take her. . ." she informed the guard.

"But the others?" I asked hopefully.

"I will take them too. . ." The guard went back to the table and collected our files. "Let's go. . ."

The woman glanced at her watch. "We have a long ride back to Pasneck. . ." We gathered our bundles and followed her towards the door where the woman signed for us and some others she had also decided to recruit. Suddenly she noticed me limping and called me over. My purple heel and the blister of puss were plainly visible because I did not own stockings and the clogs were open in the back. She bent down and examined the sore. I could plainly see her hesitate, but then she shrugged.

"Have the others help Zofia to the truck," she ordered the guard. I noted that she remembered my name. I cast a last glance at the hall and we were out in the chilly brisk wind. The sun was going down and the world seemed very strange after being indoors for three days.

The truck kept rolling for hours. We left Saxony behind and entered Thuringia. It was night as we arrived at our destination but could see very little because of the blackout. The woman led us to what she referred to as the Barracks, but which was actually a part a the factory. We went up a flight of stairs to a huge chamber inside which were rows of triple-layered bunks. It housed at least a couple hundred women. Everybody referred to the German woman as Frau Koenig. We immediately went through disinfection and showers. The de-lousing was very thorough and it also included our clothes. Sometime during the procedure I was separated from my friends and Frau Koenig intercepted me at the shower door. I was instructed to follow her. She had a small private apartment at the front of the floor where our barracks were situated.

Between her apartment and our quarters was a guardroom policed by two armed guards. Behind her apartment was a small storage room which was empty except for some old chairs. It was there that Frau Koenig told me I would be staying for the next several days. She informed me that she was the Commandant of the women's camp and that every chamber on this floor of the factory served as a women's barracks.

The large elongated chambers housed hundreds girls of various nationalities. The one I briefly saw was occupied only by Russians and Ukrainians. Beyond, were the Polish women and behind them, the French, Belgian, Yugoslavs and Checkoslovaks. I would be joining the Polish girls as soon as I was cured.

Frau Koenig still had a lot to do and I was instructed to stay in the storage room for the time being. She would attend to me later. I found a chair and made myself comfortable in the windowless room. My head and body burned from the shower and disinfectants, but for the first time in months I was actually clean.

After a while two Russian girls brought in a strawfilled burlap sack upon which to sleep. One of them, a tiny blonde in her mid thirties informed me that she was a physician. She was very friendly and wasted no time examining my foot. She shook her head and told me that she got to me barely in time. I was in a terrible shape. The other girl brought some instruments and Marushka, the Russian physician, lanced my heel and cleaned it up. She worked very carefully chatting all the time, very pleased that I could understand her. She was from the city of Odessa and had been here a few months now. She was an epileptic and suffered from seizures. I was not familiar with such an affliction and she explained about it as she soaked my foot in hot water.

Later Frau Koenig stopped by and brought with her a large jar of salve (probably sulphur compound). It was then applied to my entire body. It had a terrible odor, like rotten eggs and it was black. Marushka assured me that it would cure the scabies and the infection.

Mrs. Koenig remarked that it cost her five marks out of her pocket. "A young life was well worth five marks," as far as she was concerned. I was immensely grateful and even more so when I was given a bowl of hot soup. I was drowsy and Marushka covered me with clean burlap sacks. "You will be just fine in a week," she reassured me. But then I remembered Kazia and Maria.

"What about the others?" I asked anxiously. Marushka looked very uncomfortable. "Could do nothing for Kazia; she was too far gone," she said regretfully. "She will be leaving tomorrow on a garbage truck."

"A garbage truck?" I sat up in horror. Marushka explained that this meant being taken away because of inability to work; being discarded. "This is not a hospital, it is only a labor camp..." she added.

"And Maria?"

Marushka was not certain. "She will be attended to tomorrow." I was very fortunate that she got to me just in time!

"But where do they take those on the "garbage truck?"

Marushka leaned close to my ear. "I am not sure," she whispered. "But I think it is a crematorium and keep it to yourself."

I had trouble sleeping, after what she told me but eventually fatigue took over. I remained in the storage room for a whole week. The treatment was repeated twice. Marushka changed the dressing on my foot and brought me hot soup three times a day. I would not be eating so well later on, she told me. Marushka listened to my chest for rales. She worried about tuberculosis and suspected that Maria had it. There would be nothing she could do for me if this was the case.

I learned that the camp was called *Maihak*, that Frau Koenig was a very good person who did as much as she could for the girls. She was fair and we were lucky to have her as our Commmandant. She was a fanatic about cleanliness and for a good reason. In the past many girls succumbed to typhus. Our hair was checked for lice and even the floors had to be spotless. The girls had to keep very clean.

At the end of my stay, Marushka brought me a dress made of blue burlap-like material and led me to the Polish barracks. My foot was very much improved and for the first time in months, my skin did not itch and burn. It was a feeling of blissful relief.

I immediately looked up Maria and found her in an isolation bunk. She was sad but her face was very calm. She was saving her bread rations for me now that Kazia was gone. She no longer wanted to eat. She gave me a letter to send to Josef so that he would know that she was gone. Otherwise, he might wait forever and she wanted him to find a good woman some day and marry. Maria had been coughing up blood. She would be leaving tomorrow... She left with a guard when it was time, very guietly and without a backward glance.

Mrs. Koenig called me into her apartment and examined my hands including the spaces between my fingers. She was satisfied with my progress and had a present for me, — a fine toothed comb, some hair pins and needles and thread. She felt very badly about my two companions or anyone she had to send away and I knew that she really meant it. We chatted for a while and I felt very comfortable with her in spite of the picture of Hitler displayed on the wall and her SS insignia. I had very strong conviction that these meant very little. Frau Koenig was certainly not what the Nazis stood for. In fact, I liked her very much!

Maihak was a large factory which produced various metal components. I couldn't exactly tell what they were, except that they had to be very precisely made. The huge chambers were filled with rows of machines mounted on wooden platforms. Most were manually operated and were quite complicated. Our foremen were mostly friendly and older men.

I learned how to operate these machines pretty fast but it was very hard work. We worked twelve hour shifts, six days a week.

The factory was noisy, and production continued around the clock. I learned that the entire plant had been transported here from the city of Hamburg, including the Germans. They were a different breed; very cosmopolitan in their outlook, and mostly reasonable to deal with. Most of the women workers were Russian but not the men. Most of the male workers were from Holland. They worked elsewhere in the plant and we only saw them as they passed us by. We usually waved to each other.

The food was quite inadequate. For some strange reason our soup mostly consisted of turnips. It is still a mystery to me how there could have been such an abundance of turnips anywhere. We received one bowl of soup and a ration of bread, which tasted like sawdust and looked like mud. But here there were no pig-pens to clean and no Willi, the bowlegged foreman with a horse whip. I felt optimistic. I knew that I would have died of filth and disease on that farm. Here, if I did not perish of malnutrition, I had a chance. And I was clean! The bunks we slept in were three layers high and mine was on the top level, which meant that no one climbed over me.

I tried not to become friendly with the Polish girls. Those here were not simple peasants, but mostly sophisticated city girls. There might be questions hard to answer and they might guess something about me.

Anything could trip me up; a wrong answer to a difficult question could mean disaster. I was assigned to the night shift and spent my free time with Marushka, the physician.

I had learned how to take care of her when she had a seizure so she would not swallow or bite her tongue. We had become good friends, and I had a chance to practice my Russian. I learned a lot from her about Russia and the conditions there. She was an intelligent and wise person. The Polish girls considered me to be a bit strange because none of them associated with the Russians as I did. Here, they were considered the lowest on the social totem pole.

It was my job to deliver some of the finished components to a room where the German women worked. One of them had a daughter approximately my size who just began to outgrow some of her dresses. Unexpectedly the woman brought me a blouse and a skirt as a gift. I was overjoyed. It immediately occured to me that I could sneak out of the camp now that I actually had a decent dress to wear. If I only had normal shoes I might pass for a German. Of course, all the slave workers in Germany had to wear identification patches sewn onto our dresses.

The Polish girls wore a yellow triangle with the letter "P" in purple. The Russians wore a white square patch with the letters

OST, and so on. But my new blouse had nothing sewn upon it as yet.

I had been here a few weeks only, but already began to feel claustrophobic. My old restlessness invaded my soul. There was another girl in the camp named Adela, who also had a presentable dress and an adventurous spirit. She was from *Byelorusia* (White Russia). I looked her up without delay and we made plans. There was a world outside and we wanted to explore it. It was not very hard to get out.

Paesneck was a small town but there were shop windows to see and just the ordinary joy of being able to freely walk down the street. I, of course, insisted upon inspecting the railroad station. For me, this was imperative. "What if, for some reason I needed to run away again? I thought prophetically. One could not forsee the future. It was Hitler's Germany and I was Jewish.

We roamed around for awhile, undisturbed, enjoying our freedom. Adela confessed her ambition to me. She had a yearning to see a movie. Well, why not, we had several marks between us.

The movie theater was on the main street of Paesneck. There was no line. I approached the ticket window and made the purchase. After all, the seller could not see our feet and the clogs we wore. It was easy. We marched right in and found a seat close to the screen.

At first there was a political news reel. It was all about the *Neue Waffe*, (new weapons) and we sat through it. Then the movie began. It was a political-romantic-spy adventure. On the screen a very Germanic looking Brun Hilde, blue eyed and blond, was suffering persecution by communist agents. She was kidnapped, tied and threatened, until a dashing young SS man came to the rescue of this damsel in distress. It was a nauseating movie of pure propaganda, but the musical score was very nice. It all went pretty smoothly until the SS man appeared on the screen. Then Adela expressed her sentiments.

"Sobaka!" she hissed very loudly, which in Russian means a dog. She seemed to have forgotten where we were and since she did not speak German, wanted to know what this *sobaka* was saying.

"*Chto on Gavorit?*" (what is he saying). She asked me loudly in Russian. Heads turned towards us in the darkened seat row. I was horrified and pinched Adela as hard as I could to shut her up. Now I knew why Marushka said that Adela had the brain of a squirrel. Shortly thereafter a flashlight shone in our faces. Police!

We were escorted out and led straigt into the police station. The policemen were just simple, law and order sheriffs. They were older men since the young were all serving in the army. One of them, a rotund, white haired old-timer with a pink, cherubic face felt rather badly about the whole thing, especially when I told him that we were just dying to hear some lovely German music. . . We were put into a cell and Adela began to wail and cry.

The policemen tried to reassure us and after a while the old timer brought us two large pieces of cake, compliments of his wife, who had already heard about our plight. The policeman wanted us to have a positive impression about German culture, after all. We licked our plates clean and decided that this was just as much fun as the movies.

Eventually a call was put through to Maihak and Frau Koenig arrived with a guard to collect us. Our hands were tied with string behind our backs and we made a small procession on the way back. The policeman explained carefully to Frau Koenig how we were practically begging to return to camp in order to minimize our subsequent punishment. Frau Koenig looked very grim. "*Dumkopf!*" she told me. "I expected you to be smarter than that!"

If we were taken to the Security Police for our offense, she could not help us. It would have been out of her hands. It would have been our first stop on the way to a correction camp called *Buchenwald*, which was just a short drive away from here. "And there, things are different!" she said ominously.

We found out later on that the police did us a great favor by calling Frau Koenig directly instead of the security police manned by the SS. Frau Koenig had an investment in me, namely five marks worth of sulphur salve and the effort she extended in curing my infected foot. She did not wish for it to go to waste. Besides, for some obscure reason, she liked me. I kept a very low profile after that.

I also found out more about the security building. People did not return as a rule once they were taken there.

I was very uneasy when Frau Koenig called me in to her apartment and told me that I had a new assignment. I was to become an assistant to *Herr Meissner*, who ran what was called the "Lab." It was a room full of the most important machines in Maihak, which were fully automated and very sensitive. He specifically requested someone who spoke German and would be easy to supervise. His last assistant left via the "garbage truck" a few days before because of tuberculosis.

Herr Meissner, I was told matter of factly, was "crazy." His mind broke during the Hamburg bombing but he was a trained engineer and the only person who knew how to set, adjust and fix these machines. I ran to Marushka in consternation, convinced that this was now my punishment, but she reassured me that the last assistant had no complaints about the man. Still, I was very apprehensive when I reported to my new station the following evening.

# 19

## JUST SHOOT HER

It was a lonely feeling, not knowing what to expect. Up to that point I had worked at a long row of machines surrounded by other girls. Now I would be alone, condemned to a separate chamber, "The Lab," for a twelve hour shift. And the person I was going to work for was a "madman" this Herr Meissner. How did one deal with a madman?

I put on the jigsaw puzzle boots my friend Ignac had so lovingly made for me. They fit and it made me somehow feel more secure wearing them. Frau Koenig suspended Adela's and my food rations for two days just so we would think twice the next time we got a notion to do something foolish. Marushka gave me half of her bread ration, but it was not much and my stomach felt very hollow.

The room I entered was long and narrow. Twelve mammoth machines hummed steadily in a row. The front of the room was lit up brightly and contained a large work table, a couple of chairs, an open closet and a shelf. On the shelf were various tools arranged very orderly. There was also another personal shelf upon which were several photographs, a chess set, several coffee cups and a lunch box.

The "madman" himself was bent over one of the machines. The rest of the room was very dim because the machines were lit up from within under their plexiglass hoods. By the wall were various long metal ingots and a cart full of trays ready to be loaded with finished components.

I will have to be very careful now, I thought. I was here only because the man thought I spoke German. Supposing I disappointed him and was very slow to understand what he said. Then he would get rid of me and request another assistant. I was going to play very dumb, make him repeat everything several times over and over again. But what if he became angry? He was, after all, a madman. I braced myself.

After a while the man retrieved a finished component and examined it carefully running his fingers over its edges to test for smoothness. He looked in my direction.

"Good evening" he said. I only nodded. He was tall, slightly bent and had very blue eyes under shaggy grey eyebrows. His face was actually handsome for a man his age, almost classical, but it was criss-crossed with lines and furrows, sort of weather beaten. He looked me over very carefully from head to toe and immediately noticed my peculiar boots. He continued to stare at them with amazement but made no comment about them. Instead he asked me my name. I pretended not to comprehend. He repeated the question very slowly and only then did I tell him. It went on like this while he tried to explain my duties and showed me the machines. Finally, he threw up his hands in exasperation, went into a corner and got a broom. He bowed in front of me and extended it to me.

"May I have the great honor, to present the honorable young lady with this humble object in my possession" he said. "With this 'Thou' might sweep the floor..." He surely had a sense of humor and I found myself unable to keep a straight face in spite of a great effort. I accepted the broom and spent the next half hour sweeping.

Afterwards, Herr Meissner kept a straight face but continuously made funny remarks about my boots. What feet must be hidden under such a patchwork of leather, or was it possible that these were actually not boots at all but museum pieces. My face cracked from ear to ear into a reluctant smile.

"Aha, so you do understand me very well!" he said when he saw my smile. I was cornered. Besides, he told me, Frau Koenig did assure him that I did. "Why did you pretend not to?" he continued looking hurt. "Don't you want to work for me? It is not all that hard. Maybe a little boring but a lot less strenuous than operating a manual machine. However, if you miss being with your friends, I will be glad to arrange for your transfer."

Suddenly I decided that I liked the man and assured him that it would be fine if I stayed. I found myself telling him all about my boots and about Ignac. Then I told him about the movie escapade much to my own surprise. It was much more than I cared to tell a stranger. As soon as he heard about the "no rations" punishment, Herr Meissner reached for his lunch box.

I was embarassed. This was not why I told him the story. It was simply because I felt comfortable talking to him. I firmly declined to accept half of his lunch and assured him that I could easily last until midnight when soup would be served. I returned to my duties which were to remove the shavings out of the machines and load the components into the trays. It was very easy work and it had accumulated while we talked.

When I glanced back a while later, Herr Meissner was sitting in a chair with his eyes closed in the brightly lit up part of the room. Thinking that he was asleep, I approached closer. Then I saw it. Herr Meissner was not asleep at all, he was crying silently. The tears were streaming down his cheeks, trickling down the deep groves of his face.

Now I understood. The man was suffering from sadness. My mother used to call such a condition melancholia. This was what Frau Koenig meant when she said that he was crazy and had lost his mind during the Hamburg bombing. He was no more disturbed than I, only we had the opposite reaction. He could not help sheding tears while I was completely unable to do so.

It is strange how the tear ducts reflect our state of mind. They are the fountains of the inner soul which either burst forth from sorrow or shut off as if frozen. Frau Koenig simply did not comprehend it.

I tried not to look at Herr Meissner until midnight when I left to eat. When I returned, he was at his table working on a piece of machinery, measuring the components. We did not exhange another word until morning, when he told me that he was glad to have me work for him, and he hoped I would choose to stay. I was touched that he gave me a clear choice. He treated me with respect and consideration, as a person rather than a slave worker.

The ingots consummed by our automated machines were made of a totally different alloy than those used in the rest of the plant where it was mostly light aluminum. Our ingots did not come from the warehouse on the premises, but were trucked in to us from somewhere else and carted in by Russian prisoners of war. Usually the delivery was made during the day shift but on that particular day, we expected them at six in the evening. The place on the floor where they were stored has been empty all day because of a delay in shipment.

Herr Meissner arrived carrying a brown paper bag and appeared to be less apathetic than usual. He took four small, stapled packages out of the bag and placed them on the floor.

"These are for the Russian prisoners," he said. He explained further that he will engage the guards downstairs in a conversa-

tion so the prisoners could pick up these small parcels undetected. I was supposed to point them out to the Russians as
they brought in the ingots. The Russian men were not a part of
our camp and I had never seen them before.

They lumbered in, carting the heavy ingots, and I immediately ran forward to meet them. The prisoners looked terrible.
The rags they wore hung loosely on their skeletal frames. Their
worn out shoes were reinforced by strips of cloth. Their faces
were gaunt, like skulls covered by sickly pale skin.

"*Pajausta. . .*" (Please) I said pointing to the parcels which
quickly disappeared inside their rags. Their smiles seemed un-
natural on their starved faces. They could tell that I was a Polish
national by the yellow diamond shaped patch of cloth I wore with
a purple "P" printed in its center.

"*Kak wam zdies idziot?*" (How does it go for you here) I quickly asked.

"*Plocho. . .*" (badly) they answered sadly. We had no time for
further conversation because the guards collected them and
rushed them out.

Meissner came up anxiously wanting to know if there was
enough time for the prisoners to hide the parcels. I nodded and
he sat down relieved. It was hard for him to stall the guards even
for a moment.

"Did you see what they look like?" he asked bitterly. "Like old
men; and those were just young boys. . . They are being starved
to death!" Meissner wished that he could do something more for
them. He was very upset about the condition they were in, could
hardly stop talking about it. "These young men should live,
marry and raise families like all human beings." I found it impossible to cheer up Meissner for the rest of the night. Every time I
looked at him his eyes were red and wet.

I wheeled a supply of components to the German women
workers next door and we had nothing to do for several hours. I
remarked that we even had enough time for a game of chess and
Meissner seemed surprised that I knew about the game. Not very
well, I told him. He would be sure to beat me every time without
a doubt.

Meissner showed me a picture of himself next to a trophy. He
used to be a national champion and actually was very famous at
one time. He told me about chess championship contest matches
in which he had participated. He had represented Germany
against England and France.

"Why cannot the nations compete peacefully and confront each other in sports or chess, rather than on a battle field. But then, this was how the human species is; cruel to each other," he said.

Meissner showed me the history book he was reading. This is how the world has been all along, he explained. Germany was not the only nation singled out to be warlike. . . He spent an hour reading it to me. He was trying to somehow justify the present; he was ashamed of it.

"It is an affliction of all mankind," he said persuasively. When I had a chance, I finished reading the chapter by myself, but there were words I did not understand. Meissner brightened up. He would be giving me German lessons from now on; bring me a notebook and some more books to read. Might even teach me a little math. I appreciated this very much.

I told Marushka about my encounter with the Russian prisoners and how badly they looked, but not about the parcels. I did not want to compromise Herr Meissner. It could have been dangerous if anyone found out about it. But I did tell her how sorry he was. Marushka fell silent. She had brothers in the army and one of the half starved prisoners could have been one of them.

## RECOLLECTION

*It is during my fourth week in Maihak that lightening strikes out of the clear blue sky. I am awakened from my sleep during the day by our guard and told to report to the security building. I feel my stomach tightening in a knot. What do they want from me! Could it be still due to my having sneaked out with Adela? But she is not called. I am taken there by myself! It is a brisk sunny day and I feel as if I am being led to the gallows. It is warm inside the building but I feel ice cold; I am shivering.*

*A short, stocky SS man looks up at me from behind a desk with pale blue eyes. He has my file and pasted on it is a large red dot. It is tagged.*

*"Your papers are not in order!" he growls accusingly. He goes on to tell me that every person in this camp must have a picture identification called* Ausweiss. *But there is nothing in my file to justify his giving me one. My file is empty except for the typed out christening certificate and this is insufficient.*

*I tell him that my other papers must have fallen out somewhere but he gives me a very suspicious look. It is listed here that nothing else has been received! He is uncertain about what to do with me.*

*He walks across the narrow hallway with my file in hand. "Herr Ober!" he yells, "I need to ask you something." I clearly hear the conversation taking place while I stand rooted to the floor.*

*The man called Herr Ober tells him that the women's camp is none of his concern. He is only sitting here, killing time, until his charges, the Russian prisoners' transport, arrives. But the SS man with my file persists. Should he issue me an Ausweiss?*

*"Absolutely not!" says this Herr Ober, in an annoyed tone of voice. Where there is a question, it must be checked out! I also hear that I have points against me. It means that Frau Koenig issued a report after all. Perhaps this is how they spotted that I have no Ausweiss!; I stand there and shudder. I brought it on myself. What I would give to undo it!*

*The SS man, called Kurt, returns with my file, sits down again and chews the tip of his pencil while he ponders the problem. I have a feeling that he would much rather not be bothered. Then the questioning starts. What was my address in the city of Bochnia. I thank my lucky stars that I still remember the lies I told the official in Krakow when he questioned me. I did make a point to memorize it all, just in case.*

*"The precinct number. . ." The man called Kurt checks it off and complains that it should be Otto's job to do this. He is just sitting in for Otto. "We will have to check it all out," he tells me. He hopes for my sake that the information is all correct. Behind me, the man called Herr Ober, stops at the door on his way out and tells Kurt to take his messages for him.*

*"Just shoot the damn* Stucke *(livestock or a thing), if there is a problem and save yourself the bother," he advises Kurt. I am afraid to turn around and look at the man who is causing me such trouble.*

*"You heard what Herr Ober said," laughs Kurt, as if it was a big joke. He closes my file and stands up. "Now beat it, back to work with you!" He does not know that I work a night shift.*

*I return to the barracks scared to death, and of course I cannot sleep at all. I feel dazed and distraught when I arrive at the Lab that evening. Herr Meissner has a notebook and an engraved beautiful book for me to read but I cannot concentrate at all. I excuse myself saying that I had little sleep today, because my identification papers are being checked out, but do not go into detail.*

*Was it the 'pig-dog' Otto I saw, asks Meissner with concern. I should try to stay away from him. He is bad news, a very dangerous man! As if I only could, as if it was up to me!*

*Now what should I do? My mind keeps churning. I will have to make a run for it. I have absolutely no choice. I hear this Herr Ober's voice. "Shoot her, shoot her. . ." It plays like a record in my mind. I have a dress but my shoes would not pass inspection. Ignac's boots would only draw attention; they would attract a crowd around me.*

*I need money. I weigh the idea of asking Herr Meissner and discard it. How would I explain it? I will just have to steal it. Herr Meissner gets paid on Fridays. He usually naps in his chair each night. His jacket hangs in the open closet. It will be very easy. I feel badly about having to do it. He is the one person I would hate to steal from. . . but I have no choice.*

*On Friday, I wear my dress under the blue burlap camp smock with the yellow patch with the 'P' sewn on its front. I find about a hundred marks in Meissner's wallet but cannot bring myself to take it all and settle for sixty. Still it is a fortune.*

*I try to cheer myself up. I have spent months on the trains; what is one more trip. Of course, I cannot take the train from Paesneck, it is too close to the camp. I will walk to the next town and buy a ticket there. I remember what Ignac had told me, that it is impossible to get out of Germany. With two and a half million Polish slave laborers here, they have to be on guard, or half of them would have tried it. But clearly I must. I fear this Otto instinctively. He surely is "bad news" if even Meissner knows about him and he is in charge of my file. It is very easy to get out of Maihak right now because of construction going on.*

*On Saturday morning I make my escape as planned and trudge wearily down the road. It is windy and cold and I feel very alone. It takes all day to make it to the next small town. Darkness falls as I arrive there. But there are police at the station. I have not been missed yet, still, I cannot take the chance. I am wearing just the dress which the German woman gave me and my wooden clogs. I had no chance to get my jacket because I snuck out right after work, afraid that it would have been impossible to leave the barracks undetected. Now I am freezing and my jacket is at the foot of my bunk back in camp.*

*My bunk! How I wish I were in it! Where can I run, where will I sleep? "Just shoot her!" I can hear the voice of Herr Ober, ringing in my ears. "Just shoot her." It is all the fault of the restless creature within me. A movie! A life for a movie. . . Very expensive entertainment! The creature has done it again, gave me no peace, interferred with my reason, bent on destruction and now I have had it.*

*I go back to the station and peek through the door. It is almost empty but the gendarmes are still there; two of them. I walk down the windy street and past the town. Thuringia is hilly and full of forests. I go into*

the fir trees and choose a spot to sleep on. It is dark and cold and I know
that by now they must know I have run away. Meissner will realize that
he is missing his sixty marks. Frau Koenig will issue another report.

It is too far to walk back. I must finish what I have embarked upon.
Even if I get back to Poland, where could I hide. . . There is not even a
Ghetto left by now to sneak into so that I might die among my own people.
I feel trapped and shiver from the cold. The wind rustles among the
branches of the pines. I gather together a small heap of mulch and try to
burrow myself within it, but it is all pine needles. I roll up into a ball
with my knees against my chin and amazingly, I fall asleep. It is a fitful
sleep and the cold goes right though me. I wake and I doze. It is a relief to
see the light of day again.

Pale sunshine streams from above. I brush the pine needles off my
wrinkled and damp dress. I am back where I started the night I left the
ghetto. . . Just like then I am wearing two dresses and before me is an
empty road with drainage ditches on both sides. A melancholy road, a
road of sadness. Only now, I am in Germany. But what difference does it
make? A lonely road is the same anywhere. The whole world is full of
lonely roads which crisscross plowed fields. I keep walking, one step after
another. The clogs make a loud echoing sound against the asphalt in the
stillness of the morning. I feel hungry.

A wagon appears around the turn and passes me by. German
farmers. I try not to look at them hoping that they also will ignore me.
Suddenly I hear them yell, "Halt!" I want to run but it is hard wearing
clogs. They are off the wagon in a flash and approach me. It is amazing
how fast they move considering they are both old men. They grab me by my
shoulders.

"Where are you going?" they ask me loudly. No point answering. "Are
you a foreign worker? A fugitive?" They have mean, hostile faces. One of
them sticks his hand in my pocket where I keep my money. "Sixty marks!"
he yells at me. They practically drag me towards the wagon even though I
do not resist them at all. They are very agitated.

"She must be one of the Maihak workers. . . It is a matter for the
police. . . Let's just take her in and they will decide what to do with her.
A damn lazy foreigner. Nothing but troubles!" Very well informed old
bastards. They whip the horses into action, very much in a hurry. One
of them finds a string and ties my wrists tightly. "Russian?" they keep on
asking. "No," I say. "I am Polish".

"Verfluchte Polake!" (A cursed Polak) they screech. I sit stiffly in
the wagon burning with hatred. If only I could kill them! Two old grey-
haired men acting as if I were an infiltrating enemy ready to attack them.

*I crank up all my courage and say, "shit!" One of them whacks me across my face as hard as he can. We arrive in Paesneck and the two farmers drag me triumphantly down from the wagon like a trussed up animal and up the steps into the police station. Pedestrians stop to stare at the spectacle.*

*At the station I am confronted by the same chubby policeman who apprehended me in the movie theater. They are amazed and look embarrassed by the rough treatment and insults I receive from the farmers.*

*As soon as the farmers leave, the white haired policeman with the cherubic face loosens the string on my wrists. "Oh, it's you again!" he says mournfully. "Frau Koenig is not going to like it one bit. She is a very nice lady but she will be very upset. This time we have to take you straight to the Security Police station." He looks very concerned.*

*"But if you are a good worker they might go easy on you. . ." he adds hopefully.*

*Before we leave they give me a hot cup of erzatz coffee to warm me up. I do appreciate the kindness, but soon it is time to leave. I remember Herr Meisner's advice "stay away from this Otto. . ." but how? And I remember Herr Ober's voice, "just shoot her and save yourself the bother."*

# 20

## A GAME OF CHESS

### RECOLLECTION

*I remember the sunny morning of November as I am brought in to the offices of the Gestapo for "processing and interrogation", my face flushed from the brisk cold wind. The two corpulent policemen give me a reassuring smile and leave.*

*There is nothing immediately threatening about the room into which I am ushered. It even looks like a homey, unpretentious office. There are file cabinets against the wall, with military propaganda posters above them. There is, of course, a picture of Hitler displayed in a prominent gazing fixedly with lofty, inspired expression as it might be expected in a Gestapo office. I have been told that they will be in charge of all questioning and disposition; this is also to be expected. There are two desks standing about five meters apart and between them stands an old-fashioned, ornate, pot-bellied stove radiating warmth, with a large, steaming pot of erzatz coffee bubbling on its top. It almost looks cozy. There is a clutter of papers and a telephone on each desk.*

*There are two uniformed men seemingly at work. One of them immediately catches my eye and I instantly fear him. He is of medium height with sparse blond hair. His face is flat and pug nosed. There is something about his light blue eyes that worries me. It is a smirk, an expression that is unpleasant, and threatening. That must be Otto. I heard about him already and he fits the description only too well!*

*"It is bad oh, it is bad," says that insistant little voice in my head. "You are in for it. . ." I try to shut off this inner little voice, to silence it. Now what can they do to me? Usually , if someone breaks the rules they are sent to a correction camp, the "Buchenwald" about which I have heard vague whispers. I know people dread the very thought of going there, but now it is too late to worry. Whatever will be, will be. There is nothing I can do now. Not a thing. Just try to keep very calm.*

*The other of the two men inserts a file noisily into a drawer, slams it shut and gives me an appraising look. He is a nondescript man, perhaps in his thirties, like Otto. I try to avoid looking too close. They both wear SS insignia, and that is very bad! That is all I really need to notice about* them. He places a file on his desk, opens it and glances at it, then at me. It must be my own file, the sum total of my person and I know there is hardly anything in it. There is a backless stool in the empty part of the room and he orders me to sit on it.

"Alright, now. . . Where were you going?"

"I wanted to go back home. . ." I answer, trying to keep my voice pleasant.

"Why?"

"I missed my family."

He looks at me scornfully, doesn't buy it at all. . . "Didn't you know it is against the law to run away?" The voice is high pitched even though he is not yelling. Strange about the German language. They all have these nasal high-pitched voices, monotonous and flat.

"I am very sorry I did it. . . I beg your pardon," I answer, trying to sound convincing and apologetic.

"You will find out very soon how stupid you were. . ." he says derisively. "When you get to where you are going now, where we will send you, you will wish dearly you were back at Maihak Lager again. Your transfer orders are ready. . ." He picks up a piece of paper and shakes it at me.

So, — I think to myself, they are not going to kill me. . . I even relax a little bit. As long as they do not find out that I am Jewish, nothing else really matters. But if they will continue to check my papers, the truth will come out most certainly. Then they will really let me have it. I would be lucky to just get a bullet in the back of my head. That at least will be fast. I know it can be much worse than just being dead. It's how much one suffers in the process of being killed. Maybe if they will send me to this "Buchenwald" they will not bother to continue checking my papers after all.

I might have succeeded in distracting them by running away, might have interrupted the process. My mind is very clear. I am trying to keep very alert, but this little strange voice in my head keeps insisting, "it is bad, oh, it is bad!" I have heard this little voice before and it is always correct, a kind of intuition.

The blond fellow, Otto, takes a club from his desk and runs his hand up and down over it. At first I think it is made of wood, but it is flexible. It is rubber. He gives me an ugly little smile and puckers up his lips. "There is the matter of the sixty marks, you know. We want to know where you got it from."

I try to ignore this rubber truncheon, to deny it has anything to do with me.

*"As I told the police already, I stole it." I go over my story in detail and describe how my boss, Her Meissner, hung up his coat in the open closet and how I got his wallet out of his breast pocket where he usually keeps it and took out the money. It is easy recounting it exactly because it is perfectly true.*

*Otto gives me an angry look. "Stop lying! We already know that you are. . . We called Herr Meissner and he said he is not missing any money. We want to hear the truth from you right now. Nothing but the truth!"*

*My mind is reeling. Surely it cannot matter to them so much. They already have my transfer papers filled out and ready. Very soon they will be sending me away. What could it matter to them how I got the sixty marks. It is hardly a matter of importance for the Security Police. I am certain that by now Herr Meissner must know I stole the money from him, but he doesn't want to have me punished for stealing. That's a very serious offense... so he feigns ignorance and denies it. It would be very much like him, just trying to protect me. Suddenly I feel terribly sorry to have stolen from Herr Meissner. I am also frightened, I feel cornered. The whole room turns very threatening.*

*The other SS man, whose name I do not know, takes a piece of rag and ties it over my eyes. He pulls the ends as tightly as possible. It feels like my head is squeezed in a vise, the terrible tightness makes my eyeballs hurt. I am told to take off my dress which I do and it is taken away from me. I experience a terrible feeling of shame at being exposed. I know I must look like a scrawny, boney, pitiful creature. Yes, a creature!*

*The creature is not really me. My real self, "I", just exists submerged inside it and look at the world through the eyes of the creature. They are like small openings through which I see the world without ever being noticed. The creature within which I live is just a hiding place for my real self. But now I am threatened also. Something can happen to destroy my shell when the creature is in danger. Then, I too, will be naked and exposed before them.*

*I feel as if my body and I are not the same. It is a strange sensation. Now they have blocked the eyes, the two peeping holes I had. Now I cannot see out of the creature, I am plunged into total darkness. These thoughts jumble in my mind uninvited.*

*I feel my wrists being roughly tied with a string. No hand cuffs, but this is much worse. The string, or rope, feels very tight, just like my blindfold. It hurts and digs into my flesh. I feel myself being pushed backwards and am told to sit on the stool. It is not too high and my feet reach the floor and I am somehow grateful for that little bit of security.*

*I still have this sensation of my inner self hiding within my body. The two men are laughing. They are laughing at the creature, the scrawny* creature sitting naked on the stool. I hear them walk around. They are pouring coffee, chatting, they are in the room, but I cannot see them. I am straining to hear or guess exactly where they are, as if my life depended upon knowing it. After a while, I hear footsteps coming near and my flesh cringes as if straining to pull back, anticipating the pain I know will be inflicted upon me.

"Where did you get the money, let's have the truth!" Otto repeats the question.

"I stole it, I am telling you the truth!" I shout, wishing desperately that there was something I could think of saying that would get me free, but I know there is not.

The first blow falls on my back. I feel more impact than pain. I am knocked off the stool and I wiggle instinctively trying to protect my face as I fall and land on my side. Oh, how I wish I could just lie there forever.

But a gutteral voice shouts in my ear "Get up and get back on your stool again." I know that if I do not hurry, I will be kicked. It is very hard to get up with my hands tied behind my back. I am disoriented, try to find the stool and almost knock it over. Now I feel almost completely disassociated from the creature I reside within, it feels more and more real. Somehow it gives me a feeling of protection, it helps a little.

It is a cruel hide and seek game they are playing with me. I never know when or from which direction I will be hit. They sneak upon me and suddenly when I least expect it, I feel a blow fall at my head or back. It does not always knock me off the stool depending upon what they have in mind. I see splatches of light in front of my eyes, even though I am blindfolded. At first they are bright yellow, then purple and dimmer as they drift across my field of vision. I try to anticipate the next blow to come. I brace myself against it but it does me no good.

One catches me on the side of the jaw just as I moved my head instinctively to protect it. It feels as if my head is being knocked off my shoulders. I feel certain my jaw must be broken. The game continues. They take time out in between these assaults on my person to chat, even to work. I hear drawers of the filing cabinets being opened. They are laughing, having fun. The phone rings from time to time. I even hear them pouring coffee. My suffering is a diversion to them in what otherwise might be a boring daily work routine.

My perception of the passage of time is all distorted. How long have I been here; has it been for hours? How many? I feel very dazed, I have been knocked off this stool repeatedly, my face is battered, my knees are sore, but it is my back which hurts most of all. That is where the blows fall most of the time.

*I develop a terrible fear that they will push me against the hot, pot bellied stove, will burn me against it. I am afraid to think of it, as if they could hear my thoughts or read my mind. But they linger on obsessively, no matter how I try to banish them. What if they guess what I fear the most? They will then burn me. I imagine feeling myself pulled toward it and shudder but I remain very, very quiet. Not a sound comes out of my mouth. I am hoping I could faint, but cannot afford to permit it to happen. I have to be careful how I fall or the creature will be injured. It will break. I can only stand it all because it is not I, but the creature that is being battered and I am only within it. But I have a need to know what happens to it; must keep awake.*

*Twice I feel a cigarette touch by body, my right lower breast, but it is brief and the worst of it is the odor of burned skin and the fear that they will do it again. I begin to feel numb. After a while I cannot think and grow increasingly weaker. Another blow and I will not be able to get up and sit up again, even with assistance or prodding. I am afraid to cry out by mistake, to make a noise of any kind, or they would make a game out of this also. What if the creature will break like an egg and I will be exposed. I will spill out of it. Maybe if I am very quiet they will never guess that within the battered creature someone is hiding.*

*The door opens and I hear a conversation taking place, but do not catch the individual words because the blindfold also partially covers my ears. I think feebly by now, my mind is very sluggish. Have they come to take me away? Oh, how I hope so! Or will they finish me off? Even that would be a relief; a small caliber pistol, a soft lead bullet. I know they don't like to make a mess. This way, there is no blood splattered. The bullet would not even come out. It would stay inside the skull, a souvenir from life. I heard it is sometimes done like this. I try to imagine every step of the process so I will be prepared when it happens.*

*Then suddenly, without an explanation, I feel the blindfold being untied. It takes a while because it is tangled up in my hair. I sit still trying not to flinch while it is being done. When finally the pressure of the rag is gone, I am actually afraid to open my eyes. I really do not want to, but I force myself. Everything is fuzzy at first and I cannot see very well. The blindfold was too tight for so long. . . My eyeballs hurt. I hear a command.*

*"Get up and move your ass! Herr Ober wants to see you. . ." What now? The dress is thrown over my shoulder, but my hands remain tied. I have no feeling below my wrists at all, they feel completely numb.*

*"Come on, move!. . ." Otto prods me forward with the tip of the truncheon. I am making a terrific effort to maintain balance. The room is spinning, the floor seems to curve as if it was tilted. I put one foot after*

*another making slow progress, but I have no balance at all. If only I could manage somehow to remain conscious for just long enough to get out of here. As I go through the door, I see that someone else is being brought in, but cannot focus my eyes enough to tell whether it is a man or a woman. I wonder for what crime will the next person will be punished and I feel very sorry.*

*I manage to stay on my feet and make slow progress. It feels like I cover a great distance but I only go across the hallway. They open a door for me. "Go on in bitch!" They sound very angry because I move so slowly.*

*I feel a nausea rise in my stomach and make an effort not to vomit. I cannot quite make it through that door. I feel a boot connect with my backside and propel me across the threshhold. the room is very bright with sunlight. It is startling. I careen inside it from the impact of the shove and come to a stop against a desk trying to steady myself somehow. It is very difficult without being able to use my hands, which are still tied behind my back. I do not make it and fall backwards. I find myself sitting on the floor unable to see over the top of the desk. I hear a voice but do not see the man it comes from.*

*"Get up!" I make an effort but do not succeed. I hear footsteps coming from around the desk. "You are bleeding all over the damn floor!" The voice sounds very annoyed.*

*Now I am indeed aware that I am bleeding profusely from my nose. There is a sticky wetness of blood on my chin. It is oozing over my mouth. There is no way for me to wipe it off, so I stick my tongue out and let it drip in. It tastes salty in my mouth.*

*Suddenly, I remember that when I was a child, I used to suffer from frequent nosebleeds. They came at the most inopportune times, when I was skipping rope or playing. Mother used to make me lay down and used to apply pressure or stuff my nose with soft wet cotton. I remember how I hated it. She used to tell me that I would outgrow it someday, and stroked my hair. Was there really a time in my life when I had a mother? It seems so very long ago.*

*I keep telling myself that I must not faint, have to try to control the weakness spilling over me. I try to focus my eyes upon the man behind the desk. His outline is fuzzy but I see that he is coming towards me. He has something in his hand that glistens in the sunlight. It looks like a dagger. I feel a burst of panic explode in my brain, — fear of death!*

*The figure of the man is bending over me, the hand with the dagger comes nearer. I freeze, but the creature that is also me does not. It wants to struggle to hang on to life. The man's face is only inches away. I can actually see his eyes. I am like a cat cornered by a huge dog and just like a cat, I spit. It is not a gesture of defiance or bravery, just of pure instinct, the only defense I have. I see the spittle splash on his face and it is mostly the blood my mouth was full of. Horrified at what I did, I shut my eyes and throw myself to the side trying to escape the pain which I am certain will follow.*

*Now I am really scared. . . I feel a hand on the top of my head pressing it down and my flesh cringes to anticipate the dagger plunging in. For an instant, I lose all sanity. But all I feel is a tugging at my wrists. The string is being cut and my hands are freed. They feel numb and there is a dull pain in my wrists. There is also a sensation of pins and needles in my flesh as the circulation starts again. I move my hand clumsily towards my face to wipe off the blood from my mouth and chin.*

*I feel a piece of cloth being stuck into my hand a handkerchief. Then there are footsteps moving away from me. I hear cursing. No wonder. . . this man did not try to kill me at all. I am so ashamed of the way I look and acted, ashamed of having lost all my dignity. I cringe on the floor hoping not to vomit. If I befoul the floor it will make the man angrier and he will surely punish me for it. My stomach is shuddering with the effort of not throwing up.*

*I hear footsteps leaving the room and all is quiet for a while. Then he returns again. He must have gone to the bathroom to clean his face. I lie very still making believe I have fainted, but I am very much alert and watchful. The telephone is being dialed, then I hear the man's voice:*

*"Meissner, you old fart, I have your Stucke here." There is a pause then he continues. "Yes, she is alive," pause again. "Yes, I have her transfer slip right here." Pause again as Herr Meissner must be talking on the other side. I wonder what he is saying.*

*"Take my advice Meissner," continues the man. "It might be wise for you to get rid of her. We can send her out today on the Garbage Truck, she is not going to be able to do any work for a while." Pause, then: "No trouble, the Russians are already on the way to take her away and clean up the mess." He must be meaning the blood from my nose on the wood floor.*

*His voice continues very cheerfully. "I am looking forward to it, Meissner. It has been ages since I have played a good game of chess with anyone who could beat me, especially with a champion. Well, — soon we shall see if you still have your cunning, you old dog."*

*Suddenly my mind cleared. So it was Meissner's doing, that I am still alive. He used his connections to get me out and away from those two monsters; used his having been a chess champion at one time. So this is how he pulled it off. My life for a game of chess!*

*I am filled with such a shame, so ashamed. . . I did steal from Meissner, took his money, sixty marks of it! Of course he couldn't guess my reasons, still he forgave me. More than that, he tried hard to save my life in spite of it.*

The Russian girls came over and half dragged me to the barracks. They were shocked at the shape I was in.

"Now what did you do to get hit like this?" they wanted to know. But I couldn't tell them. I was vomiting all the way back to the barracks, and later must have slept for hours. All I remember is having snow applied as a compress on my head and vomiting from time to time with great force. It splashed across the wall. I remember the wall being washed and sleeping again, and the terrible pain in my back; not being able to bend or get out of bed without hurting.

I remember being helped to the latrine and the women saying: "Now what did you ever do, — fight the German Army?" I remember kind hands forcing some soup down my throat and some water and being totally, completely unable to talk. Not one word came out of me for days, or any other sound. It took a week before I gained enough balance to walk around and by then I had to somehow make it back to work.

I remembered the story of the Garbage Truck only too well. I had no doubt as to where it would take me if I were not able to work. I had to become useful again to survive. Slowly the splintering of my personality began to lift and the creature and my inner self began to fuse again into one person.

On the day of my return to work, two Ukrainian girls helped me across the narrow bridge to the factory. I entered again the world of ceaseless noise; machines humming and clanging busily. I was still on a night shift, twelve hours of it every night but Saturday, and I wondered how I would make it. I still felt very shaky. My right knee buckled under me when I least expected it and I had sharp pains in my back as I changed balance.

Meissner was already there when I arrived. He looked at me and his expression showed astonishment. I knew that I was a sight to behold. My face was full of bruises and one eye was still swollen. He should have seen me a few days ago when it was almost completely shut. Well, at least he could see that I have already been punished for stealing his money. I knew that during my absence a Russian woman worked for him. It would only have taken a simple request to transfer me elsewhere and he could have kept her. It was a very coveted job, much easier than operating the big machines on the main floor.

I tried to form a cheerful smile.

"Good evening, Herr Meissner," I greeted him. The long room with the twelve automatic mammoth machines looked very good to me. It was almost like coming back home again. I was glad that the back part where I usually worked was dimly lit. I could work in the semidarkness back there where nobody would see my face.

Meissner brought me forward to his work table. "Dear God!" he exclaimed. "You look terrible." His weatherbeaten face was more mournful than usual. He told me that I should rest and try to recuperate in the back room behind the machines until I felt better and offered me the blanket he kept around to keep warm in case of an air raid.

"Now you see what you have done," he chastised me. "You almost got yourself killed. They almost sent you to "Buchenwald," — did you know that? Your papers were already stamped. You don't realize what this would have meant. You would not have lasted one week in there."

He wagged his finger at me and I have never seem him so angry. "Why did you have to make a run for it? Don't I treat you well here? Are you stupid enough to think you would have made it? There are many camps around here and everybody is on the lookout for fugitives!"

After he calmed down, we sat down and I heard his version of what had happened. He didn't notice that his money was missing until the next evening. He quickly put two and two together and made a few phone calls. He had to be very careful about asking questions. He received a phone call from the Security Police, the SD, about the 60 marks and was certain that I was in trouble.

He had no influence at all; there was nothing he could do to help me, with one exception. He knew an SS man, Hans Von Ulrecht, who had rank. Meissner considered turning to Hans for help to be a matter of last resort. He knew him very well personally and for many years. They had competed against each other at a chess tournament before the war and subsequently Meissner had even met Hans' family. But he heartily disliked the man and considered him to be the most irritating opponent against whom he had ever played.

Recently, Hans had tried his darnest to talk Meissner into playing a game of chess with him, which Meissner steadfastly refused to do. But now he had no other choice but to ask for his help. He practically had to plead with him. Hans was very reluctant to get involved in my case but when Meissner suggested that they get together really soon to play chess, he changed his mind.

Hans was not even certain that it could be done and complained that everyone would wonder why he would bother to interfere with the transfer of a *Stucke.* He didn't promise anything but he knew the moron, Otto, well and outranked him considerably. Meissner knew that there was hope. Hans was a fanatic about chess and he knew that Meissner would owe him a game for this favor.

Meissner said he stayed up all morning, tired as he was after 12 hours of night shift work without an assistant. Finally, Hans went in during his lunch hour and managed to release me. Meissner received the call shortly thereafter and finally was able to get a little rest. He was not at all angry about the money, hardly mentioned it at all. But there was the matter of having now to play chess with Hans, who wasted no time in exacting his pound of flesh.

He was free to enter the factory whenever he wanted because his Russian prisoner charges occasionally assisted with the delivery of metals and other necessary work. So now Meissner took his lunch break at 8:30 p.m. instead of midnight in order to accommodate Hans. He pointed to his shelf where there was a chess board with a game already in progress waiting to be continued during the next visit.

"Now I am stuck with that 'pig of a dog,' Hans, and he's been here almost every day for a week! If he doesn't play, he just visits and talks endlessly," he complained.

Evidently Hans had arrived here to work at the Russian Prisoners of War Camp after he was wounded at the Eastern Front. It was not clear whether he had been fighting the Russian Army or chasing the partisans. He's been very bored since his return. He was divorced and didn't like any one around here. He considered the engineers to be very uninteresting and the guards to be a bunch of meatheads. Hans was an intelligent, well read man, like Meissner, but very much younger. Maybe Meissner reminded Hans of his father who had been killed, and whom he missed a great deal. In any case Hans was very eager to re-estab-

lish their friendship. Meissner, however, was not nearly as enthusiastic.

"That pig-dog has access to my personal file too, not only
yours!" he said meaningfully. "And that pig-dog cannot be
trusted!" This summed up his sentiments about Hans very completely.

I thanked Meissner from the bottom of my heart for his kindness but he soon lapsed into the silent, depressed mood which
came over him so often. "Now you are stuck with him too," he
finished glumly.

"Neither of us will have any peace, he will be here every evening. He will plague us with his presence. The man is a pest, he
will talk us deaf, dumb and blind. Wait until you see how he is.
This place will never be the same."

There was work to do and I was not much help in my present
condition. Poor Meissner did both our jobs and it was not easy.
He was pretty old, after all, and looked exhausted towards the
end of the shift. But he insisted that I rest behind the machines,
until I recovered a little more.

Every few hours, he personally wheeled the cart full of the
finished parts to the next room through the double doors, where
the German women workers completed the next step in production. Usually it was my job, but now Meissner told me in no uncertain terms not to even show my face there until I looked
human again. My appearance would scare the poor German
women half to death, not to mention the questions they might
ask.  If I gave them a truthful answer, I would be accused of
spreading bad propaganda about the SS and this alone could
send me straight to "Buchenwald."

For the next several nights, I dozed gratefully behind the pile
of metal ingots. I was getting better, but still obsessed and worried practically day and night. My papers were still being checked
as far as I knew. I kept wondering if right then a letter was being
delivered to the SS from the city of Bochnia in the District of
Krakow in Occupied Poland. I knew without a doubt what the letter would say.  No such person ever lived there. There was no
such address, no such precinct number. I could not be issued an
identification card with the stamp of the SS police affixed on it,
because all the information in my file was false! They would very
quickly guess everything. I did not have a chance!

I dreamt about it whenever I closed my eyes, thought about it
during all my waking hours. My fourteenth birthday was just

around the corner but I would not live to see it. It was like being a prisoner on death row. It was just a matter of time... All of Meissner's effort had been wasted. The hours were ticking away. I could not run anymore, not with my battered face, without money.

It began to snow and winter arrived again. I didn't believe I would live to see the spring, maybe not even the next day. It was a time of dread and fear. I collected a sharp metal shaving and carried it everywhere I went. If discovered, I would use it to cut my wrists, and beat them to it. It would be better than what they would do to me.

Somehow, once I had made this decision, my fear lessened. I even relaxed a little bit. I had made my choice. They could do nothing to me after that. All I had to worry about was to do it in time to prevent falling into Otto's hands again.

Of course, no one knew what I was going through at that time. The bruises and my physical condition were nothing compared to the agony of waiting.

Hans did not come around since I returned and Meissner gave a sigh of relief. Maybe he found himself a woman to spend his time with and wouldn't bother us again. But one day, at 8:30 p.m., he just showed up without warning. I was in the back of the room when Meissner came to let me know that Herr "Ober" Von Ulrecht wanted to see me. He didn't belive that I was actually back and able to work. This, he had to see for himself.

"Now you must stand straight, at attention," Meissner whispered in my ear. "Have to humor the pig-dog. And be sure to thank him. You wouldn't be here if it were not for him, but don't overdo it."

I could see Hans standing in the well-lit part of the room, peeling off his coat. He was of medium height and not at all the prepossessing figure I remembered. He took off his gloves, stuck them into a pocket of his coat and walked over to the open closet to hang it up. Now I noticed how much he limped. Meissner did mention that he had been wounded and transferred back to Germany. The wound must have been serious enough. I hesitated, now I could clearly see the insignia he wore. The death head!

How well I remembered and loathed it, how many times have I seen it. In the Ghetto, in Czestochowa, in Praszka, in the miserable camp in Silesia. Men who wore it, swinging a whip, a truncheon, pointing a gun, killing people, screaching in that high pitched tone of voice at us "Cursed Jews!" —"Always watch out for the arm eagle, the SS."

Why should I continue this charade? My days were numbered anyway. I will be discovered any day now I thought. Then, one of those elite corps, — death-headwearers, will pump a soft lead bullet into my head if I am lucky! They used to put a death's head and cross bones pictures on boxes of rat poison.

"What is the matter with you. . . Go on, for God's sake," whispered Meissner into my ear. "For God's sake", no less. Well I was not about to displease Meissner. None of it was his doing. I swallowed and entered the lighted up part of the room and approached closer rehearsing my "thank you" speech.

Hans turned around and we looked at each other. I snapped to attention and was about to say "Herr Ober. . ." But nothing more came out of my mouth. There was a funny expression of incredulity on his face. His mouth twitched and then he began to laugh. He was practically shaking with laughter, he was holding his sides.

"Hah, ha, how funny, what a fright! *(shracklicheit)* Hah, ha, what a face. . ." I knew, of course, why he laughed. Meissner had brought his shaving mirror the other day, especially so I could see what I looked like. As the bruises began to fade, they turned multicolor, greenish, yellow and purple. But worst of all was one eye where a blood vessel broke, turning the white part around the iris a solid tomato red. It didn't hurt and I could see well enough, but it looked almost gruesome. A terrible, bloody red eye. . .

Suddenly I was overcome by a flood of self-pity. What ever else I suffered, in addition, I looked like a monster. I would have cried if I could, but I had been unable to shed even one tear for years. Not since the time in that slimy camp in Silesia. My tear ducts have not functioned since then, I only cried inside. The creature never cried. It could not.

"What an ugly face. . ." continued Hans, greatly amused. "Damn, Meissner, you bugged me for hours about this horrible *Stucke*. . . Look at that eye!" I looked wearily at Hans; he surely had no pity. He knew exactly how I got to look this way. Now I noticed his appearance. He had grey blue eyes and sandy blond, curly hair. His face was not really handsome, just very cheerful. He had large, even teeth, very prominently visible as he continued laughing at me. He had a straight nose. He was probably in his late thirties. His face seemed ruddy — maybe just flushed from the cold and the laughter.

I couldn't continue to look at his face and lowered my gaze to his feet. There was something unusual about them. Of course, now I knew; I could tell! Hans was missing one foot. I realized that it was a prosthesis I was looking at. Now I remembered the unevenness of his footsteps. Soo, I thought, my eyes glued to his foot. I wondered how much of his leg was also gone. Of course, I could not tell.

Hans noticed me looking at his foot and abruptly he stopped laughing. We just stood silently like this for a moment.

"So you notice that my foot is missing," he finally said. "It's somewhere in Russia, you know." Now I was speechless, what could I say to him.

"Don't let it worry you, *Stucke*. . . I get by very well without it." He laughed again. "Fortunately for the ladies at home, it is just my foot that is missing and not my tail. I don't do it with my feet, you know, and as long as my tail is intact, the ladies are very satisfied. I do my patriotic duty anyway, as long as I have to be stuck back home. Somebody has an obligation to do it with all the husbands gone! Meissner, you can vouch for that! My tail is half worn off in the process, but I never shirk responsibility. The ladies all have had to sacrifice by not having their men around and I do my very best to keep them happy." He laughed again.

Meissner cleared his throat uncomfortably, and I thought this was my cue to deliver my "thank you" speech. "I wish to express my thanks Herr Ober. . .", I said stiffly.

"Don't you have some duties for your scrawny *Stucke*, Meissner?" said Hans, obviously ready to dismiss me. "Now that you have your *Stucke* back, let's see her do some work!"

He made himself comfortable in a chair, and I returned to the dimly lit part of the room. I had to start removing shavings out of some of the machines and it was hard to bend. I had to crouch to manage it. Hans surely surprised me. For a moment I even forgot to worry about my papers being checked out; about being discovered. I could see Hans and Meissner sitting and talking and though I could not catch a word of their conversation because of the noise the machines made, I did hear Hans laughing. He stayed for about an hour and left.

We were caught up with our work for a little while and Meissner moved his chair into the back of the room where he could rest. "Hans makes me tired," he complained. "Tired and mad. Now you know what a pig-dog he is. He did bring me a small flask of schnapps. It is very good for my nerves to take a mouthful now and then. But now you can see for yourself what you got us into by your foolishness!"

I was very pleased that Herr Meissner could at least take a little nap. I could manage alone feeding the metal ingots into the machines and making sure all were running smoothly. He very much deserved to relax a little. I thought about Hans and did not feel so sorry for myself any longer. He got his too, I thought. I was not the only one.

# 21

# PASSPORT TO LIFE

## RECOLLECTION

*Time has a certain peculiarity about it. We measure it by the clock
and the calendar, but neither really reflects our true perception of its passage or the way we remember it. I can see myself as I was then:*

*I trudge across the bridge to the factory building, always tired. It is
like living under a sword of Damocles poised to fall upon me. My back
does not seem to improve and I am always in pain. My knees are better
and I am grateful to be rid of at least some of the constant discomfort. My
jaw locks painfully when I eat so I mix my brown bread ration with water
and chew it very slowly. I have lost a lot of weight. The stress is taking its
toll.*

*Nobody knows what I am going through, I can never confide in
anyone, that I am waiting to be executed. I keep very much to myself, cannot trust any of the Polish girls. They might draw me into a conversation
and I will give myself away. Even the expression on my face or the wrong
word could arouse suspicion. It is hard to carry such a burden of loneliness on my soul.*

*There are a thousand girls around me and yet I am so very lonely;
can talk to no one. There are two sisters from Warsaw who love to describe
with relish how the Jews were wiped out in the Ghetto. They think it was
just great! Hitler deserves a medal even if they personally are just slave
labor living on watery soup made of turnips, working a twelve hour shift.
At least there is someone else they feel vastly superior to; the pleasure of
seeing someone else die and feeling safe.*

*Since nobody knows who I am, I hear the unveiled truth. I am as-
tounded at the depth of racial hatred and antiSemitism in particular. The
Ukrainian women rank next on the ladder of bigotry. The Jews are no
more, but they still remember how to hate the Jews. The indoctrination is
centuries old. Still, I feel safer associating with the Russian and Ukrainian girls. They are less likely to spot something about me or ask questions. I like their music and singing, and I do speak their language. It
makes the time pass faster. If I have to be a part of a group, I chose them
as less dangerous. I avoid answering questions about my bruises, which is*

*not easy. It is common knowledge in the barracks that I tried to escape. I
am considered odd, a little crazy and that is just fine with me.*

*I communicate mostly with Meissner. I feel real affection for him. He
is a rare person, truly kind, but even he has not the vaguest idea about
my predicament or why I tried to escape. He has been in and out of
depression. There are nights when he just works and stares into space as
if he were miles away. Sometimes he sits in his chair and tears run down
his face. He does not sob or cry, just the silent tears.*

*Occasionally, he sort of wakes up and makes an effort to joke. He
must have had a fine sense of humor once upon a time, before he lost his
wife and the niece he adopted. He must have been a handsome, impressive man when he was younger. He still has a sense of fairness and decen-
cy and his fine vocabulary indicates his intellectual level. I know how
badly he is going to feel when they find out who I am and shoot me. He is
the complete opposite of a Nazi.*

*As much as he dislikes Hans, he does brighten up a little when he
does make his appearance around 8 p.m. as usual. They have been at
one game for a week and afterwards Meissner complains bitterly about
Hans' bad manners but even that is better than the usual silent depression. I am quite used to him by now.*

The second time Hans visited since my return to work a habit
was established.

"Meissner!" he yelled, "doesn't your *Stucke* have any manners?
Have her come here instantly so she will learn how to greet and
welcome a visitor." I came out and waited to see what happens
next.

"Come here *Stucke!*" Hans took off his hat and plunked it on
my head. "You do not have any lice do you?" he asked with a tone
of concern as an after thought of having his hat upon my hair.

"No, I do not Herr Ober." I stood there feeling very foolish,
the hat with the SS insignia slipping down over my eyes. I was
horrified to wear such a cursed thing on my very own head, even
as a joke.

"Now hang up my great coat properly," Hans instructed me.
"Didn't anybody, including this old fart, Meissner, ever bother to
teach you some good manners?"

The great coat was remarkably heavy with all the various
things sewn onto the lapels, the thick lining and belt. I gave
Meissner a questioning glance then shook off the snow from the
coat and hung it up in the open closet. I placed the hat carefully

on the shelf. Hans had a very unnerving way of watching a person. He smiled with approval.

"That's better *Stucke*, now look inside my left pocket and see what's in it." I hesitated, worried that it was a trick and that Hans was up to something.

"Go on, do as Herr Ober tells you," Meissner reassured me. I stuck my hand in gingerly and brought out a small parcel carefully wrapped in white paper.

"It is a present for you!" Hans laughed at my consternation as he and Meissner sat down to play a game of chess. I retreated behind the machines in the back of the room and unwrapped the package. It was a sandwich made with white bread. When did I taste it last? How long has it been? But I could not bite into it, my jaw was still dislocated and painful. I filled my aluminum cup with water and soaked the bread until it was soft enough for me to chew.

Just then one of the machines pinged loudly indicating a problem which meant that Meissner had to interrupt the game and attend to it. Hans got tired sitting by himself and walked over to where I sat. He immediately noticed what I was doing and frowned.

"Don't you like the sandwich?" he asked. "Aren't you satisfied with the way I prepared it for you? Are you making soup out of it?"

I was embarrased and felt obliged to explain my problem. Hans told me to follow him where it was light enough to see and examined my jaw. He found my predicament actually amusing.

"Otto surely did a job on you!" He laughed as if it was very funny; no sign of sympathy on his part. "Very good man on the job," he continued. "I should have sent my ex-wife to him for a treatment. That might have shut her up for a while!"

He had me open my mouth as wide as I could and examined my teeth. "You were lucky that he did not knock out your front teeth. It would have been part of the procedure if he had enough time to get around to it."

It could have been worse, I agreed. It was bad enough to have a constant toothache in addition to a very sore jaw.

It felt good to be able to complain to someone about my discomfort. Hans was actually interested in my troubles, but it struck me as very strange that I found it so easy to talk to him. Just a few days ago, I was so afraid of him.

Meissner joined us, his hands full of grease. The machine needed to be worked upon and the game couldn't be continued. They turned their attention temporarily to my dental problem.

"Your *Stucke* will croak if nothing is done about her infected molar," said Hans. In her condition an infection would finish her off." Meissner agreed unhappily, I was very scrawny indeed, but he didn't know what to do about it. "Why don't you just yank the tooth out?" Hans suggested. Meissner was very uncomfortable at the prospect and Hans shrugged his shoulders. He made a decision.

"Tomorrow I will pull out your teeth," he announced with finality. "Somebody has got to do it. Otherwise, Meissner would not have a *Stucke* who speaks German."

True to his word, he arrived at eight the next evening looking very enthusiastic. He brought a paper bag containing a flask of schnapps and a pair of pliers. I was instructed to fill my mouth with the alcohol and hold it until it felt numb and anesthetized. Then I swallowed and was given some more.

The flask was passed around as if it was a jolly party. At last I opened my mouth as wide as my injured jaw permitted and Hans examined my teet with a flashlight. He shook his head. "Both molars will have to go," he announced. Out came the pliers, but at that point I wasn't feeling much pain. I was blissfully drunk and Hans was very efficient. He placed the extracted molars on a piece of paper for me to see, very proud of himself. I was given another mouthful of schnapps which, according to Hans, was a cure for all ills.

Afterwards, I was barely able to stagger behind a machine where I happily passed out for the night. I woke up the next day with a hangover but I felt enormously better. At least one discomfort was gone, though my jaw was still badly dislocated and my back still sore. I was very grateful to Hans.

He, however, did not believe in half measures, and a week later, I was taken to a real dentist. Hans and Meissner escorted me out of the camp on a Sunday morning.

It was all arranged for. The dentist came in especially for me and Hans paid for it by giving him a package of something. My teeth were x-rayed and filled where necessary, and I was given a brace to support my jaw until it healed.

Hans explained that my condition was the result of a fight with the Russian women in the camp who attacked me. The dentist patted me on the back sympathetically as we were leaving. I was unobtrusively deposited back at the camp. The guard asked no questions.

## RECOLLECTION

*It has been a month since my papers are being verified. A person can hold their breath for only so long and I begin to hope that I was simply forgotten. All this fear and suffering and they have simply mislaid my file; I tell myself. But then, unexpectedly, I am called in to the Security Police office. At last! I am so relieved that the waiting is over, I almost no longer care what will happen to me. The waiting has been unbearable, like being on death row. I go across the courtyard on shaking legs, clutching the sharp piece of metal shaving in a sweaty hand. Will I have to use it? It is a sunny day and I know that for the rest of my life, I will remember every stone along the way to the Security Police building.*

*I go inside and report to a man at a desk. He gives me a bored smile, trying to remember what it is all about. "Oh, yes", he opens my file and hands me a passport. It has my picture on it and my finger print. It has my real name, but my mother's maiden name is spelled Borkiewicz, which is typically Polish, and not as it really was, Berkowicz, which is a Jewish name. How thorough the Germans are! Even the mother's maiden name has to appear on the  Ausweiss. It states that I have been born in the town of Bochnia, a place I have never seen. My age is given as three years older than I really am. There is even my phoney last address, a make believe street and precinct number.*

*I am so stunned that my feet are practically rooted to the floor. They do not intend to keep me. I can simply leave and return to the barracks very much alive. The uniformed guard gives me a questioning glance. I thank him politely and make a quick exit, the prescious Ausweiss in my hand.*

*The sense of freedom is so sweet. It feels as if I am floating on air. Happiness! The sky is suddenly blue and beautiful! I am going to live! I am no longer the only inmate without an identification card in this lager. I can hardly restrain myself from singing. I know only too well what this blue covered passport-identification really means. To have one means exemption from death, from deportation, it means being human. People in the Ghetto would have given and done anything in the world to have such an Ausweiss, and I just got it by default, by accident. I was given life!*

*As soon as I am alone, I examine it minutely. My hands shake as I hold it. There is a swastika stamp on the front and a red stamp inside. It reads "Issued by the SD," an abbreviation for* Sieherheitsdienst

*Policei, an arm of the Gestapo; the dreaded SD. There is a signature and it is at first hard to decipher. It is signed by Hans Adolf Von Ulrecht!*

*I feel a little dizzy. Hans! It took a whole month of agony and it is signed by Hans! I don't know whether to laugh or cry. It is morning and I have the whole day to sleep. Sleep! I have not really slept peacefully in so long, I had forgotten how it feels. I rest on my bunk, as tired as if I had been running, but I feel so good, even my back hurts less than usual. I decide not to mention it to anyone, not even Meissner. The happiness in my face would give me away. They would get suspicious.*

*I go to work happily that evening, ready to clean all the machines until they shine. Meissner is his usual gloomy self, but today he, too, has a surprise for me. On the shelf there is a notebook and a pencil. Meissner decided to give me spelling lessons and to teach me a little mathematics. We have several free hours each shift and he is concerned about my missing an education. Without it, he explains, my life would have less quality. At my age, I must retain an instinct to learn. It is a sure sign that his own depression is a little less severe. Both of us, in a sense, are making a recovery at the same time. I feel very touched by this and assure Meissner how eager I am to learn and I thank him. I get so carried away I even shake his hand. We are both smiling. It is a very good day.*

*Hans drops in the next day and brings some Slivovic liquor, his favorite, in a flask. In his left pocket, as usual, I find a sandwich. I wish I could express my gratitude to him also, but decide to say as little as possible. However, he knows. "Did you get your* Ausweiss Stucke*?"*

*"Yes", I answer noncommittally.*

*"I completed your file . . .," he continues, "so you wouldn't get into a hassle with the asshole Otto, or Meissner would be banging at my door in the middle of the night again.*

*"I just got it yesterday . . ." I probe cautiously to see what else he will be willing to say on the subject.*

*"Well, you know how slow the channels are these days," he adds apologetically. "You had to be checked out, you understand; — verified. You were the only Stucke in this place with nothing in your file to base issuing you an identification."*

*I can see that somehow Hans is enjoying the subject by the way he goes on and on about bureaucracy and the headaches caused by endless "paperwork these days." There is no chess game today. Instead the flask is passed back and fourth a couple of times. Hans is in a talkative mood, not unusual for him lately. He exhausts the subject and switches to his favorite topic about his escapades last weekend. Both Meissner and I lean back and listen patiently; we are used to it by now. Hans describes graphically his difficult plight in manless Germany. He almost makes it sound heartbreaking. Poor Hans! All the women from miles around are chasing him without a pause. With all the men off to war it is downright dangerous for a man like himself in Germany these days. He would be safer on the Russian front, than under the stampede of love-starved females. He actually had to ration his services in self-defense. A man can only do so much for his country and still be fair to all. Women are trying to sneak in through the cracks under his door. He had to barricade himself, but one has to have a heart. Under present conditions, even the ugly ones deserve a break. One has to take the good with the bad. They are all German women after all and with the men shortage, he, Hans, has to do his share. His "tail" is frazzled. He is worn out. And here Meissner is of no help at all, shirking his duty to the* Vaterland, *and moping around instead. What a shame! It is true that Meissner is an old "Fart" but he still has an obligation to try. He could at least warm up somebody on a cold winter night.*

The flask of Slivovic went back and forth and nobody was sending me to the back of the room that evening. Meissner was getting tipsy. His eyelids drooped sleepily and we still had lots of work to do; the parts had to be loaded into trays. They were piling up. Shavings needed removal, and what if a machine went on the blink. I got up reluctantly to do some of the work, but before I left Hans held out the flask.

"Here, *Stucke,* have a little sip. Now that you have an *Ausweiss,* you can also take a little drink, you are almost a person." Very well said, I thought and politely took a small swallow. I was getting concerned about Meissner who looked as if he were half asleep. I could hear Hans laughing as I loaded the ingots into the machines. He had no audience any longer and left shortly thereafter. The evening had an air of celebration but I had an uneasy feeling about that *Ausweiss.* I kept wondering if Hans knew a lot more than he let on, but I couldn't be certain. Well, I had it so why should I continue to worry? But being worried and suspicious had become a part of my nature.

It was a strange sensation waking up from my sleep for the next several weeks. I used to experience such a dread for so long that at first it assaulted my consciousness every time out of habit. It was only after I remembered that I had the *Ausweiss* that the old feeling lifted. The dread was a phantom sensation now. I sewed a pocket onto my dress where I kept my *Ausweiss,* touching it to reassure myself from time to time. The nightmare was over.

For the first time since the Praszka Ghetto days, four years ago, I felt safe. If I were to be killed during an air raid, it wouldn't matter. My chances were the same as for others. I was not singled out for death. I had a sense of happiness and it was overwhelming. Happiness is such a relative thing. A piece of white bread was happiness, having a notebook and a pencil was pure joy. And now I even had an *Ausweiss.*

# 22

# EDUCATION

Happiness is relative to how deeply depressed a person can be. If someone crawled out of a pit, the ground level would appear as high as a mountain top. This probably best described my state of mind. I have not suffered hunger pains, or gone to sleep craving food for weeks. I could stand the smelly turnip soup every day if now and then I received a sandwich made of white bread.

I never cried once in three and a half years. I was unable to shed one tear when my parents were deported, when I was hungry, frightened, or had no place to sleep. Not even in pain when I was beaten. It was as if all strong emotions were frozen and suppressed within me. I became emotionally numb. I experienced sadness, but only as if all these terrible things happened to someone else and I was very sorry, very sympathetic but only as an observer. The tender, sensitive part of my person that could laugh or cry was submerged, maybe destroyed. I was simply a creature that existed and was happy just to survive.

Now I began to enjoy things for the first time in years. I became a member of a Russian singing group. My voice was just right; mother had brought me up on Russian ballads. I wished also to participate in the dancing we organized to make our lives more bearable within the bleak routine of a labor camp, but my back still hurt too much. The Russian girls accepted me very readily, and the Polish girls did not particularly miss me. I was still considered "the crazy one" who tried to escape and almost got killed in the process. Being on the night shift also helped a lot since most of the Polish women worked during the day.

Herr Meissner brought me a small German-Polish dictionary. Learning made me very happy; I looked forward to it every day. I eagerly did my lessons, though lately we had less free time. The air raids began in earnest now. The sirens wailed almost each night and day. We were herded off into the air raid shelters. Herr Meissner was terribly affected, having lived through the Hamburg bombing. His nerves were shot. If a few bombs fell in the vicinity, he could not calm down for hours and only then with the help of a little schnapps.

I, however, derived the deepest pleasure from the bombings. It was as if my personal safety was not at all affected. It simply did not matter. Each time a bomb exploded, I experienced a sharp thrill. Of course, I kept this psychological phenomenon very much to myself.

I kept myself very clean, even attempted to curl my straight hair by wrapping it around thin strips of cloth as if it were a curler. I felt very lucky and fortunate to be alive; to have made it. My new state of mind was reflected by cheerful smiling and friendliness. I suddenly changed from silent timidity to being very outgoing. It was a very drastic change of behavior.

Now, when I wheeled my tray cart loaded full of instrument parts to the German women workers, I always stopped to chat. Some became very friendly and even confided their troubles to me. Some had sons in the service and worried constantly. One woman told me a story about children being indoctrinated to report their parents to the Gestapo if they did not follow a strict party line. The younger women mainly bemoaned the fact that there were no men around. There was a desperate boyfriend shortage just as Hans had explained so graphically. Suffering is also a relative thing; boyfriends versus survival.

My gregarious new mood especially extended to Hans, the supplier of my white bread sandwiches. I began to refer to him as Hansi, adding the "i" to his name as a token of my affection. At first it was accepted with great reservation, and when I dropped the usual respectful "Herr Ober" it was as if I practically dropped a bomb.

"Good evening, Hansi," I greeted him at the door during the usual ritual of hanging up his coat. He gave me a threatening look, and his eyebrows went up in injured indignation.

"It's 'Herr Ober' to you *Stucke,* don't you forget it!" I smiled sweetly and hung up his coat.

"My name is Zofia, Herr Ober." I reminded him, which did no good at all. He never once stooped so low as to call me by my name, and I never called him Herr Ober again. My daring familiarity escalated even further. When I was told as usual to look into his left pocket for the sandwich, I even ventured a joke.

"Hope you didn't forget the mustard and the pickles, Hansi..." He retaliated by putting both on a strawberry jam sandwich next time and I quickly became more respectful again.

I was now permitted to hang around and take my break, if possible, at the time of his visits, which became very routine. Occasionally the two men discussed politics and I was banished to the back room for the duration. I was very curious and usually tried to catch a word or two. It made Hansi very mad.

"Put your nosey *Stucke* to work Meissner," he growled. "Her ears are sticking straight up like a rabbit's!"

Meissner, nervous as the air raids made him, was very much improved; he did not have a crying spell for months. He told me much more about himself as time went by. He lived nearby with a family whose sons were off to war and whose house was now half empty. It was very convenient. He had the house all to himself during the days while every one else was at work.

Meissner was never a member of the Nazi Party until he was forced to join it under threat because of his work. "Eventually, it became no longer a matter of choice," he explained. He had an engineering degree and worked as a consultant for various manufacturing companies. His field of expertise was structural engineering and avionics. He did not go into details about that.

He was in Hamburg with his family during his summer vacation of 1943. They were discussing plans for his retirement which had already been postponed because of the war. Like everyone else, he was expected to help out at an air defense station.

Meissner begrudged missing time together with his wife. They were separated often due to his work. He left for the air station reluctantly that day but had no premonition of what was about to happen.

The Hamburg bombing was a retaliation for raids against London but it was also a devastating psychological blow. There were 40,000 dead and many wounded. Meissner's neighborhood was demolished during the first assault. It was in flames; he couldn't even get near his house. His wife's and niece's bodies were never found. There was nothing left. Meissner was dazed and sick from smoke inhalation. His world had collapsed. Nothing was left of his past, not even photographs and belongings. He later got some snapshots from a cousin.

The second wave of planes swooped down and finished the city off with incendiares. It was an inferno, a hurricane of wind and flames. The fires created a powerful draft as the air was sucked out by the flames. Sick as he was, he tried to help the wounded and then he became one also. He remembered only a searing pain and flaming debris and glass falling from above. He woke up in a hospital bandaged and unable to move. He didn't even want to recover. What for? Now he had no one. But he was a tough old guy and had made it inspite of the way he felt.

Afterwards, he found himself unable to function. He suffered blinding headaches, couldn't think clearly. But there were others worse off than himself. He decided to accept a position which required little stress or decision making. It was a part of the War Effort Program. For him, it was a rehabilitation of sorts. Work kept his mind off his losses. He suffered uncontrolable crying spells. It was an embarassment to him, but he could not help it at all. Well, I knew the rest very well.

Meissner was very close to his wife. They were happily married for forty-two years and her loss was devastating to him. But it was the accumulation of things which caused his melancholia, as he referred to his deep depression. These included ideological differences, an arrest at one time and the injuries.

His tongue loosened by a little bit of schnapps, he even told me about having been a member of the Opposition Party many years ago. Now, of course, it no longer existed at all. This was a politically unhealthy involvement and it almost had cost him his life.

Meissner never asked me much about myself. Like most depressed people, he was very inward oriented. I believe he talked about himself not because he liked to, but because he had to. He also confessed that whenever possible, he sneaked food to Russian prisoners of war when they delivered and unloaded the metal ingots to the warehouse. They were in terrible physical condition and Meissner felt guilty about the cruel and inhumane treatment they received in his beloved Germany. Meissner was a patriot but there were tears in his eyes as he spoke about it. He still had this problem of crying easily and I envied him, because he was able to cry.

He confessed that he owed it to me and to Hans that he now felt better, but on one subject he did not change his mind at all. He liked Hans, even felt affection for him, but trust him? No, never! I didn't understand his stubborn stand until later and it became a part of my education.

Hans noticed my notebook and dictionary on the shelf and immediately was very interested.

"Wonderful that *Stucke* is learning a little something," he noted. "Anyone this ugly needs to acquire some knowledge. . . Imagine having nothing in the front, nothing in the back and nothing in the head. A disaster of a person." But maybe still there was a glimmer of hope for me if I managed to put a little something into my head. In fact, it was a necessity considering my numerous short comings. He went on and on in his usual style.

In view of my pitiful prospects, Hans offered to bring me a book. "Knowing math will never do a *Stucke* any good anyway." We were all only slave labor, after all. What I needed was to learn what the world was all about since even a *Stucke* had to live in it. One had to acquire a little wisdom. Of course, he informed me grandly, that I could never dream of getting a degree from a learning institution even if there was no war. In his opinion I was definitely much too stupid for that.

I timidly expressed a mild difference of opinion. It was not wise to argue with someone who was the deliverer of white bread sandwiches, but somehow starting then we began to talk more to each other.

He avoided asking me any personal questions, except if I had a sister or a brother. I told him about Wladek being in Siberia. This brought a strong comment from Hansi. "Ah ha, then my brother was learning first hand about what subhuman barbarians the Russians actually are." Hans had an all consumming hatred for all Russians. He stated, with great satisfaction, that he had personally "done in" enough of them, as he put it, to make all the deportees to Siberia smile with happiness. At least he did his share to cleanse the world a little, and protect it from the Russian menace.

There was a hard glitter in his eyes as he spoke about it. He had lost his father on the Russian front, and part of his leg was left behind in Russian soil. He had to be bitter about that. Now I had a glimpse of the serious part of his nature. He was not really able to carry on with his clowning where the Russians were concerned. He was deadly serious, and "deadly" was the word for it. I had a small glimpse of what Herr Meissner meant.

It actually surprised Hansi that I could read and write, and even more that I liked ancient history and mythology. He found it amusing that I enjoyed poetry; "a *Stucke* had little use for that." But he grandly decided to indulge this foolishness and brought me a book. He made it a point to inform me that he was not about to offer me a college course.

He, of course, had his favorite subject. Did I know anything about the evolution of the species? Have I ever heard of Darwin? Now, here was a subject every one should be informed about, in fact, the more the better; even a lowly *Stucke* should be enlightened. The fate of the whole world depended upon this subject. The selective development of the species was the most crucial matter. Hansi practically delivered a sermon on the subject. It was the greatest cause; the fate of humanity hung in the balance. It was the greatest dream Germany had. More than that, it was a goal. If Germany failed, there was no other nation which could, at present, bring it to fruition. The world would be doomed!

According to Hansi, the world, the whole planet, was fragile and vulnerable to destruction; it was dependent on how men evolved. Like all creatures, humans evolved by selection. Primitive man had to be strong and healthy. The simple process of obtaining food and surviving the harshness of nature eliminated the weak and the imperfect.    Only the best matured to reproduce. There was natural selection at work, and nature had its way most of the time.

Even in recent history, only the strongest survived a war fought hand to hand with saber. Even those who had weak eyesight did not make it. Even eyesight became a part of selective evolution. Now men wore glasses and survived to propagate. Result: more and more children were sired with weak eyes. This was just a small example of more and more imperfect humans beings born to reproduce again. Eventually, most men will be "half-blind" and wear glasses.

Evolution became very complicated now, he explained, and could no longer be entrusted to nature alone. Overpopulation was another example. . . Imperfect babies survived to give birth eventually to even more imperfect ones. It became a terrible flaw in the evolution of the human species. Men had to be bred like horses or dogs to evolve the most perfect strains. "We could no longer afford to let the mongrelization of humans to run rampant," he said with conviction.

It might take centuries to have the selective breeding take effect, but it was already almost too late to start the process. An imperfect, overpopulated human race will eventually destroy itself and the planet. Even deer cannot survive overgrazing by ruining their habitat, and that is a simplistic example, he explained. Nature is ruthless and unyielding and men must learn its message and be equally ruthless. Eventually the race has to be completely streamlined and only the most superior should reproduce — the best, the most stable and the strongest and eventually out of those the most honest and beautiful. No infant who is not perfect should be permitted to live long enough to have the mother form an attachment and nurture it to adulthood.

Hansi envisioned an underpopulated world occupied by perfect Homo sapiens, as perfect as breeding could assure. The others — well, they could be made sterile and used as labor to construct cities to prepare the world for its perfect masters. It was a grand plan, so inspired that most people could not even grasp it. Of course, religion was an obstacle, the whole superstructure of nonsensical ideas that men were equal in the eyes of God. God was nature and nature abhorred imperfection.

"Just look around and see how unequal men really are," he scoffed. What about the stupid and the misshapen, were they equal? Yet it was the weak and the parasites, the dependent blood suckers who were having the most children, draining and burdening the good and the strong and limiting their reproduction. True, there will be a great outcry when the majority of people will find themselves phased out, but in five hundred years nobody will miss or even remember them. They will just be a historical phenomenon, an unfortunate phase of human evolution. Humanity must cleanse itself and if it does not do it now, then someday in the future nature will raise its angry hand and wipe it off the face of the earth. "What is a little blood leting to assure such a vital cause!"

Of course, Meissner and I had no comment. You don't argue with the Pope about religion. Hansi brought me a couple of books next time he came around. I was to read only the passages he underlined for me with yellow pencil because my German was not all that sophisticated. Hansi was now all business on the subject. He established a new and quite unnecessary rule: My sandwich now depended upon my having done my homework.

Actually, I read all the underlined passages and then some. If only my German were better! The evolution of the species theories were very fascinating to me. I was gaining a new freedom for my mind to roam. It was the first book I had held in my hand in years; since the Gzestochowa Ghetto. It was even better than white bread. It was food for the soul, for a starved mind.

I can hardly put into words the feeling it awakened in me. It was sadness for what might have been, a wistfulness.

It made me remember Uncle Stecki's attic and the books in our home when I was a little girl. The Darwinian theory was very logical, it surely made sense, it made me wonder if all the struggle for survival was just a microscopic part of "the evolution of the human species."

Neither Meissner nor I accepted Hansi's sermon, but we had to admit that in his own misguided and fanatical way, he was sort of an idealist.

Hansi, of course, did not let me keep the books. I had to return them to him when finished. I began to view him now as an old friend; someone who talked to me, no matter what the subject was. There was a tie developing between the three of us. He and Meissner were actually pretty close now and even saw each other on Sundays.

Hansi followed a routine and I thought him to be a creature of habit. He started his work day very early, got home at about 4 PM and strolled over the short distance to visit us at 8 PM, at least two or three times per week. He usually stayed an hour or two. For a man under the obligation to keep all the lonely ladies in Germany happy, it was remarkable that he so consistently afforded us his time.

He was an eccentric person, I thought, especially since Herr Meissner told me what he did in addition to his present occupation. Hansi was a cartoonist, and a good one at that. Occasionally he also did posters for the SS on a special assignment basis.

Meissner said that Hansi got restless spending an evening at the drawing table. He needed to get away and refresh himself. We were easy to visit and he did not have to make an appointment or stay very long. Besides, in his own way, he liked us. I hoped that he would continue to do so. It always worried me that he would become engaged or married, would not come back again one day, and neither would my sandwich in his pocket. I knew I would miss him very much and no matter how much he denied it, so would Meissner.

Evolution. Now that I knew all about it, how did it apply to me? I was evolving too, growing up. I would be fifteen next year. But what would become of me when I grew up? The book was a painful reminder that I had missed school for so long... Where would third grade grammar school education get me when the war was over, no matter who won? But how could I even worry about such trifles, did I really feel safe? I had a painful reminder about the realities.

I went to the dining room one midnight shift to get my bowl of soup. There was no line at all during night shift servings. We ate on our side, at a long table. On the other side of the dining room sat the Germans.

Suddenly, there was a tap on my shoulder, and I almost fainted. There was Otto, my nemesis, a broad smile on his unpleasant face. "How are you?" What a question for him to ask!

"I am fine. . ." I spluttered.

"Glad to see that you are still with us. Decided against going over the hill again, ha?"

"I like it here very well," I assured him. He nodded approvingly.

"You will give my regards to Herr Ober Von Ulrecht, will you?" Now I didn't know what to say. Otto waited. . .

"Sure," I said. Anything to get away from this man.   The palms of my hands began to sweat. "Sure, I will give him your regards. . ."

"That means you will see him soon?" Otto stood his ground.

"I am not sure. . ." I stuttered.

"See you around," he said smiling broadly like an old acquaintance.

If I needed a jolt of reality, I received it alright. . . and here I worried about education! I fretted until I saw Hansi again, that I might have said something wrong. But when I finished telling him about the meeting he burst out laughing.

"You said exactly the right thing to him, *Stucke.* Now that he thinks you have contact with me, he will do anything for you. The jerk will shine your shoes. You are safe from now on as far as he is concerned."

"But why?"

"Because Otto spends all his time and energy collecting favors. If he will be nice to you, he will have a 'favor point' with me, it's that simple. He thinks that once he has collected enough 'favor points' with people or enough information about them, he will get places. He is right in a way. He knows he is too stupid to make it any other way."

"Hansi, is that how you you got me. . ." I knew it was a taboo subject.

"A *Stucke* does not mean anything," Hansi reassured me. "Once I told him my friend preferred to keep you working for him, it was all done. . . The easiest 'favor point' he ever got. Nobody really cares about a skinny *Stucke* like you. . . Unless, of course, you cannot work. . ."

"But why did he want to know if I ever saw you?"

"Just nosey," Hansi shrugged his shoulders. "Always fishing to see if he could discover some new information about anyone, or get some goods on you, that's how he is."

"You seem to know him well Hansi. . ." He gave me a surprised look at having asked such a stupid question. . .

"Sure, Otto is a very good man when you need something done. He knows how to follow an order alright. Just another way he accumulates his 'favor points'. Yes, he has done things for me; always writes the longest, most detailed report. In some respects he is a very good man."

Funny after all this time I learned to ignore Hansi's insignia. He still was an SS with a death head on his cap, just like the label on a box of rat poison, — cross bones and all; very depressing.

Still, in spite of everything, time passed and I was growing up. I was leaving my childhood behind me. I remember this time of transition:

## RECOLLECTION

*For almost a year, my back ache still lingers on. It is not as bad as before, but if I move suddenly, I feel a sharp pain. I still have trouble getting out of bed after spending a few hours in one position. It is cold again and I have been coughing constantly. I have lost weight again. Meissner and Hansi are concerned. There is practically an epidemic of tuberculosis, especially in the Polish barracks. They arrange another trip to town for me to see a doctor this time. Again on a Sunday I am accompanied by the both of them to a small medical clinic.*

*Herr Doctor turns out to be a very pleasant man who came in especially to examine me. He has an x-ray machine and lots of up to date equipment. He does not think that I have tuberculosis, but tells me that I might need to come back. Until then I am to take fish oil daily. He brings out a bottle of it and gives it to me.*

*Hansi pays for the visit but not for the fish oil, he does not believe in its beneficial effects. Herr Meissner has to pay for that. Now, if it was schnapps, Hansi would be willing to pay. He opens it up and takes a swig, then spits it out. None of his good money will be spent on such a stinking concoction. However, since the doctor ordered it and the visit was paid for, I am to follow orders and take my medicine. Meissner keeps it on his shelf so I do not have a chance to cheat.*

*As for my cough, it would help if I had a sweater to keep me warm. I suggest that I could crochet one easily enough, but I needed the needle and the yarn. Hansi volunteers to supply both.*

*The following week he brings a paper bag. I am overjoyed until I see the yarn. It is yellow. Yellow is the color of the Jewish Star I had to wear in the Ghetto. Yellow is conspicuous, I am allergic to anything which makes me stand out in a crowd. It is almost a reflex gut feeling. The words pop out of my mouth before I have a chance to think. "I don't like it!"*

*Hansi gives me an angry look. "You what. . .? The* Stucke *has a lot of nerve. . . I picked the yarn out myself. It is very pretty," he complains to Meissner. "It matches her freckles." But I still look unhappy about that yarn. Hansi puts it back into the paper bag and stalks out without a word, not even a goodbye to Meissner. I am very depressed over it, especially since he does not return for days.*

*"What if we never see him again?" I wail to Meissner.*

*He shakes his head. "We couldn't be that lucky!" But I miss him and keep watching the door every day at eight. Finally, he visits again and appears to be in the best of moods. There is a paper bag in his hand. I promise myself never to complain again. Yes, I will crochet a yellow sweater! But there is no yarn; this time, instead, there is a sweater inside the bag. It is brown and hand knitted.*

*"I want you to know before you start complaining that it is too large," he warns me, "it will keep you warm and I did not have to shop for it. I stole it from Hedwig." Meissner bursts out laughing, a rare sound to come from him.*

*"She is still looking for it," continues Hansi. "She will, of course, never find it unless she comes here to join us."*

*I wear that sweater all winter and it is much too large. Hedwig must be a proper woman; well rounded. It keeps me warm, but I find myself hating this Hedwig. I am jealous! It must be fun to date a man like Hansi who can be so funny. What if they get married. . . Hedwig will end up with Hansi and I with her sweater. I confide it to Meissner who gives me a look of utter disgust.*

*"Stucke, you must have lost your mind, you cannot mean it!" But I do, and Meissner is the only person I can discuss it with. Hansi has been very nice to me. Maybe, is it possible, that he likes me because I am a girl!*

*Meissner has no problem answering this question. "Not a chance," he states flatly. But I do not want to give up. "Then why is he so nice to me?" I plead. "There must be a reason why!"*

*Meissner is doing his best to set me straight. "Lets put it this way; you are his pet canary. It is not because of anything else. People can be very nice to a pet canary, treat it very well. Now wear the sweater, keep youself warm, and stop this nonsense!"*

*But it's easier said than done. I am still hoping that Meissner is wrong. I catch an opportunity when Meissner is out of earshot, and confront Hansi. It might be the only chance I will ever have, and next time I will surely not have the nerve.*

*"Hansi," I say flippantly, but I am actually very nervous. "Can I come to your apartment one day and clean it for you?"*

*He sits down theatrically as if I pinched him.*

*"You want to be my* Putzfrau *(cleaning lady)? You must take me for a fool! You cannot be trusted. You would burglarize my apartment. I would have to nail my socks to the wall and lock my closet, considering how you burglarized poor Meissner. Besides I don't need a* Putzfrau. *Women pay me to have an opportunity to clean my apartment. Hedwig would do it with a toothbrush if I let her, just so she could have a chance to sniff my bed linens to see if anyone else was there lately. . ." He goes on and on. "Besides, how do you get such a silly notion?"*

*I try to make it into a joke but it comes out half baked. "You have so many girlfriends, Hansi, so maybe I too. . ."*

*He does not let me finish, gives me an incredulous look, then seems down right insulted.*

*"What did you say? This calls for a special action. Meissner!" he bellows on top of his voice. Meissner comes out of the back, tools in hand, looking alarmed.*

*"Let me tell you Meissner, what the* Stucke *just said. She wants to be my girlfriend! Now tell me, how do I look to you? Don't I look like a man?" He flexes his muscles. "And then look at the* Stucke. *She looks like a stick. Nothing up front, nothing in the back and nothing in her head. Can you imagine anything so ridiculous! And look at that face. Ugh! Nothing but splatters of freckles. . . The nerve!"*

*I am so embarrassed! If only the lights would go out, an air raid come. . .*

*"Just imagine," continues Hansi, "me taking a skinny* Stucke *out on a date." He shakes his head. "To a movie?. . . To a party?. . . Now where could I take her!"*

Meissner comes to my rescue. "There is a machine in the back that needs some attention." I practically run into the welcome darkness in the back of the room and stay there until Meissner joins me later on.

"You are really out of your mind," he admonishes me. "You don't know how foolish you are, asking for trouble."

The night drags on endlessly, and I have nothing to say. I have been warned. There is no air raid that night, no bombs fall, but I surely wish they would. My spirits are very low for the rest of the week. I do not dare show my face next time Hans comes around and surely do not want to see his.

Meissner brings my sandwich to me. Oh well, might as well be practical, so I take it. It is neatly wrapped in white paper and something is written on it: "Girlfriend No: Three." Meissner has a warped sense of humor. He actually thinks this is funny. I hate Hansi for weeks after that but then decide to dismiss the whole thing from my mind.

There are now air raids very often and we are very tired. The British come at night and Americans during the day. We get very little rest or sleep. Hansi came along to our air raid shelter which is only a reinforced tunnel which shakes and threatens to collapse just from the concussion of nearby explosions. We hear the roar of an engine and a shrill whine. We know by now that when we hear it, then it falls somewhere else. People are hysterical. The lights go out. It is pitch black and noisy. The planes roar overhead at different frequencies. Flak and explosions.

Hansi walks back with me and we find Herr Meissner stone drunk. It must be very hard for him. The war cannot last much longer. . . There is a food shortage and our soup is thinner than ever. I feel very cheerful again. A good bombing does wonders for my state of mind.

We have a temporary shortage of ingots and spend our time cleaning the silent machines. We welcome Hansi and sit around talking. Now I decide to give him a dig.

"Herr Meissner tells me that you draw cartoons when Hedwig gives you a day off. . . I cannnot imagine how anyone with fingers like these could even hold a pencil. . ."

"What's wrong with my fingers?"

"They look like knockwursts," I say boldly. He laughs.

"The Stucke is learning, picking up bad habits, I knew this would happen sooner or later. All right, I will bring you some of my work so you can see for yourself."

He comes back the next day with a folder full of comic strips. "Actually, you both are the main characters of these masterpieces," he tells us and spreads the sheets of paper on Meissner's work table under a light.

*The first is about Meissner, and he is quite recognizable. His white hair is twice as bushy and the lines of his face exaggerated. He is sitting in his chair and huge teardrops splash all around him.*

*The next scene is of Meissner blowing his nose, then the handkerchief gets all soaked up with tears and he squeezes it dry making a huge puddle.*

*Next, Meissner washes his handkerchief in the accumulated tears.*

*Next, there is a light bulb glowing above his head indicating that he got a great idea. He is now washing his socks in his tears, and there is a caption: "It works."*

*Next, there is a storefront with a smiling face of Meissner in the window and a caption: "All natural resources must be utilized in Time of War." Above the store there is a sign, "Laundry done in soft water."*

*Next, there is Meissner again scrubbing coveralls on a washboard, the tears splashing out of his eyes and overflowing the tub. There is a caption: "Business Could Not Be Better." There is a line of ladies with laundry baskets and money in hand waiting their turn. The sketches are simple but very good and comical. Meissner gives me a look of sheer disgust but he is laughing.*

*Next, there is a picture of a rabbit like creature done in a Walt Disney-style. The rabbit has a face that is somehow familiar. It has long eyelashes and freckles. It is a caricature of me. The rabbit is holding a half eaten gigantic sandwich.*

*Next is a picture of the rabbit (me) again, sandwich in hand, walking in front of a firing squad; bullets flying all around.*

*Next, the rabbit is still there but the sandwich is full of holes. The rabbit has a big smile on its face and a caption, "I made it!"*

*Next, the rabbit walks right through a guillotine. There is a mean looking figure behind it dropping the huge blade shut.*

*Next, the rabbit makes it, almost losing its tail. There is a caption "Ouch, this was close!" The rabbit examines its tail to make sure it is still there and still has the sandwich full of holes in its paw.*

*Next, there is a drawing of Hansi sitting at his desk wearing his hat and coat with all the insignia. It is a very elaborate sketch and a very funny caricature of Hansi. It is possible to recognize his face.*

*Next, the same drawing only the rabbit is in front of the desk. It now has a bucket, mops and brooms. There is a caption "Can I be your Putzfrau?"*

*Next, there is the same drawing of Hansi at his desk, only his hat had flown straight up in the air as if he was frightened out of his wits. His hair is standing on end. There is a caption above "Mama, help me!"*

*Only the profile of the rabbit is visible; turned up nose with freckles and long lashes. It is very funny!*

*Meissner is practically choking with laughter. Something strange is happening to me! I begin to giggle. It sounds terrible, I am making a whizzing, hysterical sound. I realize that it is the first time in four years that I am laughing out loud. I cannot stop and cannot catch my breath. I am laughing and shaking and laughing. I am getting hiccups. Tears are running simultaneously down my cheeks. Not one tear in four years, but now I am laughing and the tears are rolling down my face. I experience an attack of full blown hysteria, I am a strange spectacle.*

*Meissner slaps my back, he thinks that I might be choking. I cannot even see. My eyeballs hurt terribly. The tear ducts that have not worked in years are now functioning overtime. Ashamed, I stumble away to the back of the room and lean over a machine, making wheezing noises, completely unable to gain control of myself for a while. Then it all subsides and I feel so weak I have to sit down on the floor. I see Hansi coming around in the dim light of the machines and pull myself up. What a shameful spectacle I have made of myself!*

*"Shit," he says, "nobody ever reacted this way to my cartoons before. Are you all right now?" I give him a weak smile.*

*"It is alright for you to laugh Stucke, I am very happy that my cartoons made you laugh. . . I am very glad. And, it is all right for you to cry. Sometimes it happens. . ." I refuse to leave the back of the room and after a while Meissner comes.*

*"Hans already left," he tells me. "Now what ever got into you? You are as bad as I am. . . all those tears!" He gives me a small sip of schnapps out of his flask. "Here, this should settle your nerves. It must be all the strain of the air raids. . ."*

*Again there is the wail of sirens, the slow kind, which means only an alert. It is only when the sound goes up and down frantically that a direct overflight is expected. We have time to walk to the shelter leisurely. Meissner fortifies himself with a quick drink just in case it might be the real thing. The night air feels cool on my face. Somehow, I feel good, better than I felt in years. There is a certain calm inside me as if a terrible pressure which had accumulated for so very long had lifted.*

# 23

# HAPPY BIRTHDAY

It was late fall of 1944. There was a shortage of ingots and we had a lot of free time on our hands. The mammoth machines were often idle. Since we sat around so much, an extra chair was obtained especially for me. We now had three chairs, one for Meissner, one for Hansi and one for me. It made me feel very official.

Hansi's visits have grown longer and one evening he and Meissner played chess for four hours straight. But this was a rare occasion. The bombings continued, fiercer than ever and Meissner's nerves suffered accordingly. He has been drinking a lot of schnapps to calm himself, which inevitably put him to sleep and rendered him hardly functional.

I even suggested that I could also try playing a game of chess, much to Hansi's indignation. He stayed insulted for days. The air raids now became almost a background to our daily lives bringing an awareness that the great machine of war was grinding inexorably ahead. The Germans whispered to each other about which city got it last night, how close to us, and how badly.

In December, Hansi informed me that in a few days it will be Meissner's birthday. He had lost his treasured collection of books in the Hamburg bombing and Hansi had a fine set of history volumes all wrapped up as a surprise present.

"Same stuff my father liked to read. . ." he said.

Now if only I also had something to give old Meissner... I thought it over and decided that I did. I had the silver crucifix Father Krzeminski gave me. There was not much choice, it was all I had. I announced grandly that I also had a present for Meissner.

"You?" said Hansi scornfully. "How could a *Stucke* come up with a present?"

"Well, you will wait and see. . ." It really bothered Hansi and for days he made a determined effort to find out what it was. He reasoned with me that after all, he had told me what his present was. He threatened to discontinue my sandwiches. He even threatened to turn me over to Otto or shoot me personally, but I held my ground. It was a surprise. . .

I obtained some special wrapping paper from Frau Koenig and brought it with me on the eve of the occasion. Hansi was there already and his present was on the table. Then I also unobtrusively placed my small package next to his. Hansi's eyes were bulging with curiosity.

Meissner arrived and we sang a "happy birthday" tune to him. He was very touched; did not expect anyone to celebrate it and immediately wanted to know how we discovered the date.

"Your file is in a cabinet at the security building," Hansi reminded him.

Meissner's eyes became very red when he saw the books. Then he opened my package and held up the antique crucifix on a silver chain. He was unable to say a word and quite predictably sat down in his chair and began to cry.

"Now see what you did?" said Hansi reproachfully. "It is going to cost me in the long run, because it is I who usually have to supply the schnapps. It will take a liter of it to dry him up this time."

At long last Meissner regained his speech. He read Hansi's card but I did not have one. Instead, I wrote on the wrapping: "With all my love to Herr Meissner." This produced more tears and Hansi indeed had to produce his flask. Even I received a swig of schnapps.

"It feels like I now have a family," said Herr Meissner emotionally. Hansi fixed me with an indignant look.

"I always choose my relatives very carefully; especially when it comes to females," he drawled.

I thought that it was the funniest thing I have ever heard and influenced by the alcohol, began to giggle. I was so loud that Meissner started the machines just to drown me out. We did not have any ingots that day and it was too quiet; but not for long.

As if on cue, the sirens came on wailing insistantly. It was against the rules but we decided to stay where we were instead of going down to the bunker.

It was a very cold evening. Hansi passed the flask around again and as soon as everyone else had left the floor, began to sing at the top of his voice with me joining right in. The lights went off and we were in the dark except for the glare from the search lights and bursts of flak. We opened the side window which was also against the rules. We could plainly hear the planes rumble overhead, and soon the explosions practically shook the walls. The flask went around faster and faster. All of a sudden, there was a terrific concussion and the smoke began to drift through the open window.

"Shit!" yelled Hansi. "The damned pigs scored a hit, I think, in some part of the complex. We better get out of here." But Meissner was out cold. Hansi leaned out of the window to look and decided that it was our warehouse.

The all clear sounded and the lights went on again. Meissner began to revive. He was not really all that drunk but fainted from sheer fright. Hansi got ready to leave and check out the damage.

"Now when is your birthday?" I asked him before he left.

"I am not stupid enough to tell you," he growled. "You might come up with another crucifix and if it touched my hand it would melt and go up in smoke. . . We have enough explosions going off here as it is."

Meissner and I sat around and talked for a while. "Germany is losing the war," he confessed for the first time to me. "And I feel sorrow to see my country lose it. If only we had hung onto our Jews, we would have been victorious. . ."

I felt a pang of fear. Was he questioning anything about me? But Meissner continued talking as if mostly to himself:

"Do you know, Zofia, what we used to call physics in Germany? We used to refer to it as *Judenfizik* (Jew physics). My best science professors were Jews. If we only kept our Jews, we would have developed our new weapons years ago. . . and now we are on the very brink of having rockets and jet engines but it is too late. What irony! The best of them ran away to America where they are working on the "super bomb". Ah, Zofia, I should know, I have spent most of my life around such research. And now, just look at me! I am just a shell of a man. My mind is just a shadow of its old self. The Jews were a catalyst. They seeded new ideas and with the German organizational know-how, we would have had such power! You probably never even heard of a man named Einstein, did you?"

No I never did, I told him. People have a tendency to become regretful on their birthdays, and think of what might have been.

"The course of history sometimes can be changed by such obscure things," he continued. "A missed phone call, one small decision, or being somewhere at the wrong time.

Everything depends on a whim of fate. . . the course of a human life or the course of history. They are all intertwined; even evolution. A chance meeting between two people produces a child who becomes a pivotal person and grows up to affect the lives of millions. When one grows old, it is all so clear. . ."

I wondered if he was referring to Hitler. I have never heard Meissner so philosophical, but then he had a very traumatic birthday. What he said, however, stuck in my mind and I discussed it with Marushka, the physician. She, too, was now thinking about the future and confessed to me that she wished it were possible for her not to return to Russia.

There were other Russian girls who felt the same way, and were actually afraid to go home. Now that they have been exposed to the outside world, they would present a threat to their own government. They knew too much, might ask too many questions and realize how bad life in Russia really was. This might mean being sent to Siberia. A closed society fears the light of day. I was astounded at what I heard. If it did not come from Marushka, whom I respected, it would be unbelievable.

It was winter time again, another year went by. But it was more than that. I, too, would have another birthday.

Of course, I did not expect to celebrate it, but to me it was a personal victory achieved against astronomical odds. I knew I was one of very few Jewish children who lived to experience growing older. I remember this moment in time:

### RECOLLECTION

*Hansi is scheduled to leave for several weeks and stops by to say goodbye, dressed in his official black uniform of the SS. He tells us that in his absence Otto will assume his duties and will bring Herr Meissner some schnapps. "Now, Stucke," he tells me, "if you need something, just ask Otto. . ."*

*"That devil?" I ask in amazement. Hansi laughs.*

*"If the devil can provide, ask the devil, unless, of course, God is available."*

*I would not ask Otto for anything under any circumstances, but this cynical advice sticks in my mind forever. It makes me feel very uneasy. I am learning very complicated concepts, very disturbing to me.*

*Hansi returns around Christmas time and brings us gingerbread cookies. He visited his mother while away and came back loaded with* goodies. Our ingot supply is spotty and some evenings we sit idly around the silent machines and talk. There is a certain expectant tension in the air. I have told Meissner that I have an uncle in America.

"Ah, America!" He has been there. In fact, he had lived in Boston for a short time. His wife couldn't get used to it, but Meissner liked Boston very much. He tells me all about it and describes the food. People drink orange juice in America! I can hardly believe that such a luxury is possible.

Meissner thinks that I should go back to Poland. "You would miss your homeland," he tells me naively, but it would be nice to visit your uncle; very educational. Of course, he knows nothing about me.

He mentions it briefly to Hansi during his next visit and we get an unexpected reaction. Hansi's eyebrows go way up.

"America?" he says contemptuously. "Stucke," you must stay away from that horrible place! America lacks civilization. It is a country without a future."

According to Hansi, America has an infantile mentality. It is a mongrelized country. Imagine such a calamity as having a large part of its population being black. In time, it will become a racial disaster. The blacks will lose their ethnic character and will become inferior blacks. Then the whites will lose what little purity they still have, through inevitable intermarriages. "America is the country of striped people," in his opinion. "Stucke, it would be the worst place for you to go!"

In America, he tells me, I will be totally lost. Nobody would ever understand or accept me. Americans are conceited people who do not understand how inferior they really are. In fact, in Hans' opinion, I should remain in Germany, the most superior country in the world. Germany is the only hope for mankind. Even if it loses this war, it will not matter. Germany could lose many wars and still win in the end. The Americans will come begging on their knees for the Germans to rescue them from the "Bolshevik menace" because only Germany can offer them salvation, according to Hans.

No, I should never go to America, if I am smart. In fact, he tells me quite seriously, I could go to stay with his mother. She is all alone now and very depressed. I would be very good for her and the house is big enough to accommodate me. He had already discussed this possibility with his mother and she would like it very much. It is all set. If I like Meissner, then I would love his mother because she is just like him, only she also bakes cookies. She would make a lady out of me; teach me some culture...

After he leaves, Meissner and I stare at each other in disbelief. "Hansi is always joking. . ." I say finally. But Meissner shakes his head. "God help us," he says. "The man was actually serious."

*In February I live to see another birthday. To my surprise, we have a small celebration because Hansi also has my file. He is under the impression that I am eighteen years old, which is not nearly the truth, but, of course, he only knows what is written in my file. Meissner has a blouse for me and Hansi arrives with a small package and his face is full of smiles.*

*"Meissner," he says, "now the shit will hit the fan. The Stucke is a woman now, which means nothing but trouble. Now nobody is safe around here any longer. We will have to fear for our lives and I cannot run fast enough, because I have only one foot, and you, Meissner, are too old to run. . ."*

*He unwraps the package he brought for me and inside it is a powder compact and a lipstick. I am told to sit up in a chair and Hansi begins to powder my face. He is putting lots of it on and keeps chatting away.*

*"I should have really gotten some paint to do the job properly. An ugly face like this has to be camouflaged so the men will not be able to see how terrible it is. Otherwise, the Stucke will never find herself a husband. Nobody would marry her if they saw what she really looks like."*

*Then the lipstick comes out and Hansi dabs it on and puts a final dab on my nose.*

*"Done by an artist!" he says and puts the lipstick away.*

*Meissner is doubled up with laughter, but then he runs frantically and gets a wet rag to wash my face. "What if the engineer comes here now and sees her," he frets as he wipes the make up from my face. It comes off but the red dab on my nose is very stubborn.*

*I experience very mixed emotions. It is the first time in so many years that anyone has remembered my birthday or celebrated it. It fills me with bottomless sadness and soon my eyes are as red as my nose.*

*We all have a drink and I am grateful that today we have ingots and I have an excuse to go into the back of the room where it is dark and I can work. I cannot talk and wish there would be an air raid. As usual, the sirens start up and Hansi leaves, but we do not have a direct overflight.*

In the meantime, history rolled ahead. In January of 1944, the Russians retook Kirovogorad on the 8th, and on the 15th the Allies renewed their advance to the Rapido River in Italy. On the 12th of January, the Russians took Sarny and on the 14th began the Leningrad offensive. On the 20th, they retook Novogorod and on the 27th, the Leningrad Blockade was ended.

On the 22nd, in Italy, the Allies began landing in Anzio. The Germans tenaciously counterattacked on February the 3rd. The U.S. Air Force pounded Germany during the "Big Week" from the 20th to the 25th. On the 12th, the Allied advance was halted at Cassino, Italy and the Monte Cassino Monastery was bombed. A vicious battle raged at Anzio from the 16th through the 29th, and continued through March when the Germans repulsed another attack on the Cassino.

The Russians kept rolling ahead taking Mikopol, Staria Russia and Krivoi Rog in February and starting the Ukraine Offensive on March 4th, 1944. On the 15th, they crossed Bug River and the Dniester River, approaching Tarnopol on the 23rd.

Hitler raged furiously, firing his best Generals; both Manstein and von Kleist. But as the spring progressed, the Russians kept on going like a steam roller. On the first of April, they entered Rumania. On the 10th, they took Odessa, on the 15th Ternopol, and Yalta on the 16th. They took Sevastopol on May 9th.

In Italy, on May 11th, the Allies attacked the Gustav line in their drive for Rome. On the 18th, they finally captured Cassino. On June 4th, the Fifth Army took Rome and headed for the Arno and on the 6th of June, 1944, on D-Day, Allied Forces landed in France on the coast of Normandy. It was called Operation "Overlord." On the 27th, Cherbourg was captured. They continued their drive in July to Caen on the 8th, to Saint-Lo on the 18th and to Avranches on the 30th.

In August, General Patton broke through into Brittany. On the 14th, the Allies landed on the Riviera in Southern France and liberated Paris on the 25th of August. Toulon and Marseille were captured on the 28th and Lyon on September 3rd. On the 5th, they reached Brussels. On the 10th, the U.S. First Army captured Luxembourg. The Airbone forces landed in Holland, near Arnhem and Nijmegen.

In October, rolling towards Germany itself, the First Army captured Aachen on the 21st. In November, the Americans entered Metz, France, close to the German border and Strassbourg on the 23rd. In January of 1945, Americans took St. Vith, Belgium and in February, the Rhineland Campagin had begun.

On March 2nd, 1945, the Americans rolled into Germany taking the Remagen bridge and Bonn on the 9th.

Now Germany was wide open and Hitler has been impotently replacing his Generals and watching his conquered empire shrink like melting snow. On the 8th of September, 1944, his first V-2 Rockets had fallen on England. A year earlier they could have been decisive, but now it was too late.

Germany had the first jet plane in the air, but there was not enough time left to use it with success. Too late now for the "new weapons." Victory, almost within Hitler's grasp, had now slipped out of his reach forever. And from the east, the dreaded Soviet army roared towards the German border like an unstoppable red tide.

On the 27th of July, 1944, the Russians took the Polish city of Lwow. On August 1st, the Polish Resistance revolted in Warsaw and the Russians stopped at the Vistula River for long enough to see the Germans completely suppress the Poles on the 2nd of October. They satisfied themselves in the interim with taking Bucharest, Rumania on September 1st, and invading Bulgaria on the 7th.

On October 18th, they attacked East Prussia, Germany, and on the 20th captured Belgrade, Yugoslavia. On November 24th, they crossed the Danube River near Bucharest and on January 2nd, 1945, Budapest was taken. The offensive in Poland continued and the Oder River near Kustrin was crossed.

On January 10th, 1945, the Russians reached my home town, Praszka, and Stalin personally made the announcement because it was on the German border. On the 7th of April, the Russians entered Vienna, Austria. On March the 27th, in a last gasp effort of the Nazi Collossus, the last German V-2 Rocket fell upon England. On April 17th, the Soviets began the Berlin offensive and encircled the city on the 27th, 1945.

On the 11th of April, the Allies reached Magdeburg at the river Elbe near the small town of Shoenebeck-Elbe, where I once toiled on a farm and had almost lost my life.

The shadow of the Swastika lifted at last off Europe, revealing the ravages of war and yielding its dreadful secrets. Six million Jews had been murdered across Europe in places like Auschwitz, Maidanek, Treblinka and the huge mass grave pits in the Ukraine.

A balmy breeze bore upon its wings the spring of 1945, a spring which so very many did not live to see. The planet Earth, hopefully turned its bloodied face towards the sun once again, as it spun through the cold darkness of space.

# 24

# FREEDOM

It was the sixth year of war, winter passed and there was a promise of yet another spring in the air. Could it really be that the war will be over? It was almost impossible to believe or imagine such a momentous happening. The girls discussed it in whispers and wondered how it would come about.

Strangely, I was afraid. Peace was such an unknown dimension to me and instead of being happy, I was depressed at the thought. There was a sadness in my heart for all those who did not make it. I had no hope that my parents had survived but no absolute certainty either. We did not know about the death camps or the gas chambers yet. The war had not yet yielded its terrible secrets. I dreamed repeatedly that suddenly my mother or father was there and we had so much to tell each other. There was an element of a blissfully happy surprise to those dreams, but just beneath it lurked anxiety. There was always an obstacle to our being able to stay together. My parents appeared but somehow I could not hold on to them and woke up feeling a bottomless emptiness.

Life in the camp retained its usual routine. We still received a supply of ingots for our machines, but it became spotty and we found ourselves often being idle. We just sat around and talked.

It was shortly after my birthday that I saw Hansi for the last time. The Russian prisoners of war were being evacuated and he came around to say good bye. He was not at all upset at the prospect; was actually cheerful. He left Herr Meissner a generous supply of schnapps to tide him over the ceaseless bombings.

"Well, you old fart," he drawled, "I'll see you again for a game of chess after this mess is over and done with — provided your brain is not pickled in alcohol by then."

They slapped each other on the shoulders.

"It is a fine time to leave," Hansi continued, "so I can get Hedwig off my back. She has been trying to snag me and I cannot stand her any longer. . . You know how women are."

"Hansi, aren't you worried about what will happen to you since you are with the SS?" I wanted to know.

"Worried? I never worry about anything. Never have before and am too old to change," he shrugged. "I would like to do cartooning full time anyway. It pays better and it is a lot more fun. Of course, the dumb Americans will probably try to recruit us to help them fight the Russians before long. They will need us, you know, will not be able to do it by themselves and we have the knowhow."

He laughed. "But I am not about to work for the damned 'Striped People'. They had their chance but have botched it up. Let them go it alone and see how they like it! By the way, it is you, *Stucke*, I am concerned about."

Hansi took a bunch of gold coins out of his pocket and casually handed them over to me.

"I want you to sew these into your clothes," he continued. "And do not let anyone see you do it, or they will take them away from you. You should exchange one of them for a gun as soon as possible. Without us being here to inforce law and order, there will be pure anarchy. Nobody will be safe any longer. And do not let anybody even get close to you; use it! If you need to shoot, never, never aim for the head, it is too small a target for someone without experience. Always aim for the chest or the stomach and pull the trigger at least twice. . ."

Meissner and I sat back and listened quietly much out of habit. We knew better than to argue with Hansi; he knew it all. Then, unexpectedly, he sent Meissner away so we two could have a private talk. I was mystified. He pulled over my chair and made me sit beside him.

"*Stucke*," he said, "I have to tell you something that is very serious. You must never, under any circumstances, return back to Poland! There are *no Jews* left in Poland, take my word for it. I know for sure. Poland is Jew-free."

I almost felt faint. The fear of being discovered had become a part of my person. I was terrified even though it was almost the end of the war. I was confronted by a man wearing the uniform of an SS officer. I cringed.

"Hansi. . ." I stuttered, "what ever makes you think that I am Jewish!"

"It's the way you speak German, *Stucke*. From time to time a Yiddish word slipped in. Now Meissner would never have spotted it. He is too stupid, but I have experience," he said matter-of-fact-ly.

We sat for a while just staring at each other. I was quite speechless. He knew about me all along!

"Now," he said, "you will have to find your way to my mother's house. It is all set. You will be very good for her to have around, just like you were for Meissner. And *Stucke*, you are not at all ugly. In fact, you are very pretty. But it will do you no good. It will only cause you trouble because you are all messed up psychologically, even worse than Meissner. You have a lot of problems. And whatever you do, forget about going to the country of the 'Striped People'. You could never make it there, you would never, never fit in."

He glanced impatiently at his watch. It was time to go. We stood up and Hansi hugged me and kissed my forehead. I felt dizzy and all choked up. I was unable to say a single word. I knew that I would never see him again.

He made me memorize his mother's address, then he called Meissner. We followed him to the door and he was gone. Only then did I feel tears running down my face. Meissner offered me a swig of schnapps. We sat silently together and the place seemed very empty. We knew that we would miss him. For me this was still another good bye. Finally Meissner broke the silence.

"Zofia, you must realize a few things about Hans. He is actual-ly a very bad person. It is hard to reconcile because he can also be very nice and pleasant. He somehow had a need for us and we for him. But you must never lose sight of the fact that Hans has an ugly side to his character. He represents evil, he has blood on his hands, believe me. . . I know a lot of things you could not even imagine."

Little did Meissner know how very well I could imagine. But I said nothing at all. I missed Hansi already and it made me feel very guilty. Of course, I could never go to his mother's house, but I hurt inside and knew that I would miss him for a very, very long time, maybe for years. Another friend was gone forever.

It was good that Meissner had an ample supply of schnapps because the bombings had accelerated. The planes came at any time of day and night, unannounced by air raid sirens which no longer functioned.

In April of 1945, work at the plant ceased altogether. The guards disappeared and Frau Koenig packed up and left without even saying good bye. The doors to the factory were locked shut, except for the kitchen, and everybody was milling around in confusion. Eventually, it became too dangerous to stay within the complex and we all took refuge in nearby woods. There was no food. The Dutch men joined us there and suggested that we hide in caves to avoid straffing. But first we needed to eat.

Adela and I volunteered to go back to the factory where in the kitchen were still some stocks of turnips and potatoes. It was a beautiful spring day and temporarily quiet, though we could hear a rumble of guns in a distance. We strolled leisurely down the empty street, there was not a soul to be seen. We ran up the stairs to the kitchen and filled two sacks with potatoes giggling foolishly all the time. It all seemed exciting and unreal.

Suddenly the planes arrived with a roar and swooped down upon us. Bombs were exploding everywhere. The kitchen shook as if it were hit by an earthquake. The potatoes cascaded upon us as the bin broke loose. We grabbed our bags and ran into the street. Bombs fell all around us churning up dense dust and smoke. Shrapnell flew through the air. Suddenly there were deep craters we had to skirt around. Within minutes it was quiet again.

Strangely, it never occured to us to ever hit the ground. We just hung onto our potatoes and ran until we were out of breath. Then we looked at each other in amazement. Our faces were grimy and we were covered with dust and pulverized plaster. There was destruction everywhere, but we were unhurt. We giggled as if we were drunk.

"Can you imagine getting killed on the last day of the war for a bag of potatoes!" I exclaimed.

And it was, for us, the last day of the war! We spent the night in a cave and in the morning we heard the rumble of tanks. They suddenly appeared from behind the trees, olive green, bearing a white star. We ran to meet them shouting and laughing with joy and practically blocking their way. There were hundreds of us; Polish, Russian, Belgian, Chech and French. The tanks stopped and the Dutch boys shook hands with the Americans, while we girls just gaped at them in wonder. The war was over!

We returned to camp and watched through the windows as countless trucks passed below. They made very slow progress, stopping from time to time. We grew bolder and gathered on the stairs and by the door to wave at them.

Suddenly there was a great commotion on the stairs. Shouts of excitement. The Russian women were dragging two struggling American soldiers up the steps. The men were black. The Rus-

sian women have never seen a black person before and rushed
over to touch them. It was a stampede.

"Can they be real? Maybe it is just a camouflage paint! They
are cute! So different!

Somebody got a wet rag and tried to wash their faces. The
girls hugged them and tried to reassure them that they meant no
harm. The black soldiers relaxed and even began to smile.
Everybody crowded around them until their comrades came up
to rescue them, with guns at the ready. The Russian women
reluctantly gave them up. There was an animated conversation
going on. Now the war was over for sure, the black Americans
were here and they were not just camouflaged night fighters.

The Americans set up headquarters a few streets away in a
large building. It was necessary for us to contact the Americans
and it was unanimously decided that we should send a small
delegation. The women elected myself and a young Slovakian girl
to represent them because we were pretty and the youngest. It
was hoped that we would favorably impress them. We needed
food, medical supplies and we wanted to request an MP guard
for our camp.

The Slovakian girl and I received a very friendly welcome and
were taken to a colonel with a Spanish sounding name, from
Texas. There was a German interpreter and we were ushered into
a large dining room. In its center was a large table covered with a
huge German flag which the Americans used for a tablecloth. We
thought it very funny. We explained that we were hungry and
immediately two plates full of food were placed before us. It was
delicious. We presented our request to the colonel and returned
to the camp with crates of rations and a Polish speaking MP. We
decided that the Americans were absolutely wonderful!

Freedom. What does one do with such a treasure! Am I finally
really safe? No more fear? I had considerable trouble realizing it.
Somehow I was still afraid. The feeling was deeply ingrained, I
had lived with it for six years. I took Hansi's advice and purchased a Luger pistol from an Italian prisoner of war. One never
knew. . .

It was a beautiful spring day and at last I could walk freely
where ever I pleased. I decided to take a walk in the sunshine.
The trees have sprouted new leaves and the breeze smelled
sweet.

What can I do with my life, where can I go, I wondered.
There was no one waiting for me or happy that I had survived.

All the conversations I have rehearsed in my mind, the things I would say to my parents when I saw them, would remain unsaid. So, I have made it. But who was there to care?

There were neat, Gingerbread, German houses on this particular street, unscathed by the bombings. Families lived inside there, how happy they must be!

A young German boy was leaning out of his window observing me as I passed by. He noticed the yellow patch with the purple "P" still sewn onto my dress. He raised his fist and shook it at me.

"You cursed Polake!" he screeched.

I tensed like a spring and charged at the window which he quickly shut. I rammed my fist right through it, feeling no pain as the glass splintered and tore into my skin. I pounced at the door and surprisingly it gave. It was open. I ran inside mindlessly but the boy was nowhere in sight. Must have run out the back door.

On the table stood a large kerosene lamp. I threw it against the wall and the kerosene splashed over the couch.

Matches! I must find matches. I ran into the kitchen where I found another bottle of kerosene. People depended on kerosene with electricity off because of the bombings. There was a box of matches on the table next to a stove. I splashed the flammable fluid all over the place and lit a match. Flames shot up so fast that I barely had time to get out of the door. I stood in the middle of the street, blood dripping from my hand and watched as the smoke began to pour out of the broken window.

The neighbors ran out and someone attempted to unscrew a water spout outside the house.

I will not have it — the house must burn!

I attacked the gray haired man who was trying to hose down the house with such fury that we both rolled on the ground. Somebody tried to tear me off his back and I sank my teeth into his wrist. Someone tried to sit on top of me and I jabbed my finger into his eye with all my might. There was screaming — a bedlam.

American MP's arrived on the scene and a bulky MP attempted to grab me and I kneed him in the groin. He doubled over. Eventually they managed to restrain me. Blood was dripping from my hand and my jaw was sore from biting people. But the house was in flames the job was done. I did not come to my senses until the Polish speaking MP arrived. I explained to him what had happened.

"I am proud of you," he grinned. He had lost a lot of buddies in this war and had no sympathy for the Germans. So much for my little freedom walk.

Later that afternoon Herr Meissner arrived on his bicycle to visit me. I tactfully declined to mention the incident to him even though my hand was bandaged. I rode on the back of his bike to his home. It was the first time I saw how he lived. We had some tea and he showed me the books he had managed to collect to seed a small library for himself. He looked aged and was very depressed again. Like myself, he was very alone.

The books reminded us of Hansi and Meissner told me that at one time Hansi used to be an interrogator for the Gestapo and other things he could not tell me before about him. This was why he avoided him in the beginning. A great sadness came over us and we both cried. I did not have the heart to tell Meissner about my being Jewish, it would have upset him even more. He walked back to the camp with me and it was the last time I ever saw him.

The next morning our Polish speaking MP brought us very disquieting news. The Americans were pulling out and the Russians were arriving. It will be their occupation zone from now on.

The Russians! I did not want to be here to greet them. Somebody else will have to do the honors.

As I ran out into the street, there were already throngs of people headed west towards Weimar. There was a German woman walking near me, pushing a bicycle loaded with a suitcase. I did not have to think at all, it was almost a reflex reaction on my part. I simply had to have a bike to get away from the oncoming Russians in time.

I said "good morning," and as she turned toward me, I shoved the heel of my hand under her nose and pushed it up. She staggered. I grabbed the suitcase and threw it at her. Then I commandeered the bicycle and sped off followed by screams of indignation.

I rode alongside the American convoy on the road leading to Weimar, all the way to a bridge. There were hundreds of refugees headed that way and the Americans were none too happy about it as we got in their way. At last we got to the bridge and it was a nightmare crossing. The convoy rode in the center and there was only a narrow strip for the civilians to use. There was no railing. I have always been afraid of heights and scared to look down at the water below. I had to discard the bicycle. By the time I made it across my knees were too shaky to walk and I sat down by the side of the road.

An American jeep stopped alongside me. There was an officer and a driver. The driver came out and asked if I was in trouble. He spoke German. I explained that I wanted to get away from the advancing Russians and was offered a ride. The officer informed me that he was a chaplain. I listened to his halting German and it sounded so strange. . . No, it was not German at all the chaplain was speaking. It was Yidish!

I couldn't believe it. I was riding in a jeep with a Jewish Rabbi! I told them who I was and they in turn were full of disbelief. My heart leaped with joy. There were still Jews left in the world!

The chaplain's name was Rabbi Schechter from Chicago and he was on his way to the concentration camp, Buchenwald, to conduct a religious service. Of course, I went along and before my stunned eyes there was a huge, German concentration camp. It was this Buchenwald I had almost been sent to if Hansi had not torn up the transfer order.

How does one describe Dante's Inferno? Hate! Even after liberation it glared from every inch of that place. It was oppressive. The crematorium chimneys, the ovens... the hooks imbedded in the wall upon which they used to hang people. The horribly emanciated faces of the victims inmates, the eyes that have seen such bestiality.

Among them I found a young man from Praszka, named Janiek. He came towards me with open arms. He remembered me well. I tried to recall his face, but all skeletons look alike and Janiak looked like a skeleton. Eyes stared at me out of sunken sockets. They smiled at me. How could they have made Janiak look like this? How can a pleasant young man change into a skeleton? I had an urge to take him in my arms but I did not dare show how sorry I was for him. I was full of wonder to see someone from Praszka again and terrified to hear about what he had lived through in Buchenwald. But I did not attend the services — I could not.

I remained in Buchenwald for a while while waiting for repatriation. The old SS barracks were now available for the Jews to live in. I could hardly stand being there. The place choked me. But I was told soon there would be a children's transport leaving for Switzerland under the direction of the UNRA, a refugee relief organization. Children under sixteen were eligible and I did qualify. The Swiss Government offered us rehabilitation and free education.

Rabbi Schechter promised to track down my uncle Ludwig in Asbury Park, New Jersey and to notify him that I was alive. He did indeed keep that promise.

Finally the big day arrived and I left Germany. During a stopover in Metz, France, a young woman approached me. She was very anxious to go to Switzerland but she was over the prescribed age of sixteen. She confessed to me that she was pregnant. I was very touched. A Jewish baby was on its way into this world. What a miracle! It made me think of cousin Isidor's baby. There were no Jewish babies, they did not survive.

Something very strange happened to me then. Something I never quite understood. I really wanted very much to go to Switzerland. It was an opportunity of a lifetime. But instead, unexpectedly, I stood up and gave my approved place to this pregnant girl.

It was not an act of kindness and I couldn't help it at all. The creature within me took over. Just as it happened on other occasions in my life. The creature-part of my personality did not want to go to Switzerland! Perhaps it needed to stay free. Perhaps it did not want to continue speaking German. I found myself walking away again from a helping hand, not understanding why, but unable to stop myself.

There was another train standing on the other side of the platform and I simply went aboard. I did not have a ticket and did not know where it was going, except that its destination was France. The creature dominated me — could not accept an offer of kindness.

The train lurched forward. I sat dazed and confused. Why was I there? What did I do to myself! I could be safe and secure, could receive an education. I would have been so happy!

The train sped through the night. Was it possible that the creature, a primitive, instinctual part of my personality still needed to run? It did not know that the war was over. Maybe for the creature-part of me it will never be. I had experienced a disassociative experience again, but then, I did not even understand it.

A conductor came to ask for my ticket and I showed him the identification card I received from the UNRA. He spoke to me in French which I did not understand. He smiled and shrugged his shoulders. People were feeling mellow and charitable those days. The war was over.

I remained on that train until the last stop, feeling hopeless and helpless and again very much alone. The train stopped in Marseille, France. I was here illegally. I did not speak the language and had no French money. The creature within me destroyed all my chances. The war was not over for me because the creature part of me did not know it. I was still on the run.

I spent one year in Marseille instead of acquiring an education in Switzerland where all my expenses would have been paid.

I was very fortunate to find a job through a Jewish Refugee Relief Organization. Jobs were scarce then and I did not speak the language.

It was my first encounter with the language barrier, a very formidable obstacle. It was a little bit like being a deaf person, of not knowing what was being said to me.

I could read no signs or newspapers and books once again were out of my reach. But my job was very satisfying and healing for my soul. I worked in an orphanage where the few Jewish children who somehow survived the war waited for a passage to Israel.

Most were orphans, but a few had parents who went there ahead of them, aboard vessels which were too crowded or unsafe for children to be smuggled in.

Yes, smuggled! Perhaps the creature within me was right. Perhaps the war was not really over for many of us. The British closed the gates of immigration to Israel (then called Palestine), to the few survivors who had no other place to go. The children had to be smuggled under the cover of darkness, aboard substandard boats which somehow had to penetrate a blockade of the recently victorious and mighty British Navy. Of course, the safest boats were reserved for the children. The children were the most precious resource. A whole generation of children was destroyed, there were so pitifully few left.

The world, I soon found out, did not exactly open its arms to the survivors of the "Holocaust."

I could not bring myself to go to Israel. It was psychologically for me a replay of returning to the Ghetto. I had the fear of feeling trapped again. It was a tiny country, under siege, surrounded by enemies.

Still the year I had spent in Marseille was very therapeutic for me. Marseille is very beautiful and it was the first time that I beheld the sea. Its sight filled me with peace.

While in Marseille, I lived for a while with a young widow, Anna, who was in charge of the orphanage. Anna, who was of Russian descent, had little affection for the Poles and began to call me "Sonia."

"Do you mind if I call you that?" she wanted to know.

Well, it was not new to me. While I was in Germany, the Russian girls also used to call me "Sonia." Anna thought that the name suited my personality and she was intuitively correct. It was no accident that the name stuck. It was fitting because, in reality, I was not Zofia any more. Zofia did not actually exist any longer. She could never have survived the war.

Zofia wrote poetry and picked daisies in the meadow. Zofia was gone with her parents. I really did not even resemble her; the name only made me feel sad. In order to survive the war another personality had awakened within me. "The Creature."

It must have always been there, dormant as it would have remained if there was no war. The creature was an unborn twin of my soul. Relentless, strong and incomplete. It became my alternate self, an uncompromising force. It was primitive and restless and it did not even like Zofia very much. Yet it was very much a part of me.

When Zofia was unable to function, the creature took over because it did not care. The creature could fight back where Zofia could not stand the pain or the ugliness of the world. The creature was insensitive and uncomplicated and it only reacted.

Yes, it would be easier for me to be Sonia and infinitely more honest. Anna intuitively provided a solution and Sonia I became, exactly who I am now, — a blend of two personalities. It actually made me feel better to be Sonia.

I wonder if many of us do not have a creature slumbering within the subconsciousness. There are people who have one stable, unbroken personality, people who are predictable to themselves and to others. How peaceful and easy it must be! And there are those of us whose psyche is like the theatre mask — so intuitively symbolic of this condition, because on the stage an actor has to assume different personalities and identities. Only for someone like me, it was not per choice.

The Zen Budhists say that life is a stage. On my stage I had to play two different roles to survive.

In old Jewish folk lore, there is a superstition about having to wear a hat at a funeral. Otherwise, a *Dybuk*, the homeless spirit, might enter the uncovered head and take over. I remember hearing this old tale as a child in Praszka.

Sometimes I wonder if what it really represented was that the sorrow of a loss might have awakened a submerged part of someone's personality and altered their behavior. Maybe people close to this so-afflicted person have wondered: "What got into him or her?" What caused such a radical and sudden change in someone? Perhaps the shock of sorrow and loss had awakened someone's creature within them and they called it *Dybuk*...

A folklore is sometimes like a footprint in the sand. If something unbearable happens some people are never the same.

Working with the orphans was very important to me. They all had suffered. There was a bond between us. It was a time of healing. I understood the children I worked with. I gave and I received. I felt needed.

France was a country ravaged by war. Yet, the French were generous, giving and willing to share what little they had. And they did it with graciousness and that certain Gallic gallantry. The French were charming.

It was not legal to own firearms in France without a permit, and at last I realized that I really did not need a gun any longer. I decided to surrender my Luger to the police.

I was ushered into the inspector's office, carrying it in a small, brown paper bag which I respectfully placed on his desk. The rotund, mustachioed inspector peered inside the bag, examined its contents, then came around the desk and picked up my hand.

"Merci, Mademoiselle," he said and gallantly kissed my finger tips. "Now Mademoiselle has no further need for this ugly object," he said. "I am here now, and my very life is devoted to protect Mademoiselle's safety. Please allow me. . ." He picked up the Luger and dropped it disdainfully in his drawer as if it were a dead snake. Only a Frenchman could do it with such finesse.

I finally received a letter from America, from my uncle. Rabbi Schechter had kept his promise to contact him and the Red Cross list supplied my current address. Uncle Ludwig had already heard from my brother. He was well and had returned from Russia, hoping to get to Israel. In the interim, he was in Stuttgart, Germany with his wife and a small son who was born in Siberia. He was working as a physician for the UNRA.

I also learned that my Aunt Hela and her daughter survived the war and had emigrated to Australia. My cousins, Stefan and Heniek Stecki, Isidor's brothers, were living with their wives in Krakow, Poland. My brother had made it, what a joy it was!

Uncle Ludwig sent me all the papers required to apply for a visa to the US and I hopefully went to the consulate. Now at last I could plan ahead.

I was received politely. Yes, I had the necessary documents, but the Polish immigration quota was *closed*. I was told that the German quota was open — if only I were born a few miles further west, on the German side of the border, the council could have issued me a visa. He shook his head regretfully. The Polish quota had a long waiting list in addition, and it would take a number of years, no matter what.

I spent another year and a half in Paris and at long last received my visa. It was just in time. My job working for refugee children was at an end, they were by then dispersed. But at least I saw Paris! If I could have found a job, I would have stayed there forever!

I took the train to my port of departure, Boulogne sur-Mer, right across the Channel from England. The countryside I passed was still scarred by war, the streets jagged with ruins. I spent my last night in Europe in Boulogne.

It was a foggy March evening as I stood on the pier from where I could see the small Liberty ship which would take me across the ocean. Its silhouette looked ghostly in the swirling mist.

America, "The Land Of The Striped People," as Hansi called it. This was how a person imbued with a Nazi ideology perceived America, unable to even imagine a Democracy where people actually could blend together no matter what their origin or persuasion. To a Nazi mind it was inconceivable; everything had to be concrete. If a mixing took place it had to come out like "stripes" of different color. I imagined America very differently. It sounded good to me, but I was afraid. I did not speak English and it would take time to learn it.

I was what the war did to me and in Europe I fit in very well. Europe had more or less shared my fate. Here I didn't need to explain myself. But it would be hard to belong where people did not understand what was in my heart. I tried to imagine the future.

It might be painful, and often I would not be accepted, I thought prophetically. I had no family other than my uncle, and no education. I had only twenty-five francs to my name, and a green dress of hope in my suitcase which I bought for this momentous occasion. And what did I hope for in life what was there for me?

I knew that it would be very hard, maybe impossible for me to ever marry, that the restlessness would surge within me and destroy every bond I would try to make. If someone would extend a hand to me, the creature within me would make me run the other way. I knew that I would be very fearful of closeness or love, very sensitive to rejection.

What did I hope to achieve in this "Land of Striped People?" I wanted independence! I wanted to be free! I wanted a job, no matter how humble so that I would need nothing from anyone. And I wanted a small place of my very own, as a small animal seeks a burrow or a cave in a jungle. I wanted a place where I could heal my soul. A door which I could close against the world if I wished, or open if it was my choice. And someday, when I was ready and dared, I wished to have children. But first I had a lot to learn and understand. I hoped to be accepted and maybe, because it was a "Land of the Striped People," I had a chance.